MW00465333

Personal Financial Planning for Executives and Entrepreneurs

Michael J. Nathanson • Jeffrey T. Craig
Jennifer A. Geoghegan • Nadine Gordon Lee
Michael A. Haber • Seth P. Hieken
Matthew C. Ilteris • D. Scott McDonald
Joseph A. Salvati • Stephen R. Stelljes

Personal Financial Planning for Executives and Entrepreneurs

The Path to Financial Peace of Mind

palgrave
macmillan

Michael J. Nathanson
The Colony Group
Boston, MA, USA

Jeffrey T. Craig
The Colony Group
Hingham, MA, USA

Jennifer A. Geoghegan
The Colony Group
New York, NY, USA

Nadine Gordon Lee
The Colony Group
Armonk, NY, USA

Michael A. Haber
The Colony Group
New York, NY, USA

Seth P. Hieken
The Colony Group
Boston, MA, USA

Matthew C. Ilteris
The Colony Group
Boston, MA, USA

D. Scott McDonald
The Colony Group
Hingham, MA, USA

Joseph A. Salvati
The Colony Group
Boston, MA, USA

Stephen R. Stelljes
The Colony Group
Hingham, MA, USA

ISBN 978-3-319-98415-5   ISBN 978-3-319-98416-2   (eBook)
https://doi.org/10.1007/978-3-319-98416-2

Library of Congress Control Number: 2018957457

This Palgrave Macmillan imprint is published by the registered company Springer Nature Switzerland AG
The registered company address is: Gewerbestrasse 11, 6330 Cham, Switzerland

Acknowledgments

We would like to thank all of our contributing authors, including Michael J. Nathanson, JD, LLM; Jeffrey T. Craig, CFP®, EA®; Jennifer A. Geoghegan, MBA; Nadine Gordon Lee, CPA, PFS, CFP®; Michael A. Haber, JD, CFP®; Seth P. Hieken, MSF, CFA; Matthew C. Ilteris, CFP®, EA®; D. Scott McDonald, MSFP, CFP®; Joseph A. Salvati, CFP®; and Stephen R. Stelljes, JD, CFP®. We thank our editor, Philip Revzin, for his reviews and guidance. Thank you to Austin Linthicum on the creative design work on the cover and book graphics. Julia Geffen, Faith Hill, Edward Kelly, and Joshua Nathanson provided excellent research and editorial support. We are also grateful to Philip Palaveev for introducing us to the professionals at Palgrave Macmillan so that we can share our work with others.

Each of us experiences great meaning and joy as we work with executives and entrepreneurs and share our knowledge with others. We thank the executives and entrepreneurs who have challenged us to bring what we hope is our very best thinking and planning to their circumstances and to this book. We also thank the many business partners we collaborate with regularly as we seek to solve problems and create better outcomes together.

Finally, we thank our families and our colleagues for patiently supporting each of us as we worked on this book.

Introduction

Effective financial planning is complex, dense, and impossible to reduce to a single, easy-to-understand formula—but please don't stop reading! We understand the great challenge of writing a book about financial planning for corporate executives and entrepreneurs that reads like a best-selling novel, and we love a challenge.

Our approach is designed to keep your attention and make sure that, by the end of this book, you have a strong sense of the power of effective, targeted financial planning. We will begin by telling you a story about a fictional, but plausible, couple and their family who (spoiler alert!) do pretty much everything wrong in securing their financial future. In most cases, they don't do the things they need to do because they don't know what they are.

Then, we're going to break down this story in chapters that offer a practical discussion of all the key points. These chapters contain the tools needed to tailor a plan for virtually every circumstance and need. As you will see, there is no single plan that works for everybody—if there were, we'd sell it to you in this book! There is complicated, technical information scattered throughout the book, and we do our best to explain it all. But the best use of this information may be to highlight things you should discuss with your financial advisor. All people are different, and there always will be issues and imperfections surrounding generalizations.

Let's start with a definition of our principal subject matter: executives and entrepreneurs. For our purposes, we will focus on those employees of a business organization who are in a position of leadership or management or who have substantially progressed along a career path toward being in such a position. We will use the term "corporate executive" to describe both "executives" and "entrepreneurs," though we certainly acknowledge that there can be a distinction, with the term "executives" typically referring to the leaders of larger organizations and the term "entrepreneurs" often referring to the leaders of smaller, earlier-stage organizations. Our fictional characters will illustrate some of these differences.

Most obviously, a corporate executive might be a member of an organization's "C-suite," which can be extensive in some larger organizations (Table 1).

Corporate executives may also include the organization's President, Treasurer, Executive Vice Presidents, Senior Vice Presidents, Managing Directors, and, in

Table 1 The ever-expanding C-suite

Acronym	Title	Core responsibilities
CAO	Chief Accounting Officer	Implementation and enforcement of accounting policies
CAO	Chief Administrative Officer	Administrative and operational platforms
CCO	Chief Communications Officer	Public relations and communications
CCO	Chief Compliance Officer	Compliance with laws, regulations, and ordinances
CCO	Chief Cultural Officer	Cultural oversight and strategy
CDO	Chief Data Officer	Data mining, analysis, and utilization
CDO	Chief Diversity Officer	Human capital diversity
CEO	Chief Executive Officer	Strategic vision, oversight, and governance
CFO	Chief Financial Officer	Financial oversight and reporting
CHRO	Chief Human Resources Officer[a]	Personnel
CIO	Chief Information Officer	Information resources
CIO	Chief Investment Officer	Management of investment assets
CLO	Chief Legal Officer	Legal compliance, oversight, and issues
CMO	Chief Marketing Officer	Marketing and branding
CMO	Chief Medical Officer	Medical elements of product or service offering
COO	Chief Operating Officer	Operating oversight and efficiency
COS	Chief of Staff	Oversight and coordination of management team
CPO	Chief Procurement Officer	Supply management
CRO	Chief Revenue Officer	Revenue generation
CRO	Chief Risk Officer	Assessing and managing risk
CSO	Chief Sales Officer	Sales force and function
CSO	Chief Scientific Officer	Scientific research, programs, and operations
CSO	Chief Strategy Officer	Strategic oversight, acquisitions, and dispositions
CTO	Chief Technology Officer	Information technology and development

[a]Similar titles include Chief Human Capital Officer, Chief People Officer, and Chief Talent Officer

some organizations, Directors.[1] A General Counsel and, in some companies, a Deputy General Counsel also would be a corporate executive, as would a marketing or sales executive, a Controller, and the senior members of the human capital team.

As discussed below, corporate executives typically are among the organization's higher-paid employees, are eligible for performance-based compensation arrangements, and are likely to own equity or equity-based rights in the organization. They also may have complex employment contracts and relatively extensive benefits packages.

We'll use the term "corporate executives" for people who work for large or small public or private corporations, as well as limited liability companies, partnerships, or other non-corporate entities.[2] Throughout the book we'll try to account for the relevant variables whenever appropriate. (Again, there's that key principle: optimal financial planning requires that we consider the specific facts of each case!).

What, from a financial planning perspective, makes corporate executives different? The answer is complex, reflecting the nature of our subject matter. Here are some of the key characteristics that differentiate many (but not all) corporate executives.

They Are Leaders Who Set High Goals and Worry About Achieving Them

This select group includes people with leadership and management skills, often deep education and training, and vast business and life experience. But how do corporate executives manage their own finances? Do they follow the same patterns as others?

In general, when it comes to managing their finances, wealthier people fall into one of three commonly delineated segments: Managers; Partners; and Loners (Fig. 1).

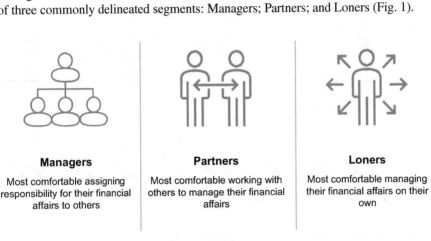

Managers	**Partners**	**Loners**
Most comfortable assigning responsibility for their financial affairs to others	Most comfortable working with others to manage their financial affairs	Most comfortable managing their financial affairs on their own

Fig. 1 Managers, partners, and loners

You might assume that the majority of corporate executives would be Managers, with the minority being Partners or Loners. Yet most tend to be Partners or Loners, with Managers representing the smallest segment of corporate executives. According to a study conducted by Fidelity Investments, fewer than 25% fall into the Manager category, with about 45% identifying themselves as Partners and 31% as Loners.[3] The same study reports that 69% of the corporate executives surveyed worked with a financial advisor.[4]

Two-thirds of the corporate executives surveyed acknowledged the need for third-party expertise when planning for their own financial futures. Yet, two-thirds also wanted to remain directly engaged in the financial planning process, as opposed to delegating it fully to others.

This apparent paradox suggests a basic reality: corporate executives worry more than others about achieving their goals because of their general knowledge levels, compulsion to set and achieve higher goals, and desire to stay involved in the execution process. Some turn to professional advisors to maximize their chances of achieving those goals; and some opt to take on all of the responsibilities themselves, again with the intent of maximizing their odds of success. Either way, corporate executives do trend toward an intensive approach, in which they often set high goals and worry more about achieving them.

The above survey also asked the executives to identify their more pressing concerns. The results demonstrated greater levels of concerns by corporate executives than other millionaires in almost every single subject area covered by the survey! (Fig. 2).[5]

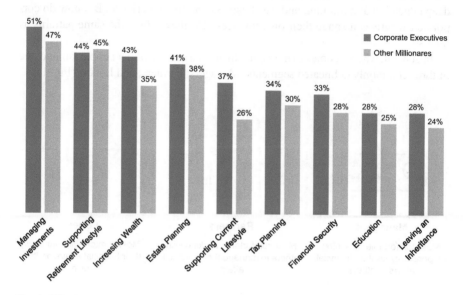

Fig. 2 What's keeping corporate executives awake at night?
Source: "Tapping into the Millionaire Professional," The Fidelity Millionaire Outlook Series (2008, 2012). © 2018 FMR LLC. All rights reserved. Used with permission

When the financial planning dynamic for corporate executives accounts for these concerns, it is far more effective. It is better tailored to identify and achieve all of the appropriate goals and take into account the psychological elements and context of the process.

They Are Paid More Than Other Employees

It may seem an obvious point, but corporate executives often can be distinguished simply by the amount of their pay relative to others in the company. In a 2013 study conducted by the Economic Policy Institute, for the 350 largest U.S. public companies by revenue, the ratio of CEO pay to the pay of other workers was almost 300 to 1—and that ratio did not account for Facebook's impact because it was considered an "outlier." If Facebook had been included, then the ratio of CEO-to-worker compensation would have risen to over 500 to 1![6]

More generally, according to the Fidelity Millionaire Outlook study, corporate executives were at the top of the list of professional categories among millionaire households (Fig. 3).[7]

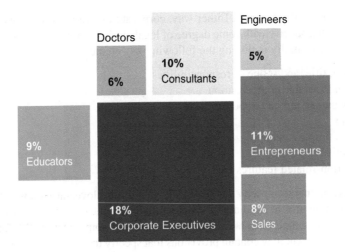

Fig. 3 Corporate executives as millionaire professionals
Source: "Tapping into the Millionaire Professional," The Fidelity Millionaire Outlook Series
(2008, 2012). © 2018 FMR LLC. All rights reserved. Used with permission

Less obvious, however, is the composition of a typical executive pay package. Often, when we read about the highest paid executives, we read that they are paid millions of dollars each year. Yet, many executives actually are paid smaller base salaries and receive a large portion of their total compensation either as variable or deferred compensation or, in many cases, as equity-based incentives such as restricted stock awards, stock options, or "phantom" equity arrangements (all of which will be discussed in later chapters).

The Economic Policy Institute study reports that average annual compensation among the country's top CEOs was over $15 million. This figure includes salary, bonuses, restricted stock grants, options exercised, and long-term incentives.[8]

In any event, corporate executives typically are the highest paid people in an organization. Of course, because they are paid so much, and because the form of their pay can be so varied, they usually require substantial and often complex planning focused specifically on and around their compensation arrangements.

They May Be Employed Under a Formal Contract of Employment

Corporate executives often have sufficient leverage when negotiating the terms of their employment to demand the protections and benefits offered by a formal, enforceable contract of employment. Conversely, their employers may see the "investment" they are making in their key employees as so important that they insist on the formality of a contract. Either way, corporate executives often have written agreements that specify with some degree of legal clarity a multitude of benefits and obligations, potentially including the following key elements:

- Position, title, and scope of responsibilities
- Base and variable compensation
- Equity ownership and opportunities
- Benefits
- Term of employment
- Restrictive covenants
- Separation-related features

The agreement may specify that the executive is an employee-at-will, which means he or she can be fired at any time for any reason, or that the executive is guaranteed a definite term of employment. In the latter case—and sometimes in the former as well—the agreement may contain provisions that specify the outcomes of events such as changes of corporate control (e.g., mergers or acquisitions), voluntary and involuntary termination, death, disability, and even personal bankruptcy or divorce.

Regardless of the circumstances, a corporate executive's employment agreement presents not only a multitude of crucial financial planning opportunities but also a maze that, if not properly navigated, can lead to a financial dead end. We will devote an entire chapter exclusively to understanding and planning around executive employment agreements.

Their Compensation Is Likely to Be Tied, in Part, to Specific Performance Goals and Standards

As suggested above, a corporate executive likely will have a component of base compensation and also a component—often a disproportionately large one—of variable compensation. Variable compensation arrangements, which can take many forms, often are utilized to provide the appropriate alignment and incentives (both long-term and short-term) to the executive while also ensuring that the executive is rewarded only when goals are achieved. In some cases, especially where payment is deferred, these arrangements are used to retain key employees.

In general, the larger the company, the more likely it is that variable compensation will comprise a substantial portion of the executives' total compensation packages. Typical base compensation for the CEOs of larger public companies has often been limited to about $1 million, in part because of federal income tax rules that have limited the deductibility by companies of executive compensation over that amount.[9] In fact, among some of the largest companies in the world, fixed base compensation for the most senior executives has been as low as $1![10] The rest is all variable, comprised of bonuses, equity-based awards, and benefits (Table 2).

This means, as we will discuss in greater detail, the executive needs to plan for multiple iterations of success and failure—both annually and over longer periods of time. In this way, corporate executives face complex planning issues that are less prevalent among employees whose pay is more predictable.

Table 2 Notable members of the $1 Club

Corporate executive	Company	Base compensation	Total compensation
Carl Icahn	Icahn Enterprises	$1	$105,533[a]
Edward Lampert	Sears Holdings	$1	$5,702,364[b]
Larry Ellison	Oracle	$1	$67,261,251[c]
Mark Zuckerberg	Facebook	$1	$610,455[d]

[a]See Icahn Enterprises Form 10-K (February 27, 2015)
[b]See Sears Holdings Proxy Statement (March 17, 2015)
[c]See Oracle Proxy Statement (September 25, 2015)
[d]See Facebook Proxy Statement (April 24, 2015)

They Are, or Will Be, Owners of Equity or Equity-Based Rights

Executives who founded their companies will likely own substantial equity in the entity for historic reasons, as well as for continued alignment of interests. Non-founders may also receive equity-based grants as incentives for future performance.

At the time of his death, Steve Jobs, who co-founded Apple, owned about 5.5 million shares of Apple stock, worth over $2 billion.[11] When Tim Cook assumed the role of CEO of Apple, the company's board of directors granted him one million restricted stock units, worth about $383 million.[12]

In general, corporate executives will own important amounts of equity—in one form or another—in their employer. In fact, at least among public companies, it has become common to impose minimum "guidelines" on the ownership of stock by executives. Typically, these guidelines are based on a compensation multiple (e.g., share value must be at least three times base salary); but they can also be based on a number of shares or a share value assigned to each position.[13]

As we will see, planning to earn, hold, transfer, and eventually liquidate this equity, which can be an executive's largest holding, can be complicated. Later in this book we'll look at:

- Investment-related considerations
- Tax implications
- Estate-planning consequences
- Liquidity and cash-flow needs
- Legal constraints and obligations

Their Financial Fortunes Are Correlated to the Company's Overall Performance

Because they typically own large amounts of equity in their companies, executives often find themselves relying—perhaps over-relying—on their employers not only for their current income but also for their overall, long-term investment fortunes. In effect, an executive's financial well-being can become highly correlated to the well-being of the company that he or she serves. This interesting but stark reality can turn out well for an executive when the company performs well; and, of course, it can turn out disastrously when the company falters.

In 2011, a flat year for the S&P 500, the CEOs of the largest 500 U.S. companies saw the value of their stock awards and stock options account for over 60% of their total pay.[14] That's great when all is well; but consider the cases of Enron, WorldCom, and Global Crossing, whose executives—even the ones who were in no way implicated in any wrongdoing—experienced unprecedented wealth destruction in such a short period of time that they had little opportunity to help themselves. By some estimates, the shareholders of Enron, including its executives, ultimately lost over $60 billion of wealth when the company collapsed in 2001.[15]

This so-called "over-concentration" phenomenon requires an executive to take appropriate measures to mitigate risk through techniques that can include:

- Strategic and tactical asset allocation
- Hedging
- Planned diversification

Yet, these techniques often are complicated by a different and competing set of considerations, making the planning process highly complex and dynamic. These competing considerations, which may include public disclosure as well as tax and securities law considerations, will be addressed in subsequent chapters.

They Have Complex, Sometimes Extensive Benefits Packages

In the case of certain employee benefits, such as health insurance, there may be legal and other considerations that mitigate any substantial differences in the benefit plans offered to an organization's executives on the one hand and non-executive employees on the other. Still, there can be dramatic differences not only in the employee benefits offered to corporate executives but also in the opportunities they are given to maximize the impact of those benefits.

We will address in detail the analysis and utilization of employee benefits by corporate executives. You'll see throughout this book that decisions that may seem small when made can lead to very large, and highly lucrative, results over time. This principle is especially true for employee benefits.

They May Be Subject to Legal Risks, Obligations, and Liabilities Associated with the Positions They Hold

With the many rewards of serving as a corporate executive come an equal magnitude of responsibilities, risks, and potential liabilities that other employees don't face. Many of these burdens are attached exclusively to the executives of public or pre-public companies, such as those arising from the need to provide holdings disclosures and comply with laws against insider trading.[16] Some only apply to select corporate executives, such as the CEO or CFO, who may be subject to special obligations and liabilities under the legal rules surrounding the audit process or the filing of financial statements and disclosures.

Executive officers can also find themselves subject to a civil lawsuit by shareholders or others who seek to hold them personally responsible for conduct that may have led to damage to shareholders or others. Equally seriously, CEOs and CFOs of public companies may be subject to "disgorgement" obligations in the event that a company is required to restate its earnings as a result of any misconduct; and they may be subject to criminal fines and penalties for improperly certifying their companies' financial statements.[17]

There are many other examples that apply not only with respect to public companies but also with respect to private companies; and a failure to address and protect against these pitfalls is a failure of adequate planning. Our discussion of these pitfalls will be centered on general compliance as well as certain risk-management techniques and measures.

***

Now that we've presented the general stakes and introduced you to the benefits of financial planning, let's consider the story of a couple of executives who got it all wrong. David and Abby didn't have this book. But you do. Read their story, knowing you'll soon learn how to avoid their mistakes.

The Colony Group   Michael J. Nathanson
Boston, MA, USA

Notes

1. Note that employees who have the title of Director should be distinguished from individuals serving on an organization's board of directors.
2. Examples might include limited liability companies, general partnerships, limited partnerships, limited liability partnerships, business trusts, joint stock companies, or even sole proprietorships.
3. In "Tapping into the Millionaire Professional," *The Fidelity Millionaire Outlook Series*, the authors refer to the categories "Delegators," "Validators," and "Soloists" instead of "Managers," "Partners," and "Loners," but the concepts are quite similar. Terms such as "Delegators," "Validators," and "Soloists" have become common within the investment management industry. We prefer the terms "Managers," "Partners," and "Loners." See "Tapping into the Millionaire Professional," *The Fidelity Millionaire Outlook Series* (2008, 2012). © 2018 FMR LLC. All rights reserved. Used with permission.
4. See "Tapping into the Millionaire Professional."
5. See "Tapping into the Millionaire Professional."
6. See Alyssa Davis and Lawrence Mishel, "CEO Pay Continues to Rise as Typical Workers Are Paid Less," Economic Policy Institute, published June 12, 2014, https://www.epi.org/publication/ceo-pay-continues-to-rise/.
7. See "Tapping into the Millionaire Professional."

8. See Alyssa Davis and Lawrence Mishel, "CEO Pay Continues to Rise as Typical Workers Are Paid Less," Economic Policy Institute, published June 12, 2014, https://www.epi.org/publication/ceo-pay-continues-to-rise/.

9. See I.R.C. § 162(m). See also, Michael Dennis Graham, Thomas A. Roth, and Dawn Dugan, *Effective Executive Compensation* (New York: American Management Association, 2008). Note that Section 162(m) was amended by the Tax Cuts and Jobs Act of 2017, under which certain performance-based compensation is now also subject to limitations with regard to deductibility.

10. Steve Jobs was among the pioneers of this trend, with others, such as Google's Larry Page and Facebook's Mark Zuckerberg joining the trend. See, e.g., Facebook Proxy Statement (April 24, 2015). Among the executive officers named in Facebook's proxy statement, COO Sheryl Sandberg had the highest base salary in 2014, $640,000, followed by CFO David Wehner at $600,000.

11. See Apple Proxy Statement (February 23, 2011).

12. See Form 8-K, Apple, Inc. (August 24, 2011) ("In connection with Mr. Cook's appointment as Chief Executive Officer, the Board awarded Mr. Cook 1,000,000 restricted stock units. Fifty percent of the restricted stock units are scheduled to vest on each of August 24, 2016 and August 24, 2021, subject to Mr. Cook's continued employment with Apple through each such date.").

13. See Jessica Yu, "Executive Compensation Bulletin: Stock Ownership Guidelines and Retention Policies—Creating Stronger Links between Executives and Shareholders," Towers Watson, published March 17, 2015, https://www.towerswatson.com/en/Insights/Newsletters/Global/executive-pay-matters/2015/Executive-Compensation-Bulletin-Stock-Ownership-Guidelines-Retention-Policies-Stronger-Links.

14. See Scott DeCarlo, "America's Highest Paid CEOs," *Forbes*, April 4, 2012.

15. See, e.g., Kenneth N. Gilpin, "Enron's Collapse: The Investors; Plenty of Pain to Go Around for Small Investors, Funds, Workers and Creditors," *The New York Times*, December 4, 2001.

16. See, e.g., Section 16 of the Securities Exchange Act of 1934 and SEC Rule 10b5-1.

17. See 18 U.S. Code § 1350.

Contents

About the Authors

Michael J. Nathanson, JD, LLM is the Chairman and Chief Executive Officer of The Colony Group, LLC. He is widely regarded as a leader in the wealth management industry and is committed to sharing his knowledge and experience with colleagues, clients, and the next generation of industry leaders. He is active in many industry-wide organizations and has served on numerous boards, including the Fidelity Institutional Wealth Services Advisor Council and the Schwab Advisor Services Advisory Board. Previously, he served on the Board of Advisors for Boston University's Program for Financial Planners and as Co-Chairman of the Boston Bar Association Tax Section.

Nathanson is frequently cited in the media as an industry expert, and he has been interviewed and quoted by many national and local news outlets, including Reuters, Dow Jones, Investment News, Financial Advisor, Financial Planning, RIA Biz, AdvisorOne, Registered Rep, Lawyer's Weekly, and the Boston Business Journal. He also has been a speaker and lecturer for organizations such as Wall Street Week, Barron's, Fidelity Investments, Charles Schwab, TD AMERITRADE, the National Association of Stock Plan Professionals, the Boston Bar Association, CompStudy, MassMEDIC, MCLE, and VC Experts. He has published articles on a wide variety of financial, tax, and legal topics in periodicals that include the Journal of Financial Planning, Financial Planning magazine, Financial Advisor, Financial Advisor IQ, the Journal of Compensation and Benefits, the Journal of International Taxation, Software Magazine, World Trade Executive, State Tax Notes, Tax Notes, Tax Notes International, Taxation for Accountants, Taxation for Lawyers, The Tax Adviser, the Boston Business Journal, Global e-Commerce, Interstate Tax Insights, the Interstate Tax Report, and IP Today.

Nathanson is also passionate about public service. He serves as the Chairman of the Board of Directors of the National Brain Tumor Society and as a member of the Boards of Directors of the affiliated Pediatric Cancer Cure and Cure GBM. He also has served as a member of the Investment Committee of the Massachusetts Service Alliance and as a Trustee and Director of the Historical Society of Needham, Massachusetts.

Nathanson has been selected six times as a "Super Lawyer," as published in Massachusetts Super Lawyers, a periodical that honors lawyers who have distinguished themselves in the practice of law. He also has been recognized ten times by Barron's magazine as one of the top 100 independent financial advisors in the nation and has been included in Worth magazine's list of the country's top 250 wealth advisors.

Previously, Nathanson served as Chief Financial Officer and General Counsel of The Colony Group. Prior to joining The Colony Group, he was a Senior Partner at the international law firm of Wilmer Cutler Pickering Hale and Dorr LLP, where he held several leadership positions. He earned his Juris Doctor, cum laude, from Harvard Law School, an LL.M. in Taxation from Boston University School of Law, and a Bachelor of Arts, summa cum laude, from Brandeis University, where he was elected to membership in Phi Beta Kappa and was the recipient of numerous academic honors.

Jeffrey T. Craig, CFP® is a Senior Wealth Advisor and a Principal of The Colony Group. He counsels clients in all areas of financial planning and executive benefits and specializes in tax planning and return preparation. Craig is a CERTIFIED FINANCIAL PLANNER™ professional and an Enrolled Agent authorized to represent taxpayers before the Internal Revenue Service.

Before joining The Colony Group, Craig was a Financial Advisor for American Express Financial Advisors, where he worked with clients to develop financial plans. Previously, he held NASD Series 7, 63, and 66 licenses. He was named a "Five Star Wealth Manager" by Boston Magazine in 2016 and 2017.

Craig earned a Master of Science in Sports Management from the University of Massachusetts at Amherst and a Bachelor of Arts in Economics and Mathematics from Colgate University. He is an active member of the Colgate University Alumni Corporation.

Jennifer A. Geoghegan, MBA is the Chief Strategy Officer and a Principal of The Colony Group. She focuses on innovative services and strategic initiatives that support the Colony team as it strives to deliver an exceptional client experience. She also engages with advisors and teams who may desire to join Colony and share its vision to help clients and employees experience meaning and joy in their lives. Previously, Geoghegan served as the Chief Marketing Officer and Advisor Coach of The Colony Group, helping to educate clients and connect them with advisors who, she believes, are some of the most talented in the industry.

Prior to joining The Colony Group, Geoghegan was the Vice President of Marketing and Advisor Coach at Focus Financial Partners, a leading partnership of independent wealth management firms, which The Colony Group joined in 2011. Before joining Focus, Geoghegan was VP, Card Acquisitions, at American Express, where she marketed premium card products to affluent prospects. During her tenure at American Express, she also worked on new product development, customer loyalty and retention, and interactive marketing, giving her experience across the full affluent consumer lifecycle.

Geoghegan holds an MBA in Marketing and International Business from the New York University Stern School of Business and a Bachelor of Arts in Foreign Affairs from the University of Virginia. More recently she received an executive coaching certification from Columbia University.

Michael A. Haber, JD, CFP® is a Senior Wealth Advisor and a Principal of The Colony Group, providing wealth management, estate, and financial planning services to clients. In addition to his client-facing role, he is also directly responsible for the development and preparation of underlying financial and estate strategies, analysis, and associated research.

Previously, Haber spent five years advising clients as a practicing attorney. His legal education and experience at leading international law firms honed his research and analytical skill set.

Haber is admitted to practice law in the state of New York. He received his J.D. from the Benjamin N. Cardozo School of Law and his Bachelor of Arts from Emory University.

Seth P. Hieken, MSF, CFA is a longtime member of The Colony Group, having joined the firm in 1994. He is the Executive Vice President of Proprietary Strategies and a Principal of The Colony Group.

With more than 20 years of experience in investment research and portfolio management, he is the lead manager on The Colony Group's mid-cap strategy. Hieken also manages a select group of large-cap portfolios while taking an active role in equity research. In addition, he holds the Chartered Financial Analyst® designation and is a member of the CFA Institute and the Boston Security Analysts Society. Before Colony, Hieken was a portfolio manager and research analyst for the trust department of Hutchins, Wheeler and Ditmar.

Hieken has been published in various trade publications, including Advisor Perspectives and the Boston Business Journal. He also has been quoted in Investment News and Bloomberg News and interviewed on multiple occasions by Wall Street Transcript. He earned a Bachelor of Science from Cornell University and a Master of Science in Finance from Bentley University.

Matthew C. Ilteris, CFP®, EA® is a Senior Wealth Advisor and a Principal of The Colony Group. He provides comprehensive wealth management and investment advisory services, including financial planning, investment management, and tax planning, to corporate executives and high-net-worth clients of the firm. Ilteris is a CERTIFIED FINANCIAL PLANNER™ professional and an Enrolled Agent before the Internal Revenue Service. He was named a "Five Star Wealth Manager" by Boston Magazine in 2016 and 2017.

Ilteris originally joined The Colony Group as a Portfolio Administrator in Colony Investment Management, where he was primarily responsible for new accounts, performance reporting, and client service requests. He earned his Bachelor of Science in Corporate Finance with a minor in Business Leadership from Virginia Tech.

Nadine Gordon Lee, CPA/PFS, CFP® Dina Lee is Managing Director of The Colony Group's Metro NY Offices and President of the Colony Group Family Office. Previously, Lee was the President and Founder of Prosper Advisors. During her more than thirty years in wealth management, Lee has spent most of her career advising wealthy family groups, corporate executives, and owners of closely held businesses. She is a former Managing Director of U.S. Trust Company and a former Partner of Ernst & Young.

Lee's planning expertise incorporates investment management techniques with philanthropic, estate, and income tax strategies to optimize family wealth while controlling risk.

As a leader within her profession, she has held the following key positions:

- Personal Financial Planning Executive Committee of the American Institute of CPAs
- Vice President and Director of the New York State Society of CPAs
- Chair of the Investment Committee of the NYSSCPA
- President of the Estate Planning Council of New York City

As a speaker, her audiences have included the Wharton School, the UJA, the Investment Management Institute, the American Institute of CPAs, the FPA, the NYSSCPA, and the Estate Planning Council of NYC. Lee is frequently quoted in the financial press and has had many interviews on network television, including hosting her own seven-part series on wealth management and financial planning on CNN financial news.

D. Scott McDonald, MSFP, CFP® As a Senior Wealth Advisor and a Principal of The Colony Group, Scott McDonald helps clients set and achieve their personal financial goals by providing individualized financial advice and service. He is a CERTIFIED FINANCIAL PLANNER™ professional with over 15 years of experience, bringing expertise in taxation, asset allocation, and retirement planning to clients' broad spectrum of wealth management needs.

Prior to joining The Colony Group, McDonald served as a Client Service Officer in the Defined Contribution Services Division of State Street Bank, where he supervised a group responsible for the management and oversight of group retirement plans. Before State Street, McDonald held accounting and finance positions at Bank of Boston and Investors Bank & Trust Company. He earned a Master of Science in Personal Financial Planning from Bentley College and a Bachelor of Science in Accounting from Providence College.

Joseph A. Salvati, CFP® is a Senior Wealth Advisor and a Principal of The Colony Group. He guides corporate executives and high-net-worth individuals and families through the creation and implementation of long-term wealth management plans. As a CERTIFIED FINANCIAL PLANNER™ professional, Salvati uses his experience in financial, investment, and tax planning to provide comprehensive wealth management and investment advisory services that are customized to meet each client's needs.

Before joining the firm, Salvati was a Senior Financial Planner at The Ayco Company, where he provided financial and investment planning services to corporate executives. He began his career as a Financial Advisor for Ameriprise Financial.

Stephen R. Stelljes, JD, CFP® is President of Client Services and a Principal of The Colony Group. Stelljes has extensive experience developing tax-efficient diversification strategies for concentrated equity positions and shaping philanthropic strategies for clients with a particular focus on charitable giving as part of a comprehensive estate plan.

Prior to joining The Colony Group in 1998, Stelljes provided financial counseling and tax services for high-net-worth individuals with The Ayco Company and the international accounting firm of Deloitte & Touche, LLP. Stelles is admitted to practice law in the State of New York and holds the CERTIFIED FINANCIAL PLANNER™ designation. He is a member of the Boston Estate Planning Council.

He earned his Juris Doctor with distinction from Albany Law School and a Bachelor of Science in Business Administration/Finance from the State University of New York with honors.

The Colony Group, LLC is an independent, fee-only, financial advisory firm with several billion dollars in assets under management and employees in multiple offices across the United States. Founded in 1986, The Colony Group provides corporate executives, entrepreneurs, high-net-worth individuals and families, service professionals, professional athletes, and institutions with expertise that goes beyond investment management and encompasses the full suite of financial counseling services, including tax, estate, retirement, and philanthropic planning, asset allocation, and cash and risk management. More information can be found at www.thecolonygroup.com.

Disclosures Regarding Awards and Recognitions Granted to The Colony Group Professionals Awards and recognitions by unaffiliated rating services, companies, and/or publications should not be construed by a client or prospective client as a guarantee that he/she will experience a certain level of results if The Colony Group ("Colony") is engaged, or continues to be engaged, to provide investment advisory services; nor should they be construed as a current or past endorsement of Colony or its representatives by any of its clients. Rankings published by magazines and others are generally based exclusively on information prepared and/or submitted by the recognized advisor. Moreover, with regard to all performance information contained herein, directly or indirectly, if any, users should note that past results are not indicative of future results. Please see below for a more detailed description of the criteria used with respect to the awards and recognitions granted to Colony's individual employees.

Barron's criteria: Advisor's assets under management, contribution to the firm's revenues and profits, and quality of service. The Barron's lists included Michael Nathanson for 2007 and 2009–2017.

Five Star Professional criteria: Credentialed as an IAR, FINRA-registered rep, a CPA, or a licensed attorney; at least five years in the financial services industry;

favorable regulatory and complaint history review; meeting firm's review standards; accepting new clients; one and five-year retention rates; assets administered; number of households served; and education and professional designations.

Worth criteria: Individual advisor's expertise, integrity, and dedication to the field of wealth management; portfolio management strategies; risk analysis; client service initiatives; and the educational and professional credentials of advisors. The Worth list included Michael Nathanson for 2008.

Super Lawyers criteria: Candidates are evaluated on 12 indicators of peer recognition and professional achievement. Selections are made on an annual, state-by-state basis. The list included Michael Nathanson from 2004–2009.

List of Figures

List of Tables

Chapter 1
The Story of David and Goliath, and Abby and Samson: A Journey with No Direction

David grew up in a rural town in Connecticut. His parents worked on an assembly line at Goliath Assembly Company, earning just enough money to support David and his two younger sisters. He lived in a modest house, attended public schools, and enjoyed a stable, unremarkable childhood.

Neither of David's parents had attended college, but they were keenly aware that the world was changing—in a way that seemed to place a growing premium on formal education. They told their children that they would one day need to attend college and that they would support them in any way they could. David's parents were firm on one point: college would not be optional for their children.

David's mother and father were both thrifty and, of necessity, disciplined about their spending. They saved what they could, but they didn't worry too much about their financial future, let alone think about retirement. Like many in their generation, they assumed that Social Security and Medicare would take care of their retirement needs, allowing them to spend their hard-earned money where it counted most: on supporting and nurturing their family. They didn't feel that they had any choice in the matter. They just didn't have much in the way of discretionary income, and, on their fixed salaries—which increased on occasion to account for the effects of inflation—they couldn't afford to worry about the future, including saving money for retirement or buying insurance for seemingly abstract concepts like long-term care, disability, or untimely death.

David was a good student, and, to the delight of his proud parents, David went on to become a three-sport varsity athlete in high-school. Smart and handsome, David was popular, had quite a few girlfriends, and generally enjoyed his four brief years in high school. At the beginning of his senior year, he became friends with Abby, who graciously agreed to be David's prom date after David summoned the courage to ask her.

Abby lived on the other side of town from David; but she, too, came from a good, hard-working family of modest means. Abby was David's natural match in almost every way. The two had actually known each other since the sixth grade, where they were both placed in their school's "accelerated track" for academically

© The Colony Group 2018
M. J. Nathanson et al., *Personal Financial Planning for Executives and Entrepreneurs*, https://doi.org/10.1007/978-3-319-98416-2_1

higher-performing students. And while Abby was David's academic equal, she was also his athletic equal, being a three-sport varsity athlete herself. Their friends and even their parents had always suggested that the two should be a couple, but it wasn't until they sat next to each other in an SAT preparatory class that they became friends and the start of something more occurred.

After scoring well on his SAT and laboring over his college applications with his guidance counselor, David was accepted into Connecticut College. Equally importantly, with some very modest help from his parents, a generous aid and loan package from the school, and a part-time job as a waiter, he found the money to attend.

In college, David excelled as a student, especially at business-related subjects like economics and accounting. By his junior year, he knew that he wanted to pursue an advanced degree in business administration and hopefully a career in business. Like many his age, he dreamed of a bright future for himself and for the family that he would have one day.

All in all, things were going very nicely for David. He took the GMAT (graduate management admission test) at the beginning of his senior year in college, and his score was in the top 1% of all test takers—on his first try! Coupled with his 3.88 GPA at Connecticut College, at which he also participated in an extensive work-study program, he had his choice of just about any business school he wanted. He knew which one he would choose before he even had to make the decision: Harvard.

An MBA from Harvard would make his parents proud (and it wouldn't look too bad on a resume either)! But even better, Abby, who had maintained a not-too-long-distance relationship with David throughout college, was living in Massachusetts and planning to pursue a master's degree herself—in Mass Communications from Boston University.

Abby, too, had excelled during her years in college. An avid reader and natural writer, she had double-majored in English and communications at Boston College. She graduated near the top of her class, Phi Beta Kappa, with highest honors, and envisioned a career utilizing her specialized knowledge and skills as an entrepreneur focused on marketing consulting and online design.

Only a year later, David and Abby were engaged. The following year, David graduated with a master's degree in Business Administration, while Abby graduated with a master's degree in Mass Communications. The newly-minted graduates were married that fall, with their friends and family now playfully (but accurately) referring to them as a "power couple." Of course, between the two of them, they also owed Harvard, Boston University, Connecticut College, and Boston College $350,000 in student debt; but they'd pay that off quickly with all of the money they were going to earn.

Abby soon started her own consulting and online design company. She wrote up a business plan, which impressed David with its bold vision and striking detail. He told Abby (and he was being sincere) that it was better and had more potential than most of the plans he had studied in business school.

Yet, Abby was equally focused on practicality and certain mundane details, such as the basic need to protect herself from potential lawsuits and creditors by creating a corporate entity to house her new business. With the help of a paralegal that she hired for a few hundred dollars, she incorporated her own company, Slingshot Innovation, Inc., when she was only 24.

As for David, he applied for and, after a series of interviews, got the job he always wanted—as a Manager at Goliath, his parents' old workplace. As a Manager of Corporate Strategy, David now had the privilege of, and responsibility for, formulating and implementing business strategy at the very company that had afforded his parents the opportunity to raise their children in such a nurturing environment.

Over the next several years, David and Abby welcomed two children (a boy and a girl) and acquired an oversized home (and an oversized mortgage to go with it), two nice cars, and a membership at an exclusive country club. They also built a successful business for Abby while working for David's eventual ascendancy to becoming a corporate executive at Goliath.

Along the way, David and Abby made—and spent—plenty of money. They also increasingly attracted the attention of many who sought to "advise" them—in areas that included investments, taxes, retirement planning, asset allocation, mortgages, education planning for their children, insurance, and even philanthropy. Sometimes they listened, but usually they didn't, especially when they felt that the "advisor" was really just trying to sell them something. They used tax software that they found online to do their own tax returns—usually right before the deadline.

When David became an officer of Goliath, he was presented with a formal employment agreement. Prior to that time, he had received an offer letter to become an "employee at will" and a series of letters that updated the original offer letter, but he had never received anything so formal until now. The employment agreement was about 15 pages long and addressed base and variable compensation, corporate benefit plans, equity opportunities, termination and severance scenarios, changes of control, and restrictive covenants. David did not feel comfortable negotiating the agreement, as it seemed fair, if not generous, and he also did not feel that it would send the right message to his employer if he hired a lawyer or other advisor to evaluate it—even though the agreement explicitly made David represent that he had been afforded the opportunity to do exactly that.

In addition to his base salary and annual incentive bonuses, David had been granted a series of "nonqualified stock options," "incentive stock options," and "restricted stock" at Goliath, which had long been a public company. These equity awards were all subject to vesting over time, which David understood to mean that if he left Goliath for any reason before the designated vesting period, he would lose the unvested portion of those awards. It seemed pretty simple. David also was given the right to participate in the company's "employee stock purchase plan," which enabled him to make regular purchases of Goliath stock at discounted prices.

David and Abby were only 40 years old when David became an executive officer of Goliath. David was earning a great salary, and Abby's income was ramping up too, after a few slower-growth years in which she simultaneously focused on her business and on the couple's growing children. In fact, Abby seemed increasingly well positioned to capitalize on the information age and the growing needs of businesses to adapt to it. Her company, Slingshot, now had 14 employees and had just leased a newly renovated office; and she was now thinking about further professionalizing the business with a dedicated management team. She and David had the sense that Abby's business was getting too large and complicated to run the way it had been run in its earlier years.

Their lives were increasingly complicated, but they seemed to be happily earning plenty of money and living the good life. As the couple made more money, they gradually raised their standard of living to coincide with their earning power. They didn't behave excessively, but it seemed to them that they never were able to build up any meaningful savings.

David did participate in Goliath's "defined contribution" retirement plan; and he did buy Goliath shares as part of the company's employee stock purchase plan. He also had his stock options and restricted stock awards. Abby had put a limited amount of money away in an individual retirement account, but she had never set up a formal retirement plan for her business; and she usually found herself reinvesting her profits back into her business. She even found it necessary to secure a line of credit from a bank, which she had to guarantee personally, to ensure that she always had enough cash to pay her employees during periods of lagging cash flow.

David and Abby often joked with their friends and family that they were "cash poor" because their money was tied up in their home, their retirement accounts, and in Goliath and Slingshot equity—and they were only now finishing the repayment of their student loans. They even had to borrow against David's retirement account to update the older kitchen and bathrooms in their home.

Still, David and Abby didn't worry too much. Goliath was a great company; David's career was going well—he might even be the CEO one day; and they had more time to save for their children's education and their own retirement. David thought that he could always work harder and that, as his parents taught him so well, his hard work would sustain all of his family's needs. He predicted that he probably could retire at the age of 50 if Goliath's stock continued at its current growth trajectory. Even if he failed, Abby's success with Slingshot offered the promise of a comfortable and strong security net.

But life is not predictable. Two years after David's big promotion, Goliath acquired one of its competitors, Samson Assembly Corp. Fortunately, David didn't lose his job when the companies began to work out the "synergies" between them (though many of his colleagues did). In fact, he was part of the integration team that was charged with creating those synergies. No, the real problems didn't start until about a year later, when it became clear that Goliath had overpaid for the acquisition—dramatically— and that the stock market was unhappy with the acquisition. Goliath's stock plunged, and David and Abby saw the value of David's equity nearly evaporate.

That, however, was only the start of their problems. David just couldn't accept the idea that the company for which his parents worked and that he had always admired above all others was in trouble. He knew that Goliath had taken on enormous debt to finance its acquisition, but he knew in his heart that the company would come back from this setback. That's why he never sold any of the Goliath stock that he held in his retirement account—or the stock that he had acquired as restricted stock or under the company's employee stock purchase plan. He thought, "If I just hold on a while longer, everything will be fine. I just need to be patient. I'd be crazy to sell at these prices when the stock was so much higher just a few months earlier."

But things did not get better. Goliath's problems got worse when a large, national bank unexpectedly filed for bankruptcy, setting off shockwaves in the global markets and triggering a major economic recession. Goliath was unprepared for the consequent tightening of the credit markets and was forced to sell itself to a competitor for a small fraction of its historic value. The day he heard the news of the sale, David was distraught. Usually not outwardly emotional, David cried while he drove home that night. How could he tell Abby that it was all gone?

Within a month, David was laid off, albeit with a severance package equal to one week of his base salary per year of employment. David argued with the human resources department and even the Chief Financial Officer that he should be paid more because his base salary typically was only about 50% of his annual compensation, with the remainder paid under the company's long- and short-term incentive plans. Nevertheless, his employment agreement, the document he had barely read when hired, was clear on the point; and David was now out of work during a major recessionary period, with only 18 weeks of severance.

His options were almost worthless, and his retirement account was decimated, as he had an overconcentration in Goliath stock in his account and had borrowed against it when times were better. Worse still, and to David's surprise, under the terms of his employment agreement, all of David's unvested equity awards would now be forfeited (though they weren't worth too much anyway).

David became depressed. He and Abby argued often. David knew intellectually that he'd be able to get another job, and Abby could always put in longer hours to preserve and continue growing her business. But how did they get here? Were all of their years of hard work for nothing? Well, at least they had their family, and at least they had their health.

And then the unthinkable happened. Maybe it was the stress. Maybe it was the extra pounds he had put on when things got bad at Goliath. Maybe it was that, with all of his hard work, he hadn't had the time to see a doctor in a few years.

At first, David didn't realize he was having a heart attack. He had developed tennis elbow while playing at the club and didn't realize that the pain he felt in his left arm was something quite a bit more this time. In the ambulance, he felt the chaos around him. He heard the technicians working on him. But he was not thinking about himself. He was thinking about his family. How would they live without him? Would he miss seeing his children grow up? How would they remember him? He heard Abby crying…

Chapter 2
The Goals of Executive Financial Planning: Peace of Mind and the Five Pillars

David and Abby often joked with their friends and family that they were "cash poor" because their money was tied up in their home, their retirement accounts, and in Goliath and Slingshot equity—and they were only now finishing the repayment of their student loans. They even had to borrow against David's retirement account to update the older kitchen and bathrooms in their home.

Still, David and Abby didn't worry too much. Goliath was a great company; David's career was going well—he might even be the CEO one day; and they had plenty of time to save for their children's education and their own retirement. David thought that he could always work harder and that, as his parents taught him so well, his hard work would sustain all of his family's needs. He predicted that he probably could retire at the age of 50 if Goliath's stock continued at its current growth trajectory. Even if he failed, Abby's success with Slingshot offered the promise of a comfortable and strong security net.

Stated most simply, the principal goal of executive financial planning is *to provide financial peace of mind* to the executive as well as his or her family and other dependents—peace of mind not only that they won't turn out like David and Abby but also that all of their financial goals and needs will be met. David and Abby could have avoided just about every one of their financial misfortunes had they just spent some time planning for their future. They could have ended up more or less insulated from Goliath's demise and well on their way to a very comfortable retirement, great schools for their children, and the attainment of all of their other dreams.

The rest of this book will offer a detailed examination of the comprehensive financial planning process, offering practical advice that should enable just about any corporate executive to identify and achieve his or her financial needs and goals. Let's start with the basics. Effective financial planning must address the following core needs and fundamental objectives of any corporate executive (Fig. 2.1):

© The Colony Group 2018
M. J. Nathanson et al., *Personal Financial Planning for Executives and Entrepreneurs*, https://doi.org/10.1007/978-3-319-98416-2_2

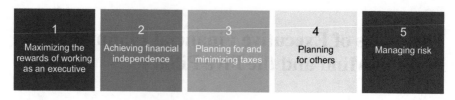

Fig. 2.1 The core needs of a corporate executive

1. Maximizing the rewards of working as an executive
2. Achieving financial independence
3. Planning for and minimizing taxes
4. Planning for others
5. Managing risk

Maximizing the Rewards of Working as an Executive

We saw that David, by dint of education, hard work, and desire, earned an executive position at Goliath. Yet, largely because of his willful ignorance, his failure to prioritize, and his fear of having important discussions with Goliath, he didn't pay sufficient attention to his employment agreement, his benefits, his equity incentives, the manner in which his compensation was paid, or his severance structure, among other issues.

Executives are, by their very position, employees of the corporations for which they work. Certain elements of the employment relationship are standardized across all employees, and these standardized elements typically are described in broadly applicable documents such as an employee manual, benefit plan descriptions, and the like. Yet, many of the critical terms that are specifically applicable to an executive will be set forth in an employment agreement between the executive and the corporation. It is the employment agreement that usually will cover such integral topics as:

- Base and incentive compensation
- Equity-based incentives
- Executive benefits
- Severance
- Restrictive covenants
- Changes of control

Therefore, planning around, negotiating, renegotiating, and understanding the employment agreement becomes central to all planning for corporate executives.

Particularly important can be the restrictive covenants that often are tied to the performance of services by a corporate executive. While less important for the position currently held by the executive, these covenants can dramatically impact the livelihood of the executive in the event that the executive leaves to work at another company. Common restrictive covenants that we will address include agreements relating to:

- Non-competition
- Non-solicitation
- Confidentiality
- Non-disparagement

Achieving Financial Independence

Perhaps the most common financial goal of corporate executives is planning to secure their comfortable retirement. Yet, when we press the question further, we see that, in many cases these executives are not precisely interested in planning for their retirement. In fact, they are more interested in planning for the *option* to retire. More specifically, they want to understand how they can achieve "financial independence," the state at which they can afford to retire or pursue other passions in life and at which the maximization of employment-related income no longer really matters as much. Planning to achieve financial independence by, say, age 60 does not mean planning to retire at age 60. It just means that retirement—or doing something other than serving as a corporate executive—will be an option at age 60.

Achieving financial independence is no easy thing. It requires a careful assessment of many variables and few constants. Some key variables are:

- Life expectancy
- Needs of dependents
- Personal goals
- Income projections
- Expense projections
- Growth of assets and liabilities
- Current and projected taxes
- Inflation
- Macroeconomic conditions

More importantly, achieving financial independence requires the creation of a plan that accounts for all these variables and that has been tested using multiple simulations. And, of course, no plan is worth anything unless it is backed up by the discipline and accountability required to ensure that it is followed, monitored, and modified as necessary to reflect changing conditions.

David and Abby never really approached financial independence. Consequently, they were unprepared for the variables of life and vulnerable both to systemic shocks (the recession) and non-systemic shocks (Goliath's poor decision to acquire Samson and David's heart attack).

Planning for and Minimizing Taxes

It seems like a simple concept: corporate executives should plan to minimize the taxes they have to pay. But, of course, it's not that simple. An executive needs to plan to minimize a variety of taxes, many of which ultimately may be a complete surprise. Even more daunting is the fact that the mechanics of minimizing taxes differ dramatically depending on the circumstances.

Most obvious are income taxes, but remember that income taxes are not just imposed by the federal government. They also can be imposed by state, local, and even foreign governments. All in, these taxes can exceed 50% in some jurisdictions, making it an absolute priority to minimize them whenever possible!

We will spend considerable time discussing techniques that every corporate executive should understand to mitigate the impact of income taxes, but we also will spend time planning for the impact of these taxes. Among the topics we will explore are:

- Deferring or accelerating income for income tax purposes
- Maximizing deductions, exemptions, and exclusions
- Planning for estimated taxes and withholding
- The difference between ordinary income and capital gain
- What types of equity-based grants lead to ordinary income, capital gain, or both
- Understanding the tax aspects of retirement planning
- Maximizing the use of specialized tax provisions that allow for lower tax rates
- The application of different types of income taxes

Corporate executives are also especially prone to a related type of tax: employment taxes. These taxes, which most prominently include Social Security and Medicare taxes, can be substantial. While they are inevitable in some cases, they can be avoided in others—with careful planning. We will discuss the circumstances under which employment taxes can be avoided, and we will demonstrate the considerable value that can be recognized over the longer term by doing so.

Like income taxes, employment taxes are imposed on earned income. In contrast, estate and gift taxes are not imposed when income is earned, but rather they are imposed on existing wealth when transferred to others. In this sense, a corporate executive is far more likely to be focused on minimizing income and employment taxes, as their impact is more current and more obvious. Yet, a failure to address the impact of estate and gift taxes could be disastrous to any executive who wishes to preserve and ultimately share his or her wealth with others, including family members and other heirs. Indeed, when general federal estate and gift taxes are considered alongside related taxes such as the federal generation-skipping-transfer, or "GST," tax as well as the estate and gift taxes imposed by many states, they can approach 100% in some cases! For this reason, the tax-planning process for corporate executives must address not only income and employment taxes but also estate, gift, and other wealth-transfer taxes.

Unfortunately, the tax-planning process does not—and cannot—end even there! Corporate executives are particularly susceptible to some lesser known taxes such as those imposed by the Affordable Care Act on higher earners. Still other taxes that should be addressed include state sales, use, and transfer taxes, as well as certain excise and other taxes.

It comes down to common sense. Some simple planning can maximize the rewards of being a corporate executive. Conversely, a failure to plan can reduce the net value of those rewards. Read on, and we will learn to avoid the latter scenario.

Planning for Others

Having just touched on wealth-transfer taxes such as the estate, gift, and GST taxes, we want to emphasize a very important point that we will revisit many times: minimizing taxes is only one aspect of planning to transfer wealth to others. In addition to maximizing the amount of wealth that can be used for, or transferred to, others, careful and thorough planning will also involve a strategy to ensure the future welfare of family members, non-family dependents, and charities or similar institutions that the executive may wish to support.

We're continually surprised by the number of executives we see for the first time who have done some rudimentary planning around taxes but who have completely ignored such basic but critical concepts as:

- Appointments of guardians and fiduciaries for their dependents
- The use of revocable and irrevocable trusts and similar vehicles to preserve and distribute wealth
- Durable powers of attorney
- Healthcare proxies and directives
- Beneficiary designations
- Forms of ownership
- Education planning
- Donor-advised funds and private foundations
- Charitable trusts

Each of these concepts will be discussed in subsequent chapters of this book.

Managing Risk

Lastly, the planning process for corporate executives must include an analysis of the short-term and long-term risks faced by the executive, with a plan for appropriate countermeasures wherever possible. Most obviously, the executive will need to mitigate *investment* risk through both traditional and non-traditional techniques that may include:

- Asset allocation
- Diversification
- Dollar-cost averaging

- Avoiding market timing
- Hedging concentrated positions
- Tail-risk strategies

Yet, risk mitigation must also extend beyond investments and focus on risks such as death, disability, casualties, litigation, divorce, and issues surrounding children and other dependents. This exercise involves the consideration of a broad spectrum of techniques and instruments:

- Life insurance
- Disability insurance
- Property and casualty insurance
- Liability and excess liability insurance
- Legal filings and exemptions
- Creditor protection, spendthrift, and other trusts
- Limited liability entities
- Protective transfers to others
- Fraud and identity-theft protection and cybersecurity

If executives cannot protect themselves and their loved ones from the known and unknown perils they must face, then all of the other planning in the world ultimately may be for nothing. We'll have much to say about mitigating risks in subsequent chapters.

The Five Pillars of Peace of Mind

As you should now be able to see, through careful, thorough, and effective planning, a corporate executive can achieve peace of mind through a focus on five interrelated goals, which we call the Five Pillars of Peace of Mind (or the "Five Pillars" for short) (Fig. 2.2):

- Maximizing the rewards of working as an executive
- Achieving financial independence
- Planning for and minimizing taxes
- Planning for others
- Managing risk

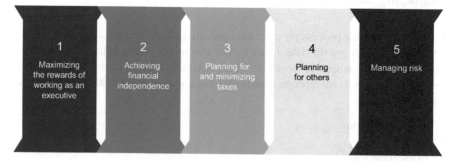

Fig. 2.2 The Five Pillars of peace of mind

You can even think of the Five Pillars as an equation. Only by calculating perfect balance among the Five Pillars can a corporate executive support a state of financial peace of mind. Conversely, a failure to address any of the Five Pillars can cause a great collapse! (Fig. 2.3).

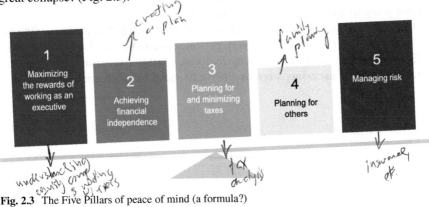

Fig. 2.3 The Five Pillars of peace of mind (a formula?)

But of course it's not quite that simple. Merely balancing each of the Five Pillars, as if they did not interact with and directly impact one another, misses the point that the Five Pillars are interdependent. For example, a corporate executive cannot effectively plan for others without minimizing risks and minimizing taxes; nor can he or she maximize the rewards of being an executive without minimizing taxes.

Thus, a better graphic illustration might look something like this (Fig. 2.4).

Fig. 2.4 The Five Pillars of peace of mind (in action)

We could propose a mathematical construct to measure the existence and strength of peace of mind. We could apply weightings to each of the Five Pillars and then combine them to derive a ratio. We could call that ratio something like the "peace-of-mind ratio," which would be pretty interesting, wouldn't it? Well, sorry, but we are not going to do that. It would be disingenuous.

Peace of mind is a concept that does not lend itself well to precise measurement. It is subjective in nature, and it is very personal. What we can do, however, is to offer concepts that can be used by any corporate executive to ensure that he or she is taking all of the necessary steps to achieve financial peace of mind.

Chapter 3
Understanding and Negotiating Executive Employment Agreements for Success

Remember David's executive employment agreement with Goliath?

When David became an officer of Goliath, he was presented with a formal employment agreement. Prior to that time, he had received an offer letter to become an "employee at will" and a series of letters that updated the original offer letter, but he had never received anything so formal until now. The employment agreement was about 15 pages long and addressed base and variable compensation, corporate benefit plans, equity opportunities, termination and severance scenarios, changes of control, and restrictive covenants. David did not feel comfortable negotiating the agreement, as it seemed fair, if not generous, and he also did not feel that it would send the right message to his employer if he hired a lawyer or other advisor to evaluate it—even though the agreement explicitly made David represent that he had been afforded the opportunity to do exactly that.

Those 15 pages made a big difference to David and his family. Given how things worked out, David should have spent more time understanding, discussing, and even negotiating his employment agreement with Goliath.

In fact, it's fairly typical that David did not do these things. It's also typical that David never had a formal employment agreement until he became an executive. Most companies prefer to remain in control of their employment relationships; and they often conclude that by utilizing basic offer letters and similar writings, they can achieve that goal while continuing to offer their employees the necessary clarity of basic terms. Smaller companies such as Abby's Slingshot are likely to avoid formal employment agreements altogether, using them only when they grow large enough to attract outside, executive-level talent or third-party investors.

A typical offer letter might be two or three pages long and address the following simple terms and concepts:

- **Employment:** brief description of job, title, and reporting structure
- **Term of employment:** recitation that the employee and the employer can terminate the relationship whenever they choose to do so or that there is a specific term
- **Exclusivity:** requirement that the employee work exclusively for the employer

© The Colony Group 2018
M. J. Nathanson et al., *Personal Financial Planning for Executives and Entrepreneurs*, https://doi.org/10.1007/978-3-319-98416-2_3

- **Compensation:** fixed and variable compensation
- **Benefits:** benefit plans and eligibility to participate
- **Paid time off:** vacation, personal time, and holiday policies
- **Restrictive covenants:** non-solicitation, confidentiality, and similar restrictions
- **Company policies:** provisions requiring adherence to company policies and other miscellaneous items

David's initial offer letter from Goliath was barely two pages long and looked like this:

Dear David:

On behalf of Goliath Assembly Company, Inc. (the "Company"), I am pleased to offer you employment with the Company. The purpose of this letter is to summarize the terms of your employment with the Company.

1. *Employment.* You will serve as Manager of Corporate Strategy, reporting directly to Abe Jones and indirectly to Sarah Smith. As Manager of Corporate Strategy, your responsibilities and requirements will include, but may not be limited to, formulating and implementing business strategy for the Company. In addition, you will be responsible for other duties as may be assigned to you by the Company. You agree that the terms of your employment may be changed in the sole discretion of the Company.

2. *At-Will Employment.* Your employment with the Company will be on an "at-will" basis, meaning that either you or the Company may terminate the employment relationship at any time, with or without cause and with or without notice.

3. *Exclusivity.* In return for the compensation payments set forth in this letter, you agree to devote all of your professional time and efforts to the Company and not engage in any other business activities without the prior written consent of the Company.

4. *Compensation.* Your base rate of compensation will be $120,000 per year of employment, paid semimonthly in 24 equal installments, less all applicable taxes and withholdings, to be paid in installments in accordance with the Company's standard payroll practices. Your base salary may be adjusted from time to time in accordance with normal business practices and in the sole discretion of the Company.

5. *Bonus and Incentive Program.* You will be eligible to participate in the Company's Employee Bonus and Long-Term Incentive Program in accordance with its terms and conditions. The rules and conditions for participation in such Program may be changed by the Company at any time without advance notice. You must be an active employee of the Company on the date that any award is distributed in order to be eligible for such award.

(continued)

6. *Benefits*. You will be eligible to participate in any general benefit programs the Company makes available to its employees, provided that you are eligible under the plan documents governing those programs. The benefits made available by the Company and the rules and conditions for participation in such benefit plans may be changed by the Company at any time without advance notice.

7. *Paid Time Off.* You will accrue 1.25 days of paid time off per month per year, to be taken at such times as may be approved in the sole discretion of the Company. Paid time off must be used within 12 months of its accrual.

8. *Restrictive Covenants*. As a condition of your employment, you will be required to execute the Company's Non-Solicitation and Confidentiality Agreement. The Agreement will be provided to you upon commencement of your employment.

9. *Company Policies and Procedures*. You will be required to comply with all Company policies and procedures. Violations may lead to immediate termination of your employment. Furthermore, the Company's premises, including all workspaces and all information technology resources, are subject to oversight and inspection by the Company at any time.

10. *Other Agreements and Governing Law*. You represent that you are not bound by any restriction preventing you from entering into employment with or carrying out your responsibilities to the Company, or which is inconsistent with the terms of this letter. This offer letter is your formal offer of employment and supersedes any and all prior or contemporaneous agreements relating to your employment with the Company. The resolution of any disputes under this letter will be governed by Connecticut law.

11. *Proof of Legal Right to Work.* You will be required to provide the Company with documentary evidence of your identity and eligibility for employment in the United States.

12. *Fair Credit Reporting Act Employment Check*. You will be required to execute authorizations for the Company to procure credit, criminal, and other investigative reports.

This offer is contingent on satisfactory reference checks. If you do not accept this offer within 7 days, it will be deemed to be revoked.

On behalf of the Company,
Joshua F. Jericho
Chief Operating Officer

Note that Goliath's offer letter did precisely what it was intended to do—and no more. It clarified three fundamental components of the employment relationship:

- The employer's expectations of the employee
- The economics underlying the employment relationship
- The employer's ability to retain control over the employment relationship

Corporate executives, however, can usually expect more than an offer letter. Market forces and the basic law of supply and demand often conspire to force companies and their executives to enter into longer, more detailed, and more balanced employment agreements that can be valuable not only for the company but also for the executive— if the executive is well informed and well advised. And these agreements can be absolutely critical in ensuring the financial success or failure of any executive. Companies and their executives must in all cases consider them carefully.

Before we get into the terms of David's 15-page employment agreement with Goliath, let's start with an outline of the key provisions of a typical agreement governing the relationship between a corporate executive and his or her employer. Certainly, agreements will differ depending on the company and the executive, but most agreements contain a universal set of provisions governing the following aspects of the employer-employee relationship.

1. Scope and nature of the relationship
2. Fixed and variable compensation
3. Equity incentives and participation
4. Employee benefits
5. Term, termination, and severance
6. Assignment and changes of control
7. Restrictive covenants
8. Reimbursement of expenses
9. Restrictions on liability
10. Ownership of intellectual and other property
11. Applicable law and dispute resolution

Scope and Nature of the Relationship

Most employment agreements begin by specifying the scope and nature of the relationship. These sections are likely to address some of the basic fundamentals underlying the relationship.

Title

David's executive employment agreement with Goliath was fairly typical, in that it began with a simple recitation of David's title and position.

> The Executive shall be employed by the Company as Senior Vice President of Corporate Strategy. Such title and position may be changed at the reasonable discretion of the Company with advance notice to the Executive consistent with its policies and procedures as adopted from time to time.

In our experience, despite the fact that it will be ever-present in their business lives, many executives fail to focus sufficiently on their title. They often believe that "titles are unimportant." At least, that's what they say. Even if they believe otherwise, they tend to think that they will appear superficial and self-centered if they pay too much attention to their title.

In fact, titles *are* important in the executive landscape. Even if the executive is not focused on his or her title, others *will* focus on it. Employees who are subordinate to the executive will focus on it, as will executives who are higher up on the corporate ladder. Customers, vendors, partners, and just about everyone else will care about titles, and well advised corporate executives should care too.

Indeed, a failure to focus on titles can have other effects on the executive. In some cases, executive benefits will only apply to people who hold the necessary title. Titles might also be relevant to compensatory opportunities, severance provisions, restrictive covenants, equity guidelines, legal requirements, and other important concepts, so they deserve due consideration and attention.

In David's case, he should have negotiated with Goliath to remove the second sentence, which created too much uncertainty surrounding his title. Alternatively, he should have requested that future changes to his title be made only as mutually agreed between Goliath and him.

Duties and Responsibilities

All corporate executives should have job descriptions, which should either be summarized or restated in full within their employment agreements. Yet, the operative provisions in an agreement are likely to reflect some tension between the executive and the employer. Executives are likely to prefer language that ensures that they are performing only the job functions they wish to perform. Employers, however, are likely to prefer the flexibility of being able to redefine those job functions as may be necessary in the future. Here's the applicable language from David's agreement:

> The Executive shall have the normal responsibilities and authority incident to his position as Senior Vice President of Corporate Strategy and such other responsibilities and authority as may reasonably be assigned to him by the Company in the future.

This type of vague clause can lead to conflicts and uncertainty, and David should have requested greater specificity regarding his responsibilities and authority as well as less discretion on the part of Goliath to make changes in the future. At a minimum, he should have requested assurances that his responsibilities and authority would remain consistent with his current status absent a mutual agreement to make a change.

Reporting Structure

Reporting structure is critical not only because it identifies the person or persons who will have control over the manner by which the executive performs his or her duties but also because it can suggest the path through which the company sees the executive advancing in the future. Needless to say, it's also important because if the executive cannot get along with the people to whom he or she directly reports, then the employment relationship may be doomed before it even begins.

Executives should seek a clear, easy-to-understand reporting structure, preferably without too many people to whom he or she must report directly. If possible, the executive also should insist[1] on seeing and understanding the company's overall organizational structure, as the indirect chain of command also can have an impact on the executive, even if that impact is only felt through an intermediary.

Exclusivity

David's employment agreement also contained a fairly standard "exclusivity" clause:

> In return for the compensation payments set forth in this agreement, the Executive agrees to devote all of his professional time and efforts to the Company and not engage in any other business activities without the prior written approval of the Company. Notwithstanding the foregoing, the Executive may serve on the boards of organizations that are exclusively philanthropic in nature, provided that such service does not interfere with the performance of services by the Executive hereunder.

Exclusivity provisions are commonplace and, conceptually, reasonable. Corporate executives usually are well compensated for their services, and, in the absence of a part-time arrangement, their employers generally are entitled to expect that the executives devote all of their business energies and efforts to the Company.

That being said, had David sought the advice of a professional, he might have been advised to request further flexibility. Agreements that are more favorable for executives might provide some additional exceptions (assuming always that the ancillary service in question does not interfere with the performance of core services by the executive):

- The ability to serve on one or more boards of for-profit organizations that are not competitive with the employer
- The ability to provide non-competitive consulting or other services to immediate family members or specifically pre-approved recipients
- Other exceptions as may be approved in advance by the employer upon request by the executive

Base and Variable Compensation

A corporate executive generally can expect an employment agreement to address three key sub-topics in the area of compensation:

- Base compensation
- Short-term incentive plans
- Long-term incentive plans

Base Compensation

While it might appear to be a simple concept, base compensation is anything but simple when it comes to an employment agreement. The agreement, of course, should specify an annual rate of base compensation, but the executive should be thinking in broader terms. While David's employment agreement specified his rate of annual base compensation, it was completely silent on the topic of future increases—or decreases—to his salary!

David could have requested a provision that guaranteed that his salary would not be diminished. He also could have requested a provision that ensured that his base compensation was, and would remain, comparable to similarly situated executives at Goliath. Lastly, he could have requested language that afforded him an annual review of his compensation, with the possibility of future increases, perhaps even guaranteeing him increases at least reflective of the inflationary environment.

Goliath certainly could have rejected David's requests; but it might very well have offered a set of compromises. For example, it is not uncommon for a company to agree that it will only reduce an executive's base compensation if other similarly situated employees are subject to the same reduction. Similarly, companies often agree that they will review an executive's compensation at least annually, though without guaranteeing that it will be increased.

Short-Term Incentive Plans

Short-term incentive plans (or "STIPs") generally are designed to offer annual rewards for achieving the company's short-term goals. These goals may relate to overall company performance. Awards usually are payable in cash but may also be payable in the form of equity awards such as restricted stock or stock options. Typical goals that form the basis of STIPs might include one or more metrics such as the following:

- Earnings per share
- Earnings growth
- Operating income
- Net income
- Revenue
- Revenue growth

They might also include goals that are more centered on business strategy and less centered on financial metrics, such as successfully launching a new product or business line or consummating a merger or other strategic transaction.

It is also common for an STIP to provide specific parameters for payouts. Specifically, these plans may offer a "threshold" and a "target." The threshold is the minimum performance level required to generate a payout, while the target is the specific performance level linked to the company achieving its stated goals. The award payable to the executive can be expected to rise as performance exceeds the threshold and approaches the target. It may even continue to rise after the target is achieved, though some companies will install a cap at some level of outperformance.

In many cases, including David's, there was no opportunity to negotiate the makeup of the company's STIP, as it was devised by the Compensation Committee of the company's board of directors and was intended to be applicable to all executives. The same plan applied to all executives, though their participation percentages varied by position.

Yet, David still would have been wise to understand all of the implications of Goliath's STIP, which was based on a combination of earnings per share and revenue growth. David should have understood that these metrics, while important, were not ones that he could easily impact with his own efforts; nor were they ones that were free of interference from market and other external forces. In turn, he needed to understand that he simply could not count on earning any annual bonuses under the Goliath STIP, a fact that became clear only when it was too late.

David also could have focused on the contractual impact of being terminated prior to the end of the year. His agreement effectively stated that if he left Goliath for any reason prior to the end of the year, then he would receive no bonus at all. He should have argued for a pro-rata bonus in the event that he was terminated without cause or that he left for good reason. We'll discuss those concepts later.

Long-Term Incentive Plans

Long-term incentive plans (or "LTIPs") can offer both cash and equity award components, but equity awards, which will be addressed separately below, are more common in this context. Unlike STIPs, LTIPs commonly are based on performance measured over a multi-year period, such as three years. Likewise, the metrics that are used under an LTIP are measured over longer periods of time, though they again can include measures such as:

* Shareholder return
* Stock appreciation
* Return on equity
* Earnings per share

As is the case in STIPs, the performance criteria can also include non-financial goals, though they will be longer-term goals.

Many companies believe that LTIPs are critical for incenting, aligning, and retaining key employees; and the authors of this book agree! Because LTIPs are often designed around metrics such as shareholder return, which can be impacted by market and other external forces, they can be difficult to rely on as an executive. As was the case with Goliath's STIP, there was little room for negotiation surrounding David's participation in the LTIP; but that did not excuse David from planning for the possibility that the Goliath LTIP ultimately could yield no payout.

Equity Incentives and Participation

The use of equity and equity-like instruments as part of an employment agreement is such a broad and complex topic that we'll have a separate chapter on it later. Nevertheless, we will address a few items in the specific context of employment agreements.

First, it is critical to ensure that an executive employment agreement adequately addresses, either within the agreement itself or as part of a schedule or addendum, the rights of the executive to participate in any relevant plans, programs, or independent grants. While the specific terms of any plans or programs may be outlined in a separate, broadly applicable document (*e.g.*, a stock option plan), the executive's rights to participate in those plans or programs should be addressed in the employment agreement (or a separate grant agreement). Most importantly, the following essential topics should be addressed:

* Nature of the grants
* Grant amounts
* Vesting schedule
* Impact of death, disability, termination, change of control, and other events

We will discuss each of these topics, but first a few words about negotiation. It is important that an executive feel comfortable with the concept of negotiating any and all portions of an employment agreement. Yet, an executive must know when to negotiate and when negotiation is inappropriate. Some provisions are more negotiable than others, and some companies are more receptive to negotiation than others. Provisions relating to equity grants are most likely negotiable by senior executives in private companies or smaller public companies. They often are more difficult to negotiate in the case of junior executives working for larger, public companies that have rigid guidelines and templates for equity grants.

Nature of Grants

The tax and other attributes of the various types of equity and equity-like instruments that may be offered to a corporate executive are addressed in detail elsewhere in this book, but it is helpful to identify the most common types of instruments so that an executive can best understand the landscape (Table 3.1).

Table 3.1 Types of grants

Acronym	Form of grant	Description
ESPPs	Employee stock purchase plans	Widely available plans designed to allow for tax-advantaged purchases of stock at a discount
ISOs	Incentive stock options	Tax-favored options that can offer capital gain and deferral opportunities
NSOs	Nonqualified stock options	Options that lead to ordinary income taxation upon exercise
N/A	Performance shares	Agreement to award vested or unvested stock contingent upon achieving certain objectives
N/A	Phantom shares	Agreement to pay cash equal to appreciation in stock and sometimes dividends, typically subject to vesting and other conditions
N/A	Restricted stock	Stock grants subject to vesting
RSUs	Restricted stock units	Agreement to award stock upon completion of a vesting schedule or other conditions
SARs	Stock appreciation rights	Agreement to pay cash equal to appreciation in stock, typically subject to vesting and other conditions

Amount of Grants

Many companies have devised formulas and guidelines for making grants to executives, and it is fair for an executive to request that his or her grants are consistent with those standards. In some cases, including with respect to ESPPs and ISOs, there are tax-related limitations on the ability to make grants.[2] Restrictions on the deductibility of overall executive compensation payable to the top executives of a public company may also play a role in limiting grants.[3] Globally, however, many companies establish clear guidelines for equity ownership by executives, which ultimately may dictate the precise magnitude of any grants.[4]

Vesting Schedule

Vesting schedules differ from company to company, but most time-based vesting schedules fall within a range of three to five years. Also relevant is how vesting occurs during a time-based vesting period. There are a variety of ways to provide for such vesting, but the most prevalent are:

- An equal percentage vesting annually (*e.g.*, 25% per year over four years)
- A certain percentage vesting after one year, with the remaining vesting ratably on a monthly basis (*e.g.*, 25% after one year and then 2.0833% per month for the next 36 months)
- 100% vesting at the end of the full vesting period (*e.g.*, 100% after four years)

Vesting also can be based on the achievement of non-temporal milestones. While this approach is less common, it can make sense in the right circumstances. Examples might include:

- Hitting a sales target
- Hitting a revenue target
- Achieving another specific goal

Impact of Death, Disability, Changes of Control, Termination, and Other Events

Virtually all employment and ancillary agreements contain provisions that address the impact of death, disability, changes of control, termination, and other extraordinary events on vesting. As David learned (too late), these provisions can be among the most important provisions in the entire agreement!

Some companies take the position that death and disability should end all vesting, with no acceleration of unvested awards. They reason that such awards must be earned through the performance of services and that, of course, this can no longer occur in the case of death or total and permanent disability. Other companies allow for acceleration in the event of death or total and permanent disability on the rationale that such events are beyond the control of the executive, who should not be penalized for events beyond his or her control.

The term "disability" is accompanied in many agreements by the terms "total and permanent" to differentiate from short-term, temporary disability events. In any event, these concepts should be defined in the agreement, often with reference to definitions used in the Internal Revenue Code or elsewhere. The Internal Revenue Code offers multiple definitions, but a common reference, which was used as the basis for David's agreement, defines "total and permanent disability" as follows:

> The Executive is permanently and totally disabled if he is unable to engage in any substantial gainful activity by reason of any medically determinable physical or mental impairment which can be expected to result in death or which has lasted or can be expected to last for a continuous period of not less than 12 months.[5]

Similarly, the agreement should address the impact on vesting of a change of control, such as a merger or acquisition. The calculus here is a bit more complicated than for death or disability, as there are many ways to deal with a change of control. In effect, the main choices are:

- Cease vesting upon a change of control, with all unvested awards being forfeited
- Accelerate all unvested awards upon a change of control
- Allow unvested awards to continue vesting in the form of substitute awards issued by the new company

Given the potential impact of a change of control, the definition of such an event again will be critical. David's agreement, which caused a forfeiture of all unvested awards upon a change of control, contained a definition, described later in this chapter, that ultimately caused David to lose some of his equity.

In any case, an executive should consider the totality of his or her compensation package and how it is structured. If an executive settles for less cash compensation in exchange for the promise of equity or equity-like compensation, then it would be reasonable for the executive to request that death, disability, or a change of control result in acceleration of vesting. If the executive feels adequately compensated through cash or other means, then the executive may feel less inclined to push for acceleration provisions. In David's case, he forfeited real value when Goliath was acquired, and he might have been able to avoid that result had he negotiated for more favorable change-of-control provisions.

As for termination provisions and their impact on vesting, they will also be discussed below; but the general considerations are similar. Vesting typically ceases, and unvested awards typically are forfeited, upon either:

- A voluntary termination by the executive
- An involuntary termination of the executive by the company for cause

Vesting typically does not cease, and unvested awards typically become vested, upon either:

- A termination by the executive for good reason
- An involuntary termination of the executive by the company *other than* for cause

The concepts of "cause" and "good reason" are among the most important in any employment agreement. The definitions assigned to these terms can have dramatic implications, and any executive reviewing or negotiating an employment agreement should think very carefully—and seek out the advice of a professional—when considering these provisions.

The term "cause" is intended to cover the circumstances in which an executive's actions or behavior justify the loss of all unvested awards—and other potentially adverse consequences. If an executive's behavior satisfies the standard of "cause," then he or she should be prepared to lose all unvested awards and, in some cases, even vested awards.

In David's agreement with Goliath, "cause" was defined as:

1. Willful misconduct by the Executive that results or is reasonably likely to result in material harm to the Company and that, if curable, is not cured within thirty (30) days after written notice thereof;
2. A conviction of the Executive of a felony or a conviction that materially and adversely impacts the Executive's ability to perform his or her obligations under this Agreement and that, if curable, is not cured within thirty (30) days after written notice thereof;
3. A material breach of this Agreement by the Executive that results or is reasonably likely to result in material harm to the Company and that, if curable, is not cured within thirty (30) days after written notice thereof;
4. A material breach by the Executive of any other agreement with, or policy of, the Company that results or is reasonably likely to result in material harm to the Company and that, if curable, is not cured within thirty (30) days after written notice thereof; or
5. Gross insubordination of the Executive that, if curable, is not cured within thirty (30) days after written notice thereof.

Under these specified circumstances, David would have been required to forfeit any unvested equity awards, which seems reasonable given the egregious nature of the circumstances identified. In fact, these provisions actually were more favorable than what one might see at other companies. At the very least, David's agreement contained fairly specific conditions for an assertion of cause. It also contained "cure" provisions, which would have allowed him an opportunity to undo the harm he had caused (if possible) and thereby avoid the consequences of a cause-based termination. Well-advised executives will seek out similar provisions in their own agreements—ones that are narrow in scope and allow for a time-limited cure when possible.

But let's suppose that David did nothing wrong—nothing that could be construed as "cause." Let's suppose that, to the contrary, he was the ideal executive who worked hard and was well on his way to earning his equity awards when Goliath decided to relocate its headquarters 200 miles away! Should David lose his unvested equity awards just because he and Abby decide that they do not wish to move? Would such a decision be unreasonable, especially when Abby was running a local business and when the couple's children were attending the local schools?

Under David's agreement, the unfortunate answer to these questions would be "yes!" David failed to request a "good reason" clause, which many companies avoid including as part of their standard employment-contract template. Had he known to ask for it, David would have requested a provision that accelerated his vesting in full if he left Goliath for "good reason," perhaps along the following lines:

> The Executive may terminate this Agreement for Good Reason upon written notice to the Company within thirty (30) days of the condition leading to such termination, provided, however, that the Company shall have thirty (30) days to cure such condition. For purposes of this Agreement, Good Reason shall mean:
>
> A reduction or diminution by the Company in the Executive's title, position, or authority;
>
> A material breach of this Agreement by the Company;
>
> A reduction by the Company in the Executive's base salary, provided, however, that the Company shall be permitted to make such a reduction if it is part of a Company-wide program of making similar reductions to all similarly situated Executives;
>
> An organizational change by the Company that causes the Executive to report to a person other than the Chief Strategic Officer or his or her regularly appointed successor; or
>
> The relocation of the Company's offices at which the Executive currently works to a location more than seventy-five (75) miles from the location of such offices.

Once again, many companies will avoid including a Good Reason clause in their employment agreements. Forward-looking executives will ask for one nonetheless.

Employee Benefits

Most companies offer a standard set of employee benefits to all of their full-time employees and then offer a series of additional benefits to their executives. Often, there is variability among the executive class, with the highest-level executives receiving the most extensive benefit packages.

David's employment agreement with Goliath stated that:

The Executive will be eligible to participate in any and all benefit programs the Company establishes and makes available to its employees from time to time, provided that he is eligible under (and subject to all provisions of) the plan documents governing those programs. Such benefits currently include:

1. *Health Insurance*—The Executive is eligible to participate in the group health insurance plan on an individual or family basis. The Company will pay such portion of the premium as is specified by the policies in effect at the commencement of employment and from time to time thereafter, which may differ based on choice of coverage.

2. *Dental Insurance*—The Executive is eligible to participate in the group dental program on an individual or family basis. The Company will pay such portion of the premium as is specified by the policies in effect at the commencement of employment and from time to time thereafter, which may differ based on choice of coverage.

3. *Disability Insurance*—The Executive is eligible to participate in the Company's long-term disability and short-term disability plans. The Executive would pay the premium, deducted after-tax from his paycheck.

4. *Life Insurance*—The Company will provide the Executive with life insurance in an amount specified by the policies in effect at the commencement of employment and from time to time thereafter. Currently, such amount equals two times (2×) annual base salary but not to exceed the limits of the Company's group term plan.

5. *401(k) Plan*—The Executive will be eligible to make elective deferrals under the Company's 401(k) plan. The executive may elect to contribute up to the maximum amounts allowed under the terms of the plan and any applicable laws.

6. *Profit Sharing Plan*—The Executive will be eligible to participate in the Company's profit-sharing plan under the terms thereof.

7. *Paid Time Off*—The Executive will accrue 1.5 days of paid time off per month per year, to be taken at such times as may be approved in the sole discretion of the Company. Such paid time off must be used within 12 months of its accrual.

The benefits made available by the Company and the rules, terms, and conditions for participation in such benefit plans may be changed by the Company at any time without advance notice.

Note that Goliath offered other benefits as well, but its approach was typical in that it chose to list only a sampling of the benefits it offered. Remember also that in our story, David made the critical mistake of not purchasing disability insurance. He had been perturbed by the fact that he was required to pay the premium himself with after-tax dollars. What he failed to understand is that, in general, when companies choose to have the employees pay for disability insurance with after-tax dollars, they do so in order to ensure that any payouts in the event of disability will be free from federal income taxation. Perhaps if David had asked for another important benefit—an allowance by the Company to pay for the costs of retaining legal and financial advisors to help him review and negotiate his agreement with Goliath—he could have avoided that mistake and all of his other mistakes as well!

An executive should understand the full menu of benefits available to all employees and whether any special benefits might also be made available to him or her. A common request is to ask for benefits that are consistent with those offered to similarly situated employees. A range of potential employee benefits would include the following (Table 3.2).

Table 3.2 Common and uncommon employee benefits

Benefit	Market usage	Description
Cafeteria plan	Common	Company offers multi-faceted plan for benefits such as tax-advantaged spending accounts or public transportation programs
Charitable contribution matches	Less common	Company makes additional contributions to charitable causes based on employee contributions
Contributions of profit-sharing to retirement plan	Common	Company makes contributions to retirement account irrespective of employee contributions
Daycare assistance	Less common	Company provides daycare facilities or allowance for childcare (in some cases solely on an emergency basis)
Dental insurance	Common	Company provides dental insurance, usually with some financial contribution for premiums; may include an orthodontics benefit
Financial planning	Less common	Company provides an allowance for retaining a financial or tax advisor
Free meals	Less common	Company offers free meals on the premises
Gym benefit	Less common	Company offers gym facilities or an allowance for off-site gym membership
Health insurance	Common	Company provides health insurance, usually with some financial contribution for premiums
Health savings accounts	Common	Company provides a tax-advantaged structure, possibly including contributions, for employees to save money for healthcare costs
Life insurance	Common	Company provides limited life insurance, usually based on the amount of salary payable to the employee
Long-term disability insurance	Common	Company provides or facilitates the provision of limited long-term disability insurance, usually based on the amount of salary payable to the employee
Matching contributions to retirement plan	Common	Company makes additional contributions to retirement account based on employee contributions
Paid time off	Common	Paid time off for vacations and holidays

(continued)

Table 3.2 (continued)

Benefit	Market usage	Description
Short-term disability insurance	Common	Company provides or facilitates the provision of limited short-term disability insurance, usually based on the amount of salary payable to the employee
Student loan repayments	Uncommon	Company offers limited repayments of student debt
Tax-preferred retirement and savings plans	Common	Company offers retirement and other savings plans that allow for accumulating savings in a tax-advantaged manner
Tuition reimbursement	Common	Company pays for some or all of any educational expenses, especially related to the company or job performance
Vehicle allowance	Less common	Company provides a vehicle or an allowance for a vehicle
Vision insurance	Common	Company provides vision insurance, usually with some financial contribution for premiums

Term, Termination, and Severance

While most employment relationships are "at will," meaning that the employer and employee are free to terminate the relationship at any time (for any legal, non-discriminatory reason), corporate executives often receive a loose guarantee that they will remain employed for a certain period of time, usually one to five years. We say "loose" because the company usually retains the right to terminate the relationship prior to the end date as long as it is willing to compensate the executive for the early termination.

Ideally, a corporate executive can negotiate for an agreement that allows for a guaranteed term of employment, with the consequences of early termination dependent on the nature of the termination. Nevertheless, even if there is no specified term, the executive should, in some circumstances, expect to be afforded certain benefits upon a termination.

To further this discussion, we must once again refer back to the concepts of "cause" and "good reason," which we previously considered in the specific context of vesting. Now, however, we must address not only whether vesting should be accelerated but also whether severance payments should be awarded to the executive. The concepts are similar. When an employee leaves because of the company's behavior, he or she usually should be appropriately compensated. When an employee leaves because of his or her behavior, there should be little or no compensation.

A common structure might provide for terms consistent with the following matrix (Fig. 3.1).

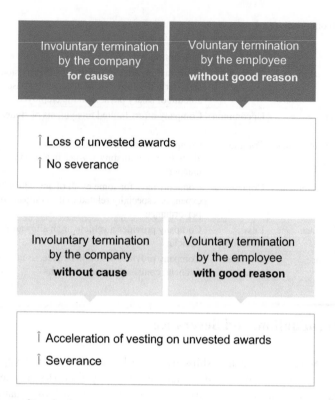

Fig. 3.1 Types of termination

As for the amount of severance to be paid, that, of course, is negotiable and depends on the circumstances. A common starting point for the executive might be an amount of severance equal to what he or she would have been paid during the remainder of any guaranteed employment term or, if there is no term, a fixed period such as six months or one year. An executive is more likely to have negotiation leverage if the executive can show that he or she relied on the existence of a longer term. For example, an executive who moves a family across the country with an expectation of being able to work at a company for several years is in a good position to ask for a generous severance package in the event of an early termination either without cause or for good reason.

Also negotiable will be the timing of any severance payments. The executive usually will want to be paid up front (though there may be tax reasons to seek deferred payments), but the company often will want to pay any severance over time in accordance with its regular payroll periods. A primary motivation of the company for wanting to defer severance payments relates to yet another issue: whether the company can deduct amounts from the severance package to compensate it for any material breaches of the agreement by the executive. Naturally, a company will be loath to pay severance when it simultaneously believes that it has the right to be compensated by the executive for damage caused by the executive.

Assignment and Changes of Control

Most employment agreements contain language that addresses the consequences of a "change of control," an event in which the ownership or control of the company changes so dramatically that the executive might now be working at a company with substantially different leadership and decision-makers than the company for which the executive initially agreed to work. An executive should pay close attention to these provisions, as the executive will want protection in the event the company changes in a manner that fundamentally changes the conditions under which the executive agreed to work for the company.

Change-of-control definitions can vary wildly and can offer different levels of sensitivity as to how much change constitutes a change of control. David's agreement with Goliath offered a long definition that can be summarized to define a change of control as occurring if there is an event or series of related events in which there is:

- An acquisition of 80% or more of either (A) the common stock of the company or (B) the combined voting securities of the company
- A merger, reorganization, sale, or other disposition involving substantially all of the company's assets unless the current shareholders of the company retain more than 20% control of the surviving entity
- A change in the composition of the board of directors in which the members who comprise the board cease to constitute more than 20% of the board vote
- A liquidation of the company

Unfortunately for David, this was not a helpful definition, as Goliath was sold to a competitor in a transaction in which certain legacy Goliath shareholders and board members received 25% of the shares and board votes of the acquiring entity as part of the sale, thereby ensuring sufficient control to avoid a technical change of control. David would have been far better served by a more traditional change of control threshold of 50%.

Specifically, had the sale of Goliath qualified as a change of control, all of David's unvested equity awards would have been vested; he would have received an amplified severance payout equal to the total amount of base and variable compensation he received during the prior year; and his employee benefits would have been continued for a year! That's because David's agreement contained a typical "double trigger" provision that offered David these benefits if two triggers occurred:

- There was a change of control
- David was terminated after or in connection with the change of control without cause

Some agreements contain "single trigger" provisions that provide for such special benefits for employees when there is a change of control even in the absence of a termination. Single-trigger change-of-control clauses are somewhat common but far less common than double-trigger clauses. Nevertheless, an executive who can successfully negotiate for the former will be best protected.

The value of these additional or accelerated benefits attributable to a change of control can be quite substantial. Many therefore call them "golden parachute" payments. That's also what the Internal Revenue Service calls them. Under the Internal Revenue Code, golden parachute payments are subject to substantial additional taxes if they are too large.[6]

Well-advised executives seek not only favorable change-of-control definitions but also favorable tax-related consequences when accelerated payments or benefits are offered. More specifically, they negotiate with their employers regarding the burden of any golden parachute taxes. David's agreement contained a "cutback" provision, which would have reduced David's golden parachute payments to the extent necessary to eliminate the additional taxes. This approach is among the least favorable for an executive, and well advised executives should negotiate for a better provision if possible. A sampling of some potential approaches to dealing with golden parachute taxes follows (Fig. 3.2).

NO PROVISIONS	CUTBACK	BESTNETRESULT	GROSS UP
Agreement is silent on golden parachute taxes	Agreement provides for cutback of benefits to the extent necessary to avoid golden parachute taxes	Agreement provides for cutback to the extent it leads to the best result net of golden parachute taxes	Agreement requires company to pay executive's golden parachute taxes (and sometimes the taxes on this extra payment)

Fig. 3.2 Options for handling golden parachute taxes

Restrictive Covenants

Executive employment agreements usually contain a series of "restrictive covenants" that require the executive to refrain from certain activities during, and sometimes after, the employment period. In reviewing and negotiating these provisions, the executive should be focused on ensuring that these provisions are customary, reasonable, and limited both in scope and time. Common restrictive covenants are set forth below (Fig. 3.3).

Non-Competition	The executive agrees, for a period of time after leaving the company, not to compete with the company.
Non-Service	The executive agrees, for a period of time after leaving the company, not to service the company's clients or customers—regardless of whether solicitation occurs.
Non-Solicitation	The executive agrees, for a period of time after leaving the company, not to solicit the company's clients, customers, employees, or other key relationships (*e.g.*, suppliers or vendors).
Non-Disparagement	The executive agrees not to make false or disparaging statements to the media, industry groups, current or former employees, business partners, clients, or customers of the company regarding the company or its employees or representatives.
Confidentiality	The executive agrees to refrain from disclosing important information to third parties unless the information already is public or there is a legal demand for the information.

Fig. 3.3 Types of restrictive covenants, from most restrictive to least restrictive

Some restrictive covenants ultimately may be legally unenforceable, especially in jurisdictions whose laws are weighted in favor of employees. Yet, the approach of ignoring such provisions on the advice of counsel or others simply because they may not be enforceable is imprudent. Even if they are unenforceable, an executive will wish to avoid the costs and time constraints associated with litigation and should negotiate for reasonable restrictive covenants at the time of entering into the agreement. It might take many thousands of dollars and many years to get a court or other decision-maker to declare a covenant unenforceable!

Executives also should think about the circumstances in which restrictive covenants should cease to be enforceable. For example, an executive should request relief from his or her covenants in the event of:

- A material breach of the employment agreement by the company
- Termination of the executive by the company other than for cause
- Termination by the executive for good reason

Reimbursement of Expenses

On the matter of expenses, David's agreement stated that:

> The Company will, in accordance with its policies in effect from time to time, reimburse the Executive for the reasonable business expenses incurred by the Executive in connection with the performance of the Executive's duties, upon submission of the required documentation pursuant to the Company's policies and procedures.

This provision is fair and customary, as it ensures that the executive will be reimbursed for all ordinary and necessary business expenses incurred by the executive on behalf of the company.[7] Importantly, the executive should be careful to understand the company's procedures for reimbursement, including all deadlines for submitting proof of having incurred the expenses.

Yet, executives also should ask about other expense-related provisions that can be of benefit to them. Among the types of additional expenses for which an executive might request specific consideration are:

- Relocation expenses if a move was or will be required
- An expanded allowance for first-class or business-class travel, especially for longer, overseas business-related trips
- An expanded allowance for business-related meals and entertainment expenses
- An allowance for limited financial, tax, and legal advice

Restrictions on Liability

Most businesses that have employees—and especially ones that have executives—are organized as corporations, limited liability companies, or some other legal structure intended to insulate employees against legal liability for the negligent or other actions or inactions of the company. Yet, these liability shields are not always fully effective and can sometimes be subjected to what lawyers call a common-law or statutory "piercing of the corporate veil." Executives of public or pre-public companies are especially vulnerable,[8] with high-level executives, such as the CEO or CFO, often facing the greatest risks.[9]

Prudent executives should do at least a couple of things to protect themselves. First, they should request proof that the company carries "Directors and Officers" liability insurance with a reputable insurance carrier in an amount adequate to protect the company's executives from any personal liability arising from their business-related conduct. Second, they should request an indemnification clause, requiring the company to protect and hold the executive harmless against any claims relating to the executive's performance of services in the ordinary course.

David's agreement with Goliath contained customary clauses intended to protect David:

> The Company shall indemnify and hold the Executive harmless against any liabilities, damages, costs, and expenses (including attorneys' fees) reasonably and directly incurred in connection with serving as an executive of the Company, whether arising prior to, on, or after the date of termination of employment. The Company shall provide the Executive with coverage under a directors and officers liability insurance policy in amounts and on terms that are consistent with those provided for similarly situated officers of the Company from time to time.

While these clauses generally were appropriate, David also should have requested a copy of Goliath's insurance policies in order to evaluate them and consider any potential gaps in coverage.

Ownership of Intellectual and Other Property

Executives also should be aware of the provisions in an agreement relating to the ownership of property—especially intellectual property. It is common for an agreement to provide that the company owns any personal property, such as computers, artwork, and furniture, afforded by the company to the executive. It is equally common for the agreement to provide, as David's agreement provided, that the company owns:

> ...all inventions, methods, discoveries, trade secrets, secret processes, technologies, know-how, copyrightable materials, developments, software, and works of authorship, whether patentable or not, that are created, conceived, or reduced to practice by or under him, or jointly with others, during his employment by the Company, whether or not during normal working hours or at the offices of the Company.

If the executive believes that there are or may be intellectual property rights that should not be the property of the company, there will need to be explicit exceptions written into the agreement.

Applicable Law and Dispute Resolution

Virtually every employment agreement will conclude with a series of legal provisions, perhaps the most notable of which address the manner in which disputes between the executive and the company will be handled.

David's agreement with Goliath contained the following clause:

> This Agreement shall be governed by, and construed in accordance with, the laws of the State of Connecticut without regard to conflict of laws principles. The parties agree that any suit or proceeding arising directly or indirectly under this Agreement shall be brought solely in the Courts of the State of Connecticut or the United States District Court for the District of Connecticut. The parties irrevocably submit to the *in personam* jurisdiction of the Courts of the State of Connecticut or the United States District Court for the District of Connecticut and agree that any process in any such action may be served upon any of them personally, or by certified or registered mail upon them or their agent, return receipt requested, with the same full force and effect as if personally served upon them in the State of Connecticut. The parties waive any claim that any such jurisdiction is not a convenient forum for any such suit or proceeding and any defense based on lack of *in personam* jurisdiction.

Well, that's a mouthful, but what it basically says is that if David and Goliath have a dispute that requires a third-party to settle it, then they are headed to state or federal court in Connecticut. That may seem simple and fair, but going to court is expensive, requires lawyers, and usually favors the party that can best afford to pay these expenses—the company.

There are a few ways that David could have sought to create a better balance in the event of a dispute with Goliath. First, he could have negotiated a provision that would have addressed the problem of legal expenses. He could have requested a provision that required Goliath to pay his legal expenses in any dispute in which he reasonably alleged and proved a breach of contract or similar action by Goliath. More common would be a provision that simply required the loser to pay for the winner's expenses. Such a provision ensures that an aggrieved executive will be properly compensated for legal expenses in the event of a successful lawsuit against the company. It also provides a disincentive against taking frivolous positions in lawsuits by increasing the potential costs to the loser.

Additionally, David could have requested that any dispute be resolved by mediation or arbitration instead of having to go to court. Mediation involves the use of a neutral third party to facilitate an agreed settlement by the parties. Arbitration involves the use of a neutral third party to make a decision in favor of one of the parties—but in a non-judicial setting. By agreement, it can be binding on the parties, or it can be non-binding, in which case the parties are free to go to court if they do not agree with the non-binding decision of the arbitrator. Both mediation and arbitration (including binding arbitration) are usually less expensive than going to court and can better level the playing field between the executive and the company in the event of a dispute.

A range of options other than simply having to sue in court could have been available, including the following (Fig. 3.4).

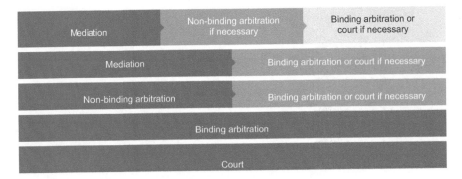

Fig. 3.4 Possible resolution structures for settling a dispute

Notes

1. When we say "insist," we understand that an executive will need to assess all of the relevant circumstances when deciding how hard to push, if at all, for any particular request. We suggest a common-sense approach and fully recognize that compromise is often necessary.
2. See I.R.C. §§ 422 and 423.
3. See, *e.g.*, I.R.C. § 162(m).
4. See, *e.g.*, John Kester, "Companies Set Strict Guidelines on Equity Compensation, Study Finds," Wall Street Journal, March 18, 2015. ("Nine out of 10 of the nation's top public companies had stock ownership guidelines on the books in 2014, according to data from consulting firm Towers Watson").
5. See, I.R.C. § 22(e)(3). David's heart attack came after he left Goliath. Nevertheless, it is important to note that his heart attack might not have amounted to a total and permanent disability, depending on when David's doctors believed he could resume his duties.
6. See I.R.C. §§ 280G and 4999.
7. Note that it is common to limit reimbursement to expenses that are deductible by the company for tax purposes. In general, expenses are deductible by a company only when they are ordinary and necessary. See I.R.C. § 162.
8. See, *e.g.*, Section 16 of the Securities Exchange Act of 1934 and SEC Rule 10b5-1.
9. See, *e.g.*, 18 U.S. Code § 1350.

Chapter 4
The ABCs (and ESPPs, RSUs, SARs, ISOs, and NSOs) of Equity-Based Compensation

In addition to his base salary and annual incentive bonuses, David had been granted a series of "nonqualified stock options," "incentive stock options," and "restricted stock" at Goliath, which had long been a public company. These equity awards were all subject to vesting over time, which David understood to mean that if he left Goliath for any reason before the designated vesting period, he would lose the unvested portion of those awards. It seemed pretty simple. David also was given the right to participate in the company's "employee stock purchase plan," which enabled him to make regular purchases of Goliath stock at discounted prices.

One of the most overlooked, but most important, areas of executive financial planning involves taking advantage of the various kinds of stock-based grants that lurk in complicated-sounding sections of employment agreements and company plans, as well as in countless human resources communications. Many executives, like David, don't take the opportunity to understand these opportunities fully until a company, career, or personal event forces them to look more closely. Since stock valuations, taxes, and careers don't move in a perfectly planned trajectory, it's important to get educated ahead of time.

Good planning is nuanced planning. Securities laws, tax laws, and company ownership and retention guidelines, as well as personal tolerances, needs, and aspirations, are critical in deciding how to utilize these arrangements.

While specific employment agreements and company plans will govern most arrangements, this chapter will explain the most common types of equity-based compensation and address the longer-term planning implications surrounding each type. We will endeavor to address the most important concepts, but it's best to consult with the company's legal and human resources departments (which is mandatory for "insiders" of a public company), as well as experienced tax and financial advisors, when considering equity-based compensation.

© The Colony Group 2018
M. J. Nathanson et al., *Personal Financial Planning for Executives and Entrepreneurs*, https://doi.org/10.1007/978-3-319-98416-2_4

Most executives have a stake in their companies through one or more of the following arrangements:

1. Directly owned company stock
2. Employee stock purchase plans
3. Qualified benefit plans
4. Deferred compensation plans
5. Restricted stock
6. Restricted stock units
7. Stock appreciation rights
8. Incentive stock options
9. Non-qualified stock options

David had access to just about all of these forms of ownership, but while he benefited from some of them, he never took the time to utilize, understand, or plan for them with care. That's an easily avoided mistake, so let's go through them one by one.

Directly Owned Company Stock

Over the years, an executive may acquire company stock through private transactions, the public markets, payouts, and, of course, through various compensatory arrangements. A buildup of company ownership may be part of a well-considered plan to create wealth, meet stock retention guidelines, and align an executive's fortunes with those of the company. In David's case, however, his concentrated buildup of wealth tied to Goliath was an unconscious act caused by indifference. Whatever was offered, he bought—and held. While directly owned shares may be emotionally painful to part with (especially compared to options), selling the shares may be one of the most efficient and effective means of raising capital for diversification. There are several ways to sell, and the specific circumstances can make a big difference. Let's go through some basic guidelines.

Shares Held in Individual Retirement Accounts

Selling shares inside an individual retirement account (an "IRA") is usually the most tax-efficient means to reduce single-company, concentrated ownership and raise capital to diversify a portfolio. Sales inside an IRA are not subject to current taxation, generally allowing appreciated shares in an IRA to be sold without generating a current tax liability.[1]

Highly Appreciated Shares in a 401(k) Plan

Similar to shares held in an IRA, company shares held in a qualified retirement plan such as a 401(k) plan may also be diversified in a tax-efficient manner. Furthermore, they can be eligible for additional tax-favored treatment under the "lump-sum distribution" rules described below under "Shares in Qualified Plans".[2]

Shares Held in Taxable Accounts

In the case of stock held in taxable accounts, it generally is best to begin by selling the shares that have the highest cost basis, since selling those shares will have fewer tax consequences.[3] It may even be possible to realize capital losses by selling shares acquired during market highs.

Holding periods also will be relevant, as it usually will be better to sell stock held for more than one year in order to ensure long-term capital gain treatment. From a tax perspective, it typically is beneficial to avoid taking gains on shares that have been owned for one year or less, as short-term capital gains are subject to higher federal tax rates,[4] and, in some states, are subject to substantially higher state tax rates.[5]

If an executive is fortunate enough to have low-cost, highly appreciated shares that have been held for more than one year, it may also be appropriate to consider using those shares to satisfy any charitable gifting plans or obligations, taking advantage of the opportunity to generate a tax deduction and avoid paying tax on the appreciation.[6] We'll talk more later about disposing of large blocks of shares that have risen substantially in value over time.

In any event, unlike David, a prudent executive should actively manage the sale of his or her company stock. A good practice is to keep, on paper or electronically, a current schedule of all the shares that have been acquired or awarded, listing:

- The date acquired
- The price on the acquisition date, as well as any associated expenses of acquiring the stock (generally the tax basis)
- Any legal or holding-period requirements that may apply
- The specific type of account in which the shares are held

If these records have not been kept up to date, then it will be necessary to recreate them with human resources or with the custodian of the brokerage accounts in which they are held. Did David keep accurate and up-to-date records of his Goliath stock purchases? Take a guess.

As we will see below, it also is necessary to be aware of special rules for any shares acquired through tax-advantaged structures such as employee stock purchase plans. Company stock ownership guidelines and disposition rules set by the SEC and the company must also be understood and followed.

Employee Stock Purchase Plans

Qualified employee stock purchase plans ("ESPPs") afford participants a regular opportunity to purchase company stock, often at a discount from the market price and in a tax-advantaged manner.[7] Most of these plans base the purchase price on the lower of the price at the onset of the offer period or the last purchase date. Current tax rules limit the discount to 15% and also limit the amount of annual participation to $25,000.[8]

These plans are a convenient way to accumulate shares at a potential discount. Yet, they can also offer substantial tax advantages. It is important to keep track of these shares and to remember that there are special tax rules that apply to disposing of shares acquired through ESPPs:

- If a participant holds the shares for at least one year after the purchase date and two years after the grant date, then any gain from the sale of the shares will qualify as long-term capital gain.
- If a participant sells the shares before the end of the above holding periods, then the discount from the initial fair market value will be taxed as compensation income. The balance of the sale proceeds will be deemed a sale of capital asset, and how long they've been held will determine whether the sale generates a long-term or short-term gain.[9]

In an ideal world, a participant in an ESPP would hold the shares for the required periods. But we don't always live in an ideal world. As we will reiterate elsewhere in this book, don't let taxes get in the way of a decision to diversify or otherwise sell the shares of a company that is or could be in distress. David did buy stock through Goliath's ESPP, but that only made his over-concentration in Goliath stock worse. Remember, even when an executive buys stock at a discount, it's still part of his or her portfolio; and it must be considered in executing an appropriate diversification strategy.

Shares in Qualified Plans

As discussed above, diversifying within a retirement plan is generally a wise move, primarily because it is an efficient one for tax purposes. Sales within the plan are tax-deferred, making diversification a less expensive proposition.[10]

In addition, if an executive has substantially appreciated company stock inside a retirement plan, there is another tax-efficient technique that may be available if the executive is separating from the company or is old enough to make penalty-free withdrawals. In such cases, the executive should consider taking the following steps:

1. Take a lump-sum distribution of the full vested balances of all employer plans in a single tax year;
2. Properly roll over the assets other than selected company stock into a qualified IRA; and
3. Take the selected company stock as actual shares, without having converted them into cash.

Under these circumstances, the executive will pay ordinary income tax only on the cost of the stock, with all of the net unrealized appreciation (often referred to as "NUA") eligible to be taxed as capital gain when the stock is sold.[11] Qualifying NUA transactions can be quite favorable, potentially avoiding ordinary income taxation on the NUA, although a complete analysis will be necessary to:

- Ensure that all of the necessary legal requirements are satisfied; and
- Evaluate the benefits against the cost of having to recognize ordinary income on the cost of the stock at the time of the distribution and foregoing the benefits of long-term deferral.

It's important to work with the plan administrator to identify and select the layers of lowest cost basis shares in order to optimize the strategy. It's equally important to engage an expert advisor to compare alternative scenarios to determine the best course of action over the short and long term.[12]

Units in Deferred Compensation Plans

Nonqualified deferred compensation plans effectively stockpile an executive's share value in the company's coffers—generally tax free—until the executive receives or has the right to receive that value.[13] When considering participating in a nonqualified deferred compensation plan, it is important to keep in mind that the executive effectively is acting as an unsecured lender to the company and that the return will be measured by the performance of the shares. David did choose to defer some of his stock grants, and when the value of Goliath shares tanked, he suffered the consequences.

Restricted Stock

A company may offer an executive one or more grants of restricted stock, which are grants of company stock subject to vesting. Vesting usually is tied to the continuation of employment over time but can also be tied to the achievement of specified goals.

As with most forms of executive compensation, there are tax rules that must be considered in order to optimize the net value of restricted stock. Most importantly, an executive who receives restricted stock should consider making an election under Section 83(b) of the Internal Revenue Code with respect to the stock.

In order to explain the effects of making a Section 83(b) election, it is perhaps best to describe what happens when a Section 83(b) election is *not* made. If no election is made, then the receipt of the restricted stock is not considered a taxable event, primarily because it might be forfeited if the conditions for vesting are not satisfied. Instead, taxation occurs at the time of vesting. The amount taxed will be the fair market value of the stock at the time of vesting, and, because the stock was granted in connection with the performance of services by the executive, the fair market value of the stock will be taxed as ordinary compensation income.[14] This income generally will be subject to withholding by the company, requiring the executive to sell some of the stock or to pay with other available cash.[15]

Suppose, however, that the executive thinks that there may be an initial public offering, a major incoming investment, or some other liquidity event in the company's future, preferably when the stock has become highly appreciated. This is when a Section 83(b) election may make sense. If properly executed, a Section 83(b) election causes the executive to include the value of the stock at the time of grant as ordinary compensation income, again subject to withholding. Any future appreciation, however, will not be taxable until the stock is sold, and the appreciation will be taxable not as ordinary compensation income but as capital gain.[16]

A Section 83(b) election can work wonders to reduce the overall tax costs of appreciating stock, but, as in many corners of life, there are also potential disadvantages to making the election. That's because the value is included in income and generally subject to withholding at the time of the grant, regardless of what happens to the share price later. Also, there is no deduction or ordinary loss recognized if, for any reason (*e.g.*, illness or resignation), the executive doesn't stay at the company long enough for the stock grant to vest. Similarly, if the stock vests and is sold at a value less than the amount taxed as compensation income, then the executive will need to settle for a capital loss, not an ordinary loss. Capital losses can offset capital gains and can in some cases offset a very limited amount of ordinary income,[17] but they generally are not as effective as ordinary losses.

For all of these reasons, the decision as to whether to make a Section 83(b) election can be one of the most important decisions an executive needs to make from a tax perspective. It is important to work with tax and financial advisors to consider all of the potential implications. Just ask David.

As to how the election is made, the basic requirements are as follows[18]:

- Must be made within 30 days of grant
- Must be filed with:

  - The company
  - The appropriate IRS Service Center (generally where the executive files his or her 1040)

- Must contain, among other items:
  - The name, address, and taxpayer identification number of the executive
  - A description of the shares on which the election is being made
  - The date or dates on which the shares are transferred and the taxable year for which the election is being made
  - The nature of the restriction or restrictions to which the shares are subject
  - The fair market value at the time of transfer of the shares
  - The amount (if any) paid for the shares
  - A statement that copies have been furnished to the company

Here's an example of a Section 83(b) election:

Election to Include the Value of Restricted Property in Income in the Year of Transfer Pursuant to Code Section 83(b)

Joseph Jacobson
123 Egypt Street
New Canaan, CT 06840
Taxpayer Identification Number: 123-45-6789

Tax Year End: 12/31/2018

Pursuant to Code Sec. 83(b), Joseph Jacobson hereby elects to include the value of certain restricted property in income in the year of the transfer.

As required by Treas. Reg. § 1.83-2(e), the following information is provided for the property that is subject to this election (for the tax year ending 12/31/2018):

Property Transferred: 100 shares of common stock of Luxor Assembly, Inc. (the "Company"), a Delaware corporation.

Date on which property was transferred and tax year of election: January 1, 2018, calendar year 2018.

Fair market value of property at time of transfer with respect to which election is being made: $10,000.00

Total amount paid for the property: $0

Restriction(s) placed upon the property by the transferor: For so long as the holder remains in the service of the Company, the shares will be subject to vesting as follows: twenty five percent (25%) of the shares shall vest on each of January 1, 2019, January 1, 2020, January 1, 2021, and January 1, 2022 such that on January 1, 2022, one hundred percent (100%) of the shares will have vested. If such service is terminated for any reason, all unvested shares will be forfeited.

A copy of this election statement has been furnished to the Company.

_____Date:_____
Joseph Jacobson   January 5, 2018

Restricted Stock Units

Restricted stock units ("RSUs") work a bit differently. An RSU represents a promise by the company to grant stock to the executive if and when the conditions for vesting are satisfied. The actual receipt of stock does not occur until the future, at which point it generally is taxable as ordinary compensation income, subject to withholding.[19] No Section 83(b) election is available upon the grant of RSUs.

Nevertheless, after 2017, certain qualified stock received under an RSU or stock option may be eligible for a Section 83(i) deferral election. The Tax Cuts and Jobs Act of 2017 provides eligible employees an election under Internal Revenue Code Section 83(i) to defer income taxes on the amount of income attributable to the receipt of "qualified stock."[20]

Qualified stock includes, with respect to a qualified employee, stock in a corporation that employs the employee if:

1. The stock is received in settlement of an RSU or in connection with the exercise of a stock option; and
2. The RSU or stock option was granted in connection with the performance of services to an employee by an eligible corporation that satisfies certain requirements, including that the corporation has privately owned stock and has a written plan under which not less than 80% of all U.S. employees are granted RSUs or stock options with the same rights to receive qualified stock.[21]

The election must be made no later than 30 days after the first date the rights of the employee in the stock are transferable or are not subject to a substantial risk of forfeiture, whichever occurs earlier.[22] The manner for making the election is similar to the manner in which an election is made under Section 83(b).[23] If it is made, the income becomes taxable on the earliest to occur of the date on which:

1. The stock becomes transferable;
2. The employee becomes an "excluded employee," generally defined as an individual:
   (a) Who owns or at an any time during the ten preceding calendar years owned 1% or more of the corporation, or
   (b) Who is or has been at any prior time for the corporation the CEO, CFO, acting in that capacity, or related in certain respects to such an individual, or
   (c) Who is one of the four highest compensated officers for the taxable year or any of the ten preceding taxable years;[24]
3. The stock becomes readily tradable on an established securities market;
4. Five years have passed since the first date the employee's right to the stock are transferable or are not subject to a substantial risk of forfeiture, whichever occurs earlier; or
5. The employee properly revokes the election.[25]

The considerations in making a decision as to whether to make a Section 83(i) election are similar, but not identical, to those applicable to making a Section 83(b) election with respect to restricted stock. We recommend a thorough analysis with the help of knowledgeable advisors.[26]

As to what to do with shares received under an RSU from a non-tax perspective, our view is that the decision should be made unemotionally and from a pure investment perspective. As discussed elsewhere in this book, however, members of senior management may be precluded from immediately selling due to regulatory and/or company requirements.

Stock Appreciation Rights

Stock appreciation rights ("SARs") are similar to options in that they're only valuable if the underlying stock appreciates. These grants also typically carry a "vesting" date, after which the executive generally is entitled to cash compensation equal to the appreciation in the company's stock since the grant date of the SAR. This cash is taxed as ordinary compensation income,[27] subject to withholding, whether or not the executive formally exercises the award and takes the cash owed. Executives should routinely consult with their advisors if offered SARs.

Incentive Stock Options

Executives like David who are fortunate enough to have been granted incentive stock options ("ISOs") must familiarize themselves with yet another set of complex rules. Like just about everything we mention in this book, careful attention to details by the executive and his or her advisors yields the best results.

ISOs offer substantial tax advantages but must meet a number of requirements in order to qualify, including the following:

- They can only be granted to employees.
- They must be granted under a written plan that, along with the applicable option agreement for each employee, satisfies several requirements.
- The fair market value of the stock underlying the options cannot exceed $100,000 for any recipient per calendar year.
- The option term must be limited to ten years.
- The option generally must be exercised within three months of separation from service.
- An election cannot have been made under Section 83(i) with respect to the stock received in connection with the exercise of the option.[28]

Assuming that these criteria and a few others are satisfied, then the exercise of an ISO can yield the favorable tax consequences described below, but only if the shares purchased are held for at least two years from the date of grant and one year from the date of exercise. Otherwise, the sale of these shares will be considered a "disqualifying disposition," leading to the less favorable tax result described below.

The taxing scheme for ISOs basically looks like this:

- The *grant* of an ISO is not subject to income taxation.
- Upon *exercise* of an ISO, the option "spread" (the post-grant appreciation in value) at the time of exercise is not subject to regular taxation at exercise, but the option spread is a tax preference when computing the alternative minimum tax ("AMT").
- Upon a *qualifying disposition* in which the above holding-period requirements are satisfied, the gain for regular tax purposes is taxed as capital gain, and the gain for AMT purposes is reduced by the tax preference recognized at exercise.
- Upon a *disqualifying disposition*, in which the above requirements are not met, the spread on the date of exercise will be treated as ordinary compensation income, and the difference between the value on the date of exercise and the sales proceeds will be a capital gain. The tax preference for AMT purposes will be eliminated if the shares are disposed of within the calendar year of exercise.[29]

Sound complicated? That's what advisors are for!

Because of the promise of significant tax savings, ISOs can be an excellent way to build wealth. In general, they should not be exercised until they have developed substantial value or in preparation for a significant capital appreciation event; but, as discussed below, strategic exercises over time can be useful as part of a long-term diversification strategy. If possible, taking into account all of the relevant considerations, executives should take advantage of the tax benefits offered by ISOs.

As we've seen, David left a lot of money on the table—money he couldn't afford to leave on the table—by not paying attention! In the case of a traditional public company like Goliath, the share price might hypothetically double every ten years, assuming anticipated annual growth of approximately 7%. Since markets (and careers) don't move in a straight line, one general rule of thumb is to consider exercising options at the earlier of the doubling in price or three years prior to expiration. The volatility of the stock in question and the executive's employment also play significant roles in determining timing.

It's in any event important to understand how the three-month rule would impact the options in the case of termination, retirement, or other early departure. Some companies provide that, three months after separation, vested options continue as nonqualified options, but at many companies vested options simply expire.

Of course, the primary benefit of ISOs is that if the requisite holding periods are met, the profit on the underlying stock is potentially taxed at favorable capital gain rates and deferred until the stock is eventually disposed. The downside is that the option spread on the date of exercise is included in the AMT calculation. Effective ISO strategies often involve layering exercises over several tax years to minimize the AMT. Exercising ISOs in tandem with non-qualified options or in a year that restricted stock vests may also serve to reduce the impact of the AMT.

Executives who, prior to option exercise, are already facing the AMT may receive reduced benefit from ISO treatment. If there isn't a clear benefit from ISO treatment, then it may be advisable to make a disqualifying disposition, *i.e.*, sell the shares in the same calendar year and treat the initial option spread as ordinary income. Complicated? Yes. Again, professional help may be required in figuring out how to navigate the complexity.

During the 2007–2008 stock market drop, there were many instances of executives getting whipsawed by the AMT. Their options were exercised when the stock price was high, and the executives were faced with a bill for the AMT; but by the time they sold their stock the following calendar year, the proceeds often weren't enough to cover the tax. By not understanding the rules, these executives ended up owing more in AMT than the ultimate value of their stock. Currently, the only way to eliminate the inclusion of the ISO spread as a tax preference in AMT is to sell the shares in the same calendar year as the exercise. Though a credit for the AMT theoretically may be available to take against regular tax in future years, the interplay of the AMT and capital loss rules can cause the benefit to be limited. Again, seek, and take, advice from qualified professionals when appropriate.

Though not practical in all cases, we generally find the following calendar useful in thinking about exercising ISOs and minimizing the AMT (Table 4.1).

Table 4.1 ISO and AMT timetable

January	• Review option positions and begin considering the implications of potential ISO exercises as early in the year as possible. • Consider financing option exercises with existing shares. • Prepare a multi-year tax projection to ensure ISO treatment is warranted. Executives who are always in the AMT may not receive a benefit from ISO treatment. • Consider a plan to exercise non-qualified stock options ("NSOs") later in the year to eliminate/minimize AMT.
November	• Run a tax projection to check for AMT implications. • If in the AMT, consider exercising additional NSOs and/or making a disqualified disposition of the ISO shares acquired by year end, especially if the shares have dropped in value.
December	• Consider making disqualifying dispositions of ISO shares to the extent they are creating AMT liability (unless it is desirable to be a holder of the stock). • Plan ahead for next year's potential option exercises.

Financing Hints

It's also a good idea to devote some thought as to how to raise the money to exercise these options, rather than just automatically writing a check. What's the best way to purchase these option shares?

If, like David, an executive already owns a big chunk of company stock but has a juicy ISO grant ripening, it may make sense to swap some of the shares already owned by the executive to finance the purchase of the option shares if allowable by the underlying plan and option agreement.

Of course, how the exercise is financed may have significant tax consequences. Many plans offer a convenient cashless exercise feature, under which the executive basically gets fewer shares but doesn't put up any cash to pay the exercise price.

However, in the case of ISOs, this feature will cause some of the options' benefits to be eliminated. Unless the intention is to make a disqualifying disposition, it is generally tax smarter to exercise ISOs with existing shares, cash, or borrowings. Again, to navigate both the opportunity and pitfalls of ISOs, we strongly encourage seeking help from experienced advisors.

Non-qualified Stock Options (NSOs)

An option that does not meet all the requirements of an ISO is a non-qualified stock option ("NSO"). These options are among the most popular for companies and are attractive for wealth accumulation but less efficient from a tax perspective.

Like ISOs, NSOs aren't taxed when they are granted; however the option spread, or the difference between the value of the stock on the exercise date and the exercise price, is treated as regular compensation income for income and employment tax purposes and is subject to income tax withholding.[30] Any further gain or loss is recognized when the shares are sold.

Executives who are granted an NSO enjoy the potential growth without risking personal capital prior to exercise. Once exercised, the executive must pay both the exercise price of the option as well as the taxes on the compensation element.

We generally recommend holding NSOs until the executive is ready to cash out. As discussed above, NSOs are often exercised in tandem with ISOs to minimize AMT consequences. Occasionally, when there is a very positive outlook on the underlying stock, it may be beneficial to exercise early by using existing capital or borrowing the funds needed to complete the exercise. A plan to realize future appreciation at capital gain rates and perhaps participate in the dividend income can be a good one. Keep in mind, however, that if the company is public, such optimism may be better placed by purchasing the stock in the marketplace and letting the options run.

Option strategies should also take into account opportunities to minimize employment taxes. The total FICA tax rate is currently 7.65 percent, payable by both the employer and the executive (for a combined tax rate of 15.3 percent); but, of that amount, the Social Security tax of 6.2 percent, payable by both the employer and the executive (for a combined tax rate of 12.4%), is paid only on a limited amount of inflation-adjusted income ($128,400 in 2018).[31] If an executive already has exceeded the Social Security cap, bunching option exercises may offer the benefit of minimizing Social Security taxes.

Here's a general NSO example to consider:

- Executive has vested options for 10,000 shares with an exercise price of $10 per share
- Stock is valued at $10 per share (no appreciation since the option was granted)

- Executive borrows $100,000 at an interest rate of 5% per year to exercise the options
- Two years later, the stock is valued at $50 per share, and the executive sells the shares
- Effective long-term capital gain tax rate is 25%
- Effective ordinary income tax rate is 40%
- For simplicity, ignore employment taxes, the potential deductibility of the interest, and the possibility of dividend payments

We will consider two possible scenarios here: the executive exercises the options immediately, or the executive waits two years to make the exercise.

Early Exercise Versus Delayed Exercise with Immediate Sale

In our example, the executive borrows $100,000 to exercise the options. Two years later, the executive sells the underlying stock for $500,000. Now let's suppose that the executive exercises the option early, before the underlying stock appreciates in value. During the two years prior to sale, the executive will have paid about $10,000 of interest and, upon sale, will owe about $100,000 in capital gain taxes (25% × $400,000 of appreciation). After paying back the loan, the executive's net profit is **$290,000**.

In contrast, if our executive exercises the option only when ready to sell the shares at the higher price, the result is quite different. The executive doesn't borrow any money and, when the options are exercised at the two-year mark, has a $400,000 pre-tax profit and faces a personal tax bill (primarily through withholding) of about $160,000 (40% × $400,000). The net profit is **$240,000**, making the early-exercise approach a better one.

But wait, there's an even better approach.

The Turbo Charge

For an executive who really believes that his or her company stock will appreciate in value, instead of using the loan proceeds of $100,000 to exercise the option early, the executive could have used it to buy 10,000 shares of the company's stock. The executive could then have sold the purchased shares and used the proceeds to pay back the loan and exercise the option after two years. In that case, the executive would have walked away with both the $240,000 from the delayed exercise and $290,000 of net profit from the purchased shares after paying back the loan, capital gains tax, and interest. The net profit: **$530,000**.

Financing Hints

Unlike with ISOs, the method of financing an NSO does not affect the tax consequences of the exercise itself. Many of our clients use a cashless method of exercise to avoid any additional investment in the company.

The following example is useful for explaining tax basis when financing the exercise of an NSO with existing shares:

- The executive has 400 shares of company stock, which is trading at $25. She acquired the stock years ago and believes that her tax basis is about $1 a share, or $400 for the lot.
- She has an NSO grant for 1,000 options that she would like to exercise with a strike price of $10 per share. No matter how she finances the exercise, she understands that she will recognize $15,000 of compensation income on the exercise (1,000 shares times the spread between the current value of $25 and the purchase price of $10).
- Since the Company does not offer a method of cashless exercise, she will finance the exercise by exchanging her 400 existing shares. (Note that this generally should be considered a tax-deferred exchange.)
- The result:

  - The executive recognizes $15,000 of compensation income.
  - The additional 600 shares received will have a tax basis equal to $25 each, totaling $15,000.
  - The other 400 shares will have a carryover tax basis of $1 each and be treated as having a carryover holding period relative to the exchanged shares.

Putting It All Together

While the tax rules are themselves complicated enough, the best way to make the most of equity compensation is to take into account all of the following: current holdings, company and market risks, career plans, and ability (both financially and emotionally) to tolerate the risks and possible losses associated with company equity.

To find the best strategies, ask these critical questions:

1. How much of my net worth is directly tied to the company stock today? What will this percentage look like in 5 years?
2. How secure is the company?
3. Am I in this for the long term, or could there be a shorter window?
4. Am I comfortable with the risks?
5. What am I willing to do about it?

Let's look at each one.

How Much of My Net Worth Is Directly Tied to the Company Stock Today?

Keeping in mind that these equity-based arrangements are designed to align an executive's interests with the company's, the executive may find that he or she has a large concentration of equity in that company. The executive may also be participating in deferred compensation arrangements and nonqualified retirement plans that, in effect, also make the executive a lender to the company. While there can be great opportunity in concentrated wealth, there are also great risks.

How Secure Is the Company?

We recommend that executives read objective research on their industries and companies. If possible, legally and ethically, we also recommend that they talk to competitors; and, as we have reiterated throughout this chapter, we also recommend conferring with financial professionals for their insight. An executive should ask whether, if he or she weren't with the company, they would be investing substantial sums in it. We often coach our C-suite executives to develop their "personal advisory board" of people they trust to give them objective views.

Am I in This for the Long Term, or Could There Be a Shorter Window?

We're talking way beyond impending retirement. By their nature, certain companies, industries, positions, and personalities are destined for shorter trajectories. Imagine having worked for a typewriter maker 30 years ago.

The investment window is critical in that volatility tends to diminish over time. An individual who has a three-year career window may not have the time to recover from a market downswing. Just look at what happened to David.

Am I Comfortable with the Risks?

Risk tolerance is both an emotional and financial barometer. Yes, the stock price imploding is going to feel awful, but, more importantly, what does it to do to the holder's financial security? Financial planning software has matured to the point where advisors can sit with clients and, in real-time, model stock price movements to illustrate risks and game out strategies.

What Will I Do About It?

If a decision is made to start reducing concentration in company stock, an integrated plan of diversification usually begins by triggering the most tax-efficient means of raising liquidity and leaving in place those positions that offer leverage, minimal personal capital expenditure, and tax efficiency. Executives should commit to evaluating regularly how their compensation plans impact financial security. A written plan with dates and/or price targets is essential to optimizing the opportunities while managing risks, minimizing taxes, and balancing the need for long-term financial security.

Special Situations, Hedging, and Rules for Insiders

Techniques for Large Positions of Highly Appreciated Securities

Holders of significant positions in highly appreciated securities may want to consider certain techniques that offer diversification while deferring taxes. These techniques are generally most applicable to positions valued at $500,000 or more and which have appreciated at least three-fold since purchase. For example, a stock that was purchased for $125,000 and that has grown to $500,000 could be a candidate for one of these techniques. We also caution that these ideas are only suitable for those individuals who have access to significant wealth beyond the particular shares and who are free of legal restrictions against engaging in them.

The financial markets have created opportunities for investors to protect against downturns without necessarily selling the underlying stock. The following is a very brief discussion of these very complex financial instruments.

The simplest example is a purchase of what is known as a "put option," which provides the buyer an option to sell the stock at an agreed-upon amount known as "the strike price" during the term of the option. Unfortunately, put options by themselves can be very expensive.

A collar, or forward contract, may make sense for an executive who remains so bullish on the company stock that the executive does not want to part with it at the current price. It also makes sense for an older (or very unhealthy) holder who would like to avoid a taxable event in their lifetime. In both cases, the executive can participate in further upside in the stock (to the extent of the ceiling) and has purchased downside protection (known as the floor). Funds are often advanced to allow for the creation of a diversified portfolio.

An added benefit of these arrangements is the deferral of the tax on capital gains until the contract is settled with shares. The downside to these arrangements include complexity, loss of upside over the negotiated ceiling, potentially higher tax rates on dividends, and fees that may not be transparent to the purchaser.

Trading Plans

There is another complicated strategy available, called a Rule 10b5-1 trading plan. This type of program allows corporate insiders to diversify their stock holdings in a predictable, convenient, and disciplined fashion, while providing an affirmative defense against insider trading. Here are the highlights:

- Pre-arranged stock selling plan, specifying dates, times, and prices or formula for sales (or giving discretion to a third party).[32]
- Trustee or third party may trade on behalf of insider.
- Plan may be implemented during an open corporate trading window.
- Plan may be revoked at any time or altered during an open trading window.
- Insider must comply with SEC Rule 144 requirements (reporting, volume, manner of sale).[33]
- Insider must comply with Securities Exchange Act Section 16 requirements.[34]
- Plan is suspended during underwriting lockup periods.
- Plan may be implemented for stock options, derivative transactions, and principal transactions.

These arrangements must be approved by the company's counsel and should only be modified or altered if absolutely necessary (Table 4.2).

Table 4.2 Tactics for "insiders"

Types of restrictions	Specific examples	Potential solutions
Regulatory (applicable to officers, directors, and owners of 10% or more of the outstanding securities)[a]	• Rule 144 (volume, notice, manner, holding period) • Section 16(a)—disclosure obligation • Section 16(b)—short-swing profits rules • Section 16(c)—prohibition against short sales • Sarbanes-Oxley—Form 4s within 2 business days of any change	Consider with proper disclosures: • Block and coordinated sale programs • Hedges and blind trusts • Monetization strategies, including prepaid forward contracts
Issuer (applicable to officers, directors, employees, and certain individuals with access to sensitive information)	To prevent individuals with access to sensitive non-public financial information from trading on inside information, companies often create: • Blackout policies • Holding-period requirements • Pre-approval processes	• Rule 10b5-1 selling plans
Contractual (applicable to officers, directors, and large shareholders)	Generally invoked by the company or underwriter as a result of a merger or other reorganization or liquidity event. Restrictions include lock-ups, vesting agreements, and restrictions on pledging for specific periods of time or by consent	In certain instances: • Rule 10b5-1 selling plans may be entered during the lock-up period • Monetization strategies such as prepaid forward contracts may also be appropriate

[a]See 17 CFR 230.144; 15 U.S.C. § 78p

Notes

1. See I.R.S. Publications 590A and 590B.
2. See I.R.C. § 401.
3. In general, cost basis is the overall investment made by the executive in the shares, subject to adjustments. Importantly, however, the rules for calculating cost basis can be complex, often requiring their application with expert advice.
4. See I.R.C. § 1.
5. In Massachusetts, for example, short-term capital gain tax rates are more than double the rate of taxation on long-term capital gain. See M.G.L. ch. 62, § 4.
6. See I.R.C. § 170.
7. See I.R.C. § 423.
8. See I.R.C. § 423(b).
9. See I.R.C. § 421(a)(1).
10. See I.R.C. § 401.
11. See I.R.S. Publication 575.
12. It may also be important to consider contributing the NUA shares to a Charitable Remainder Trust, which we'll discuss in Chap. 10.
13. But see I.R.C. § 409A.
14. See I.R.C. § 83.
15. See I.R.C. §§ 3401 and 3402. Withholding generally presupposes an employment relationship.
16. See I.R.C. § 83.
17. See I.R.C. § 1211.
18. See Treas. Reg. § 1.83-2.
19. See I.R.C. §§ 3121(v)(2); Treas. Reg. §1.451-2(a). Again, withholding generally presupposes an employment relationship.
20. See I.R.C. § 83(i). We refer repeatedly to the Tax Cuts and Jobs Act of 2017 throughout this book. Note that certain provisions of this act are scheduled to expire in 2025, potentially leading to future changes in the tax laws.
21. See I.R.C. § 83(i)(2).
22. See I.R.C. § 83(i)(4).
23. See I.R.C. § 83(i)(4).
24. See I.R.C. § 83(i)(3).
25. See I.R.C. § 83(i)(1).
26. If an employee receives qualified stock from an employer that is eligible for the election, the employer generally is required to inform the employee: (1) that income inclusion may be deferrable; (2) that, if the employee makes an inclusion deferral election, the employee must report, at the end of the deferral period, income based on the value of the stock at the time the stock becomes substantially vested, even if the value of the stock decreases by the end of the deferral period; and (3) that the income will be subject to federal income tax withholding, leading to responsibility for the employee. If the employer fails to do so, the employer may be subject to penalties. For more information, see Section 83(i)(6) and "US tax reform: Qualified equity grants by private companies under newly added Section 83(i)," Deloitte, published 2018, https://www2.deloitte.com/content/dam/Deloitte/us/Documents/Tax/us-tax-reform-new-section-83i.pdf.
27. See Treas. Reg. §1.451-2(a).
28. See I.R.C. § 422.
29. See I.R.C. §§ 421 and 422.
30. See I.R.C. § 83(a). Again, we are assuming an employment relationship.
31. See I.R.S. Publication 15.
32. See 17 C.F.R. 240.10b5-1(c).
33. See 17 CFR 230.144.
34. See 15 U.S.C. § 78p.

Chapter 5
The Story of David and Goliath, And Abby and Samson: The Aftermath

David survived—barely. He and Abby spoke at length with David's doctors and learned that David's heart attack was the result of a blockage in the arteries that led to his heart. While the healing process might only take a few months, David's heart would form scars in the affected areas; and those scarred areas would no longer contract properly with the rest of his heart. Unfortunately, his heart would be weaker for the rest of his life.

Shortly after the initial shock of the heart attack, David and Abby realized the full extent to which they had suffered not only a major health-related setback but also a major financial setback. David would need several months before he could even concentrate on finding a new job, let alone working at one, and Abby would need to put all of her energy into her company. David, however, was not in a position to take over Abby's responsibilities at home, and the couple was no longer in a good position to hire any help.

David regretted that he hadn't thought more about disability insurance when he had the chance. Goliath had offered him disability insurance, but David didn't really think he needed it. Like many of his peers, he had thought he was too young for such a thing. Plus, he had been annoyed that he had to pay for it himself and that such a benefit would not have been paid for by Goliath. Someone in human resources had told him that such arrangements were common and ensured that he would receive any insurance proceeds free of tax, but he had been too annoyed to listen. If only he had planned more carefully, he might now be eligible to receive 60% of his annual compensation (up to certain limits but free of taxes), for as long as it took for him to get back to work!

But that, of course, was only one of their problems. In addition to the impairment of David's future ability to earn income, David and Abby now had to deal with the aftershocks of Goliath's implosion. Their failure to pay attention to their asset allocation strategy—if it can be said that they even had one—in both David's retirement accounts and the couple's overall holdings was catastrophic. David and Abby had made several common mistakes. Most obviously, they had not properly diversified their holdings. David, in particular, had allowed his decision-making to be affected

© The Colony Group 2018
M. J. Nathanson et al., *Personal Financial Planning for Executives and Entrepreneurs*, https://doi.org/10.1007/978-3-319-98416-2_5

by his emotional, highly partial attachment to Goliath. Then he allowed his emotions to overcome any rational plan to divest himself of at least some Goliath stock once he realized that Goliath's stock might be heading lower.

David had heard something about "trading plans" at some point in the past. He knew that he was subject to special securities-related rules for making sales of his Goliath stock; and he also knew that a group of other executives had implemented plans to facilitate regular sales of their stock; but David wasn't among that group. David was just always too busy and too confident for these things.

Then there was David's retirement plan. He had too much Goliath stock in that plan, especially when considering his Goliath stock options, his employee stock purchase plan and restricted stock holdings, and, perhaps most importantly, the fact that David relied exclusively on Goliath for his annual compensation income. How could he have allowed himself to take so much risk—to bet so much on the success of one company?

David did have some other holdings in his retirement plan. But those holdings were not well coordinated, and only a few of them were working well from an investment perspective. Well, at least David and Abby had something left, right? Not exactly. That would have been true but for the fact that they had borrowed against the plan assets. True enough, they were really just borrowing from themselves; but it wasn't that simple. Now that they no longer could afford to pay back the plan loan, they would be treated as having received a taxable distribution of the loan balance, yielding a massive tax bill for them at the worst possible time.

And continuing with the theme of taxes, David and Abby's misery only gets worse from there. They had to pay taxes not only on their "deemed distribution" of the outstanding retirement plan loan balance but also on the vested stock options that David had accumulated and not exercised. During Goliath's distressed sale, the acquiring company had agreed to pay out cash to all holders of vested, "in-the-money" stock options. While most of the stock options were underwater and therefore worthless, some of David's options had been valuable enough to earn him a cash payout. David was of course grateful to have the cash, though it was a small fraction of what he had dreamed it would be one day. Yet, he now learned that he would have to pay ordinary income taxes plus employment taxes on the full amount of the payments. This was a great disappointment, as David had understood that, at least for his incentive stock options, he would one day have the benefit of capital-gain taxation at lower rates—if he had followed the rules for ensuring that favorable result.

David did get favorable tax treatment when the outright shares of Goliath stock he owned outside of his retirement plan were acquired by Goliath's competitor, but he was distraught when he finally figured out why. It seemed that David, on the advice of one of his friends at work, made a Section 83(b) election when he had received his restricted stock awards. He remembered that this election had caused him to pay substantial taxes when he received the stock—even though it was still subject to vesting—but he always thought he would have to pay less tax in the future when he finally sold the stock at a gain after it vested.

Unfortunately, he was now selling his vested stock for dramatically less than the value on which he had paid taxes. Even worse, when David was terminated by

Goliath, all of his unvested options and restricted stock were forfeited. Even though David had paid ordinary income taxes on the receipt of his unvested restricted stock, he never actually got the very stock on which he paid those taxes. That's right: David had paid taxes on the value of something that he never got! His only consolation now was a large capital loss that could be used to offset his paltry capital gain.

After accounting for his tax liabilities, David would have a little cash to live on while he and Abby worked to get back on their feet. But they had expanded their lifestyles so much that their expenses were now putting too much pressure on their fragile financial state. They had never planned for the possibility that they might lose their income and savings.

One big and obvious problem was their mortgage, which, because of the recession, was now greater than the value of their home. The recession might ultimately lead to lower mortgage rates, but banks generally do not look favorably upon unemployed executives who do not refinance their mortgages when they should and instead wait to do so when their homes are worth less than their associated loan balances.

Another problem was that David had a friend who had convinced him to buy a whole-life insurance policy a few years ago. David had known that he needed to buy some life insurance, but he didn't really know how much or what type he needed. His friend told him that he needed a $5 million whole-life policy, which would cost him about $50,000 per year. David knew that he could have purchased less expensive term insurance, but his friend had said something about whole-life insurance being partly for investment purposes. David didn't take the time to evaluate his choices and bought the policy from his friend, having never investigated his real needs for insurance and how he could have obtained more efficient policies for his family's particular circumstances. Now he and Abby had to face the real prospect of having to cash out the policy, which had a value of about $35,000, or else have to continue paying premiums they could no longer afford.

Yet, if they cashed out the policy, could David ever get life insurance again? He had just had a heart attack, and his insurability was now very much in question. In short, David had bought himself into an insurance trap—keep his expensive policy that he could no longer afford or risk having no life insurance at all. David felt especially guilty when he remembered that there had been an optional "disability rider" on the policy that would have paid the premiums in the event of David's disability; but remember—David hadn't believed that he could become disabled.

Of course, the expensive insurance policy was only another example of a far larger problem. Everything in David and Abby's life was now too expensive—their home, their cars, their country club, their lifestyle, and just about everything else— even their children.

And what about those children? What about saving for college? As you might expect, David and Abby hadn't really planned for that either. They had always "known" that they could just pay for college out of their accumulated wealth or high incomes. Now what would they do? David remembered what his own parents had taught him about higher education. How could he and Abby have placed so little emphasis around planning for their own children's education when it had been such a priority for David's parents? How could any of this have happened?

And speaking of David's parents, David's aging mother, who already had become frail, was now moving rapidly downhill. Forgetfulness had been leading to dementia, but the stress of David's heart attack had accelerated her condition toward an outright Alzheimer's diagnosis. She could no longer take care of herself and needed to move into an assisted-care facility. Contrary to her core beliefs as a younger woman, Medicare simply did not cover all of the associated expenses, and her assets, as well as those of David's father, would now be depleted fully in anticipation of her moving into the Medicaid system for those who could not afford to pay. And what about David's father? How was he going to get by with only the meager assets that he had accumulated over his lifetime and was allowed to keep and without his partner of five decades?

It was now up to Abby to be the sole earner for a while, and, putting aside issues of childcare, she was up to the task. Yet, while she personally was capable of playing that role, her business was at an inflection point. With a larger lease, a larger extended credit facility, and a larger workforce, Abby's ability to generate substantial income was going to require a renewed commitment that would be more difficult than ever to meet at this time of family crisis. Her forced inattention to growing the business while the children were younger, coupled with the recessionary environment, had led to a new set of challenges. Because she had hired people in anticipation of future sales, she now would need to lay people off if she wanted to make immediate room for her to draw a larger salary.

In turn, Abby now realized that her best choice might be to sell her company, leading her to have multiple consultations with attorneys and accountants (and more bills for her and David). Unfortunately, Abby eventually learned that the after-tax value of her company was artificially lower than she expected because she had incorporated it and had failed to make an important tax election that one accountant called an "S election." This mistake, coupled with the current market conditions, meant that a sale was not going to be the answer to David's and Abby's woes.

Despair set in—a feeling of increasing helplessness. David and Abby had hit rock bottom.

Chapter 6
Achieving Financial Independence: Goals-Based Planning

Along the way, David and Abby made—and spent—plenty of money. They also increasingly attracted the attention of many who sought to "advise" them—in areas that included investments, taxes, retirement planning, asset allocation, mortgages, education planning for their children, insurance, and even philanthropy. Sometimes they listened, but usually they didn't, especially when they felt that the "advisor" was really just trying to sell them something.

Before they became a cautionary tale, David and Abby possessed all the raw materials necessary to achieve financial independence. Rather than independence, David and Abby's lives and lifestyle depended on their next paycheck clearing. When the paychecks stopped, their lives came to a halt. This didn't have to be the case.

Why did David and Abby fail to achieve financial independence? They neglected thoughtful consideration of their goals and were likewise derelict in formulating a plan to achieve their objectives. Without such consideration and planning, they couldn't measure their progress and adjust their strategies, lifestyle, or expectations in case their goals appeared untenable.

David's depression over losing his job and David and Abby's arguments when things got tough might not have happened if they had possessed and shared financial peace of mind: knowledge that their financial needs and objectives could be met. So what if, instead of ignoring unsolicited advice, David and Abby either had sought comprehensive counsel from a competent wealth management professional or, at a minimum, had made a responsible effort to create and follow their own financial plan?

Achieving financial independence starts with a dispassionate, objective, and administrative census of all resources, assets, opportunities, risks, and liabilities. But the key to this truly thoughtful exercise is the highly personal definition of one's own goals. So, what is goals-based planning? How might an executive determine and advance towards his or her goals; and how are goals even identified in the first place?

© The Colony Group 2018
M. J. Nathanson et al., *Personal Financial Planning for Executives and Entrepreneurs*, https://doi.org/10.1007/978-3-319-98416-2_6

Goals-Based Planning

There are many, many different combinations and permutations of personal financial goals, but a list of goals compiled by a younger corporate executive would, in most cases, include:

1. Housing security
2. Education
3. Retirement

Indeed, these goals are so ubiquitous that we can consider them as basic elements of the larger objective of financial independence.

Most younger corporate executives intuitively understand their careers as the means by which this objective will be achieved. Even a couple like David and Abby, who spent very little, if any, time planning their financial future, achieved a certain amount of progress toward financial independence by simply following this intuition. Unfortunately, David and Abby never actively explored their personal vision of financial independence. Had they consciously engaged in goals-based financial planning, they undoubtedly would have been more prepared for the shocks they experienced because they would have been much further down the path toward financial independence.

Goals-based financial planning differs from traditional, generic financial planning in that, as the name suggests, the process elevates personal financial goals to a position of prominence. At the same time, asset accumulation is relegated to a more utilitarian role, as a marker of progress. It may seem like a minor shift, but a goals-based approach should encourage a more holistic focus and engender a greater sense of ownership in the process. With those points in mind, the first step in the process is to consider the possibilities!

This step, by nature, allows for a certain amount of dreaming, which can be fun for some people; but for others, that rather innocuous point can morph into a major roadblock. For younger executives, like David and Abby, financial independence is so far off, with so many unknown experiences and life events in between, that attempting to conceive of it might seem meaningless. In the event that this point does present a roadblock, keep in mind that an executive's vision almost certainly will change and evolve over time. The process allows for change. It expects change. In a goals-based planning process, the steps of monitoring, redefining, and adjusting are almost as critical as developing the initial framework.

To begin, it might help to consider two of the five pillars identified elsewhere in this book, specifically:

- Achieving financial independence; and
- Planning for others.

These pillars will center on asset accumulation over time and for specific reasons. The other pillars, "managing risk," "maximizing rewards," and "planning for taxes," should naturally filter through the discussion when considering asset accumulation goals. As we know, David and Abby were meandering down a path toward financial independence. They had purchased a home and accumulated some retirement savings before calamity struck. Since they had not yet begun saving for their children's education expenses, we may assume they expected current cash flow from employment income to support those expenses.

David and Abby failed to consider the possibilities, and consequently, their future financial goals were ill-defined. Because their goals were ill-defined, they had no particular sense of ownership and attachment to those goals. Without that sense of attachment, they had no specific motivation to maximize asset accumulation toward financial independence; nor did they care enough to thoughtfully and thoroughly protect their assets and their income against unexpected shocks.

Even if dreaming about financial independence comes naturally, those dreams should be tempered, to a degree, by the realities of current income, liabilities, taxes, health, and other externalities. Assumptions about the future, including income and asset growth, needs of dependents, and life expectancy, must also be realistic. If these factors are ignored at the outset, the planning process is likely to result only in failure and frustration.

Putting It All Together: The Financial Planning Process

In order to define financial independence more thoughtfully, both qualitative and quantitative information should be considered. With respect to asset accumulation goals, it is likely that some level of current sacrifice will be required in order to achieve future success. For that reason, values, interests, expectations, and motivations are at least as important as dollar amounts, target dates, and percentage allocations. These qualitative elements will serve as a bonding agent, holding a plan together when the stresses of sacrifice and temptation might otherwise pull it apart.

For David and Abby, the goal of financial independence should never have been in doubt, but they unfortunately failed to appreciate the importance of asking themselves questions like:

• What do we want our future and our children's futures to look like?
• Why is that vision important to us?
• What if one (or both) of us experiences some sort of unexpected calamity?
• How would we respond if we were unprepared?

Had they tried to answer those questions, they may have found it easier to avoid certain financial excesses, such as the country club membership, until a time when the primary goal of financial independence was more secure.

By its nature, qualitative information is personal, and the process by which this information is gleaned might feel like an exercise in self-discovery. It follows, then, that revealing this information to an advisor or any other person, even a spouse, might feel like divulging an intimate secret. But the more honest and open an executive is with his or her answers, the more committed to the goal they will be. Additionally, honest answers will uncover hidden tensions and conflicts that otherwise might have subverted the planning process. Compromise undoubtedly will be required at some point in order to agree on a common vision of financial independence. It is best to identify those tensions at the beginning of the process through honest conversation, rather than learning of them later in some other, more difficult manner.

The quantitative information, of course, is also critical. Data points such as current income, asset values, liability balances and repayment terms, interest and other expenses, and savings rates must be recorded in order to create a detailed plan to achieve financial independence. Quantitative data gathering for a corporate executive also requires submission of information regarding all employer-provided benefits, from savings and incentive plans to insurance coverages, both basic and optional/supplemental, to perquisites. With regard to savings and incentive plans, summary plan documents are vital sources for information and should not be overlooked. In addition to plans and benefits information, information such as insider status, stock ownership thresholds, specific retention requirements, blackout periods, and procedures to obtain permission to sell company stock must also be reviewed.

Much of the planning process for corporate executives necessarily focuses on weaving all such employer-provided benefits together with options available to individuals in the most efficient manner possible. Failing to take full advantage of employer-sponsored tax deferred plans will result in higher-than-necessary tax bills. At the same time, savings deposited to the wrong vehicle or too much savings deposited to the otherwise right vehicle could trigger a violation of tax laws.

Gaps in insurance coverages can be extraordinarily costly. Conversely, duplicating insurance coverages is a waste of after-tax income. Thoughtlessly timed and/or unsanctioned transactions in company stock, at the least, might violate company policy, but in a worst case scenario, such transactions can run afoul of SEC regulations. Considering the potential for inefficiencies and, in certain instances, unlawful behavior, care must be taken to accumulate all relevant information during the data gathering process.

Once goals have been discussed and data have been gathered, an advisor (or the executive if he or she does not prefer to work with an advisor) must carefully review, analyze, and synthesize all of the details in the form of a formal financial plan. The plan does not necessarily need to be in written form, but it must be actionable, complete with recommendations, rationale, and projected results. The plan should address each pillar and clearly prioritize each goal. It should assign tasks, and ideally, it should identify specific timeframes for completion of those tasks.

For example, based on what we know of David and Abby, it seems safe to assume that they never bothered to execute complete estate planning documents, including wills and trusts, financial power of attorney documents, or healthcare proxies and directives.[1] Like many components of financial planning, these documents are critically important to a family's financial viability, but rarely does the work of drafting and execution rise to the level of urgent. A well formulated financial plan should address this topic, assign responsibility for initiating the work, and identify a timeframe for completion.

Of course, even if all parties are agreed and committed, certain tasks might linger unfinished. The planning process anticipates and addresses delays during the monitoring phase. Periodic reviews are designed to reinforce goals by measuring progress and reminding the responsible parties of tasks that need further attention. Without persistent monitoring and periodic reviews, momentum is easily lost and plans fail.

As we learned earlier, even David and Abby occasionally met with advisors, it's likely that at least one of the advisors walked them through a process that resembled this one. Unfortunately, none of the advisors with whom they met were able to engage effectively with David and Abby. The topic(s) addressed might have been too narrow; the goals might have felt advisor-imposed instead of client-generated; the proposed funding levels might have been too daunting; and/or the advisor's commission-based compensation structure might have created a conflict of interest. Perhaps this point should have been raised at the beginning of the chapter, but it is critical that executives who seek professional help choose a knowledgeable, trustworthy, objective advisor to guide them through the goals-based planning process.[2]

The potential for achieving financial independence will suffer if the initial plan and those first steps are faulty. Nevertheless, the true value in the planning process is gleaned over many years. As financial circumstances evolve, a capable advisor or do-it-yourselfer executive will identify new risks of which the executive might not have been aware, adjust original plans as life unfolds, and incorporate entirely new objectives when necessary.

Financial Independence (The Goal of Goals)

Like any personal goal, financial independence is subjective and defined as the state at which an executive can afford to retire or pursue other passions in life and at which the production of employment-related income no longer really matters. We know David and Abby didn't achieve financial independence:

> David knew intellectually that he'd be able to get another job, and Abby could put in longer hours to continue growing her business, but how did they get here? Were all of their years of hard work for nothing?

Faith in oneself is not an accurate predictor of financial independence, unfortunately. With two kids, a big house and an inflating lifestyle, it would be necessary to examine, understand, and make reasonable assumptions about:

- Future income sources
- Future expenses (annual and one-time)
- Liabilities
- Inflation of expenses
- Growth of investments

In order to plan for financial independence, a detailed inventory of all these categories, and more, must be taken. Part of the inventory process is discovery and education. To that end, let's discuss some of the most commonly addressed areas.

Future Income Sources

Let's assume that David and Abby committed to achieving peace of mind while still in greener pastures. (We'll hear more about this later.) David's contract with Goliath provided for a robust (if not well-negotiated) and complex compensation package. It is often helpful for an executive to understand each component of his or her compensation separately before putting the pieces in motion. So let's look at David's package. David's income and compensation included a variety of sources, such as salary and variable compensation, non-qualified stock options, incentive stock options, and restricted stock. Planning for financial independence would also consider maximizing the value of Goliath's defined contribution plan and ESPP.

Abby's income on the other hand, would have been much harder to plan for—but not impossible. If anything, this is not unusual. The marriage of a traditional executive and an entrepreneurial executive highlights the need for planning. Busy, determined, and optimistic dreamers must mind the financial independence gap!

Future Expenses

David and Abby's expenses were inflating, not well-examined, and ultimately prohibitive. We could say their behavior was counter-productive, but without goals to measure their behavior against, it's difficult to say what's productive and what's not.

Let's dive into some of David and Abby's expenses, as might have been done had they properly set out to reach the point where employment-related income would no longer have mattered:

- Education and college
- Child-related expenses
- Liability payments
- Home mortgage and maintenance
- Travel

Saving and spending for college educations deserves a closer look. Even for high-earning big savers, accumulating the funds for two college educations can be burdensome and seem daunting. Planning to fund higher education expenses requires the examination of several variables:

- Current tuition and growth rate
- Current room and board expenses and growth rate
- Savings rate and growth of savings
- Timing of expenses

In many ways, planning to save for college is a microcosm of planning for financial independence. Typically, the goal is to solve for a steady stream of additions into a funding account either up to or through the period at which assets will drain out of the funding account for the expenses. All the while, the cost of college is rising, and the additions to the funding account are (hopefully) growing at an appropriate rate of return.

At a minimum, there are many online calculators that David and Abby could have found with even a quick online search. Let's consider how David and Abby might have saved for college.

We can begin by assuming that David and Abby start saving for college today and that their children are six and four. Also assume that the average annual cost of tuition and fees at a private four-year college stands at over $33,000, while room and board would run about $12,000, and books, transportation, and other costs might add $4,500.[3] We're up to $49,500, so let's call it $50,000—and this could be a conservative number. It would be important for David and Abby to take a look at the costs of colleges at which they could picture their children.

How much is that $50,000 going to "cost" 12, 13, 14, 15, 16, and 17 years from now when David and Abby are funding overlapping college educations? We'll need to find the future value of the $50,000 in each of those years, which requires us to assume some rate of growth for the expense.

According to the College Board, college costs have grown annually by about 5% annually over the last ten years.[4] Growing at 5% per year, that $50,000 will cost $89,792.82 in 12 years, when their oldest starts college, and $114,600.92 in 17 years, when their youngest completes college. The total estimated cost would be $813,705.90 in "future dollars."

How much should David and Abby be saving each year to meet this goal? To figure this out, we'll need to assume a growth rate for this funding account. Let's call that 6%. We can calculate that, if David and Abby were to save a fixed sum annually through each child's college education, they would need to save about $15,550 per year for the youngest and $17,100 for the oldest.

But how should they be going about it? One popular option is through a so-called 529 plan, which is a popular choice and deservedly so. A 529 plan is "a tax-advantaged savings plan designed to encourage saving for future college costs," according to the SEC.[5] Taking their name from the Internal Revenue Code section that governs them, these plans offer the following benefits:

- Tax-deferred growth on invested assets
- Potential for state tax deduction on a portion of contributions (varies by state)
- Simple and cost-effective investment strategies (varies by state)
- A disciplined and sometimes automated approach to savings
- Tax-free withdrawals for qualified educational expenses[6]

And there are several other options David and Abby could have considered. Here is a quick look at two other popular savings tools (Table 6.1)[7]:

Table 6.1 Select education savings tools

	What is it?	Pros	Cons
ESA[a]	The so-called "Education IRA" allows contributions of after-tax funds to grow tax-deferred.	• Qualified education withdrawals are tax-free • Can be used for K-12	• Income phase-outs, $2,000 limit • Beneficiary must be under the age of 18
UTMA/ UGMA[b]	A custodial account invested in the child's name	• Controlled by the custodian/ parent • Flexible—no restriction on use	• Owned by child/ beneficiary • Taxable to child

[a]See I.R.C. § 530

[b]UTMA stands for "Uniform Transfers to Minors Act." UGMA stands for "Uniform Gifts to Minors Act." Many states have adopted these acts, which facilitate the transfers of assets to minors

Liabilities (Including Home Mortgages)

Another big obstacle to David and Abby's financial independence was the liabilities they accumulated in pursuit of an ever-inflating lifestyle. David borrowed from his retirement plan, and the couple had a substantial mortgage on their home. While there might be circumstances that call for loans from a 401(k) account, they are generally best reserved for emergencies because of the embedded tax risk. Specifically, the risk is that the loans are only amortizable as long as the employee remains employed.

If an employee is fired or quits, the aggregate balance of all outstanding loans from the employee's 401(k) plan account may become taxable income in that year. The additional taxable income recognized during a year in which income unexpectedly ceased could present a major cash-flow problem.

Depending on the size of their existing mortgage, David and Abby might have been better served by a home-equity loan or line of credit. Even better, up to a certain limit, provided the loaned amounts represented acquisition indebtedness (such as for home improvements on the same property), David and Abby could have claimed the interest expense as an itemized deduction on their tax return.[8]

The potential tax deductibility of the interest expense on mortgage products contrasts with the fact that repayments on a 401(k) loan, including principal and interest, are made on an after-tax basis. Mortgage products can be much more tax-efficient options for financing home improvements than borrowing against a 401(k) plan balance.[9]

That point aside, the facts of David and Abby's life invite questions. Did they really need those improvements, and could they afford them? They made the decision without considering its net effect on their path to financial independence or placing any value on peace of mind. So, step one for them might have been simple: consider repayment of the 401(k) loan.

Financing a Home

When considering a home purchase, aspiring homeowners generally—but not always—seek financing, often after many years of saving for a down payment. The decision on how and how much to finance can sometimes be confusing. Deciding how much savings to sink into a home in order to optimize a family's path to financial independence is a multifaceted process. Acquiring a personal residence, within one's means and with prior responsible planning, can be a great step towards achieving financial independence.

When defining affordability, two questions are paramount. What percentage of income will be needed to support ownership on a monthly basis; and, what percentage of assets will be needed for a down payment to purchase this home?

David and Abby didn't ask either of these questions. They went ahead and bought a much too expensive house. Don't be like them!

First, and most importantly, work to develop a sustainable housing budget. The budget should include additional expenses, including tax and ongoing maintenance, with assumptions for future increases. After that, there will be many options to finance the home.

Generally, traditional home loans fall into one of two categories: fixed-rate loans and adjustable-rate loans. A fixed-rate loan ensures a fixed interest rate and a fixed monthly payment throughout the life of the loan. Typically, the term will be for 15 years or 30 years. This type of loan serves well those individuals who have good credit scores and plan on sticking around in their new home for a while.

On the other hand, an adjustable-rate mortgage (or "ARM") might offer a lower interest rate for a certain guaranteed period. These types of loans are often attractive in circumstances where the homeowner might not stay in the home long-term and/ or would benefit from a lower payment for the first several years of the repayment period.

Importantly, the embedded risks in an ARM product are the annual interest rate adjustments that might change the monthly payment requirements every year after the rate-lock period expires. When considering an ARM product, prospective borrowers should clearly understand:

1. The duration of the lock period
2. The maximum initial interest-rate adjustment
3. The maximum annual increase to the interest rate after the first adjustment
4. The maximum lifetime increase to the interest rate

These points will help prospective buyers anticipate the upper-bound limit (*i.e.*, worst case) on potential cash-flow requirements during the adjustable phase of the loan repayment period.

No matter the type of loan, one advantage to financing home ownership is the potential tax-deductibility of mortgage interest. Subject to limitations, homeowners who itemize their deductions currently may deduct the mortgage interest expense incurred on up to a specified amount of combined home acquisition debt on a primary residence and/or a designated second home.[10] There are other critical considerations that must be taken into consideration when determining the applicability of this deduction, so homeowners and prospective homeowners should consult with a tax advisor on this topic.

Opportunities

David and Abby left many opportunities on the table, but they did some things right, even if mostly by accident. Although they failed to maximize the potential of employer-sponsored savings plans and equity compensation awards, at least they were in a position to accumulate these benefits, which put them on a potential path towards a secure financial future. By virtue of their work ethic and talent, they were temporarily successful asset accumulators.

Defined Contribution Plans

David was participating in his company's 401(k) plan, as we read earlier. Thoughtful participation in a 401(k) plan would take into account the maximum salary deferral contribution an employee can make.[11] Dollars deferred by an employee into a 401(k) plan usually are pre-tax dollars.[12] As such, these contributions reduce the employee's taxable income (and tax liability) for that year.

However, the entire plan is subject to required minimum distributions, which currently begin the year following the year in which the employee attains age 70½. While the funds grow tax-deferred through retirement, these distributions would be taxed at David's ordinary income tax rate as he received them in retirement.[13] Planning for contributions to, growth within, and distributions from these building-block retirement plans is an essential part of securing financial independence.

Taxable Savings

Liquidity, or having cash available, was a key factor in David and Abby's financial crisis. They were at least somewhat wealthy on paper, but much of their wealth was either illiquid or, as in the case of equity-incentive compensation, not yet realized.

They were in no position to respond quickly when calamity struck or opportunity arose. They suffered from a lack of accountability—to themselves and to each other. They only considered what they wanted, and never what they might need.

How much better would David and Abby have fared, for instance, if they had saved a sum sufficient to cover three to six months of expenses and if that sum had been held in highly liquid cash or cash-equivalent investments? How would life have been different after Goliath's downfall had they maximized cash compensation and systematically sold company stock holdings to build a diversified investment portfolio?

Once executives are able to comprehend the variables in their financial independence equation, the next step is to codify everything into a dynamic, written financial plan.

An Actionable, Written Financial Plan

A written financial plan opens up the dynamic nature of a family's financial situation. When individuals ask themselves, each other, and their advisors "what if," the written financial plan lets them examine and test each consideration.

Had David and Abby seen—on paper or on a screen—the differences that saving, investing, controlling expenses, and skipping the home renovation could have made, would they have acted the same? What if they understood how a drop in Goliath stock would affect their long-term financial security? Would they have reallocated funds and perhaps exercised/sold some Goliath options/shares at appropriate points in time?

If David and Abby were asked how they were tracking their assets, liabilities, income, and expenses, what would they have said? At inception, a written financial plan aims to capture and animate those categories in the service of goal achievement—funding education, paying for a home, minimizing risk, and securing financial independence.

A walk through a written financial plan might start with a review of all the underlying assumptions, allowing David and Abby the chance to opine on what looks right and what looks wrong. It helps if all agree on the "facts" before diving deeper. Besides financial items, certain items such as retirement dates, timing of one-off expenses (*e.g.*, weddings, round-the-world trips, etc.) must be assumed.

To create a balance sheet, it is necessary to collect as much of an executive's financial document set as possible and consider each item to ensure that it is properly reflected. An example is set forth below (Table 6.2).

Next, some items will be individually scheduled—such as stock plans—according to the distinct terms of each grant (Table 6.3). As the options and shares flow into the plan, both the income and also the cost of each share (exercise cost, tax owed, etc.) must be reflected. Entries must be made for real and personal property, life insurance, and anything else upon which one can place a value or cost.

Similarly, liabilities must be reflected and modeled properly. The plan will reflect not just the outstanding balance of a mortgage but also the relevant provisions, such as interest expense, nature of the interest rate (*i.e.*, fixed or adjustable), loan term, and balloon payments.

Table 6.2 Balance sheet

	David	Abby	Joint – WROS	Total
Assets				
Non-qualified assets				
Cash equivalents				
Joint checking	–	–	40,000	40,000
Joint savings	–	–	50,000	50,000
Taxable investments				
Brokerage account	65,000	–	–	65,000
Goliath stock—outright	100,000	–	–	100,000
Insurance policies				
David's whole life	35,000	–	–	35,000
Retirement assets				
Qualified retirement				
Abby's IRA	–	55,000	–	55,000
David's 401k	250,000	–	–	250,000
Deferred compensation				
Employee stock purchase plan	110,000	–	–	110,000
Stock options				
Goliath ISOs	80,000	–	–	80,000
Goliath NSOs	450,000	–	–	450,000
Goliath RSUs	117,000	–	–	117,000
Business interests				
Slingshot	–	1,500,000	–	1,500,000
Real estate assets				
Family home	–	–	2,000,000	2,000,000
Total assets	1,207,000	1,555,000	2,090,000	4,852,000
Liabilities				
Long term liabilities				
Home mortgage	–	–	(1,100,000)	(1,100,000)
Personal line of credit	–	(500,000)	–	(500,000)
Total liabilities	0	(500,000)	(1,100,000)	(1,600,000)
Total net worth	$1,207,000	$1,055,000	$990,000	$3,252,000

Once forward-looking income and expenses are laid on top of the plan (like the education savings and expenses discussed above), it is necessary to project the plan forward in a series of tables, schedules, and charts and begin to make judgments and decisions. However, one cannot attempt to project income, expenses, and investments without first agreeing on reasonable assumptions for growth of investments and inflation of expenses and income. These growth assumptions facilitate the extrapolation of a straight-line picture of David and Abby's life—and even death. A basic example of a five-year cash-flow analysis is provided in Table 6.4.

Table 6.3 Stock plan schedule

Grant	Grant type	Grant date	Exp. date	Exercise price	Shares granted	Shares vested	Shares exercised	Shares exercisable	Market value	Exercise cost	Profit pre-tax	Est. tax	Net value
Goliath ISOs (TICKER: GLTH—Market price: $13.0000)													
ISO 1	ISO	1/1/2014	1/1/2024	$9.00	10,000.00	10,000.00	0.00	10,000.00	$130,000	$90,000	$40,000	$14,800	$25,200
ISO 2	ISO	1/1/2015	1/1/2025	$9.00	10,000.00	10,000.00	0.00	10,000.00	$130,000	$90,000	$40,000	$14,800	$25,200
ISO 3	ISO	1/1/2016	1/1/2026	$9.00	10,000.00	0.00	0.00	0.00	$0	$0	$0	$0	$0
Totals					**30,000.00**	**20,000.00**	**0.00**	**20,000.00**	**$260,000**	**$180,000**	**$80,000**	**$29,600**	**$50,400**
Goliath NSOs (TICKER: GLTH—Market price: $13.0000)													
NSO 1	NSO	1/1/2014	1/1/2024	$8.00	50,000.00	40,000.00	0.00	40,000.00	$520,000	$320,000	$200,000	$74,000	$126,000
NSO 2	NSO	1/1/2015	1/1/2025	$9.00	60,000.00	36,000.00	0.00	36,000.00	$468,000	$324,000	$144,000	$53,280	$90,720
NSO 3	NSO	1/1/2016	1/1/2026	$10.00	65,000.00	26,000.00	0.00	26,000.00	$338,000	$260,000	$78,000	$28,860	$49,140
NSO 4	NSO	1/1/2017	1/1/2027	$11.00	70,000.00	14,000.00	0.00	14,000.00	$182,000	$154,000	$28,000	$10,360	$17,640
Totals					**245,000.00**	**116,000.00**	**0.00**	**116,000.00**	**$1,508,000**	**$1,058,000**	**$450,000**	**$166,500**	**$283,500**
Goliath RSUs (TICKER: GLTH—Market price: $13.0000)													
RSU 1	Restricted	1/1/2015	1/1/2019	$0.00	6,000.00	6,000.00	4,000.00	2,000.00	$26,000	$0	$26,000	$9,620	$16,380
RSU 2	Restricted	1/1/2016	1/1/2020	$0.00	9,000.00	6,000.00	3,000.00	3,000.00	$39,000	$0	$39,000	$14,430	$24,570
RSU 3	Restricted	1/1/2017	1/1/2021	$0.00	20,000.00	4,000.00	0.00	4,000.00	$52,000	$0	$52,000	$19,240	$32,760
Totals					**35,000.00**	**16,000.00**	**7,000.00**	**9,000.00**	**$117,000**	**$0**	**$117,000**	**$43,290**	**$73,710**
Grand Totals					**310,000.00**	**152,000.00**	**7,000.00**	**145,000.00**	**$1,885,000**	**$1,238,000**	**$647,000**	**$239,390**	**$407,610**

Prepared using technology provided by eMoney Advisor. © 2018 FMR LLC. All rights reserved. Used with permission

Table 6.4 5-year cash-flow analysis

Year/Age	2018 (48/48)	2019 (49/49)	2020 (50/50)	2021 (51/51)	2022 (52/52)
Portfolio asset balances (beginning of year)					
Taxable investments	165,000	481,845	737,516	1,285,366	1,717,293
Retirement accounts	415,000	458,205	504,641	561,474	621,775
Cash accounts	90,000	90,009	90,018	90,027	90,036
Insurance accounts	35,000	35,945	36,916	37,913	38,937
Stock options/grants	647,000	260,000	390,000	130,000	0
Total portfolio asset balances (beginning of year)	1,352,000	1,326,004	1,759,091	2,104,780	2,468,041
Cash inflows					
Salary					
David bonus	460,000	472,420	485,175	498,275	511,728
David LTIP	350,000	359,450	369,155	379,122	389,358
David salary	600,000	616,200	632,837	649,924	667,472
Stock options/grants sale	1,625,000	728,000	819,000	533,000	182,000
Total cash inflows	3,035,000	2,176,070	2,306,167	2,060,321	1,750,558
Cash outflows					
Living expenses	350,000	359,450	369,155	379,122	389,358
Liabilities	194,748	194,748	194,748	194,723	59,268
Stock options/grants purchase	1,238,000	562,000	392,000	284,000	154,000
Insurance premiums	50,000	50,000	50,000	50,000	50,000
Taxes	802,942	687,589	690,995	689,010	665,236
Other expenses					
Private clubs	45,000	46,215	47,463	48,745	50,061
Real estate tax	20,000	20,540	21,095	21,665	22,250
Planned savings	24,000	25,000	33,000	33,500	34,500
Total cash outflows	2,724,690	1,945,542	1,798,456	1,700,765	1,424,673
Total inflows	3,035,000	2,176,070	2,306,167	2,060,321	1,750,558
LESS: Total outflows	2,724,690	1,945,542	1,798,456	1,700,765	1,424,673
EQUALS: Net cash flow	310,310	230,528	507,711	359,556	325,885
Total portfolio asset balances (end of year)	**1,326,004**	**1,759,091**	**2,104,780**	**2,468,041**	**2,957,211**

Prepared using technology provided by eMoney Advisor. © 2018 FMR LLC. All rights reserved. Used with permission. Note that, in this table, Total Cash Inflows less Total Cash Outflows equals Net Cash Flow. However, the calculation to determine Total Portfolio Asset Balances (End of Year) includes important inputs that are not illustrated in the table. Those inputs include, but are not necessarily limited to, portfolio growth and net stock option activity, as well as offsets for inputs like planned savings, which are illustrated in the table as cash outflows but, ultimately, are accretive to portfolio value

Now comes the real utility of the written plan. The plan must be made a dynamic tool for answering questions and forming judgments. Assumptions and goals must be tested. Suppose that David and Abby run through the numbers and happily see that their employment and compensation should last a lifetime assuming they retire at age 60. How much conviction should be placed upon that observation?

One way financial advisors attempt to achieve comfort with the conclusion of a written plan is to run a Monte Carlo analysis (Fig. 6.1). A Monte Carlo analysis acts as a stress test on the straight-line cash-flow plan by applying repeated and randomly sampled historical investment returns to a given portfolio over a defined time horizon (*e.g.*, life expectancy). Monte Carlo testing might run 100, 1,000, or 10,000 trials.

Judged against a goal, say $10 million, to be remaining at the end of the plan, each independent trial will result in either success or failure. Taken collectively, those trials will present a success rate (or failure rate, depending on how one views the output) for that specific set of inputs. It is possible that a cash-flow plan that looks quite healthy in the straight-line analysis would result in a low probability of success when stress tested in the more dynamic Monte Carlo analysis. If the results of the Monte Carlo analysis are unsatisfactory, changes can be made to the plan to create a higher likelihood of success. Of course, changes made to the plan are not worth anything unless they are carried out in real life.

Even if the initial Monte Carlo analysis produces a very positive result, however, it should not be an excuse to file the plan away and return to complacency. Circumstances and assumptions that were used in the initial plan can and will change over time. Persistent monitoring and review are necessary to ensure that progress toward financial independence is not derailed. It is worth noting that planning is not prediction. The plan must be used as a decision-making tool and a measuring stick against which to measure outcomes.

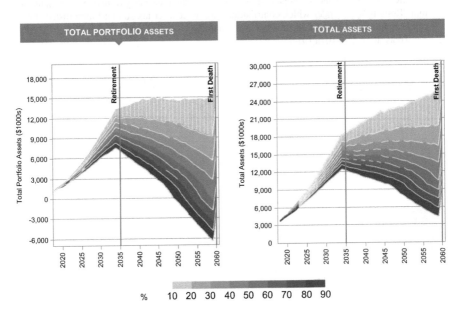

Fig. 6.1 Monte Carlo analysis
(Prepared using technology provided by eMoney Advisor. © 2018 FMR LLC. All rights reserved. Used with permission.)

Notes

1. See Chap. 9.
2. See Chap. 12.
3. See "Average Published Undergraduate Charges by Sector, 2016–17," The College Board, published 2017, https://trends.collegeboard.org/college-pricing/figures-tables/average-published-undergraduate-charges-sector-2017-18.
4. See "Average Published Undergraduate Charges by Sector, 2016–17," The College Board, published 2017, https://trends.collegeboard.org/college-pricing/figures-tables/average-published-undergraduate-charges-sector-2017-18.
5. See "An Introduction to 529 Plans," The U.S. Securities and Exchange Commission, published August 8, 2012, https://www.sec.gov/reportspubs/investor-publications/investorpubsintro529htm.html. See also Chap. 8.
6. See I.R.C. § 529. Under the current federal tax code, "qualified educational expenses" also include $10,000 a year for "elementary or secondary public, private or religious school." See I.R.C. § 529(c)(7) and (e)(3)(a). As always, professional advice should be sought to determine whether relevant state tax codes and 529 plans are in agreement with the federal tax code.
7. Additional options are discussed elsewhere in this book.
8. See I.R.C. § 163.
9. See Chap. 8 for a further discussion of the tax considerations relative to debt.
10. See I.R.C. § 163. The current limit is $750,000, but the limit is higher for home acquisition mortgages incurred prior to December 15, 2017. A further discussion is offered in Chap. 8.
11. For 2018, the contribution limit is $18,500, or $24,500 for employees over 50. Including any employer contributions (if any), the maximum annual contribution into a 401(k) plan in 2018 is $55,000, or $61,000 for taxpayers over the age of 50.
12. See I.R.C. §§ 402(g) and 414(v) and 415(c). But note the possibility of making contributions to a "Roth 401(k)," under which contributions are made after tax so that future distributions can be made free of federal income tax. See Chap. 8.
13. See Treas. Reg. § 1.401(a)(9)-5.

Chapter 7
Investment Planning in Five Steps

Their failure to pay attention to their asset allocation strategy—if it can be said that they even had one—not only in David's retirement accounts but also in the couple's overall holdings was catastrophic. David and Abby had made several common mistakes. Most obviously, they had not properly diversified their overall holdings. David, in particular, had allowed his decision-making to be affected by his emotional, highly partial attachment to Goliath; and then he allowed his emotions to overcome any rational plan to divest himself of at least some Goliath stock once he realized that Goliath's stock might be heading lower.

*   *   *

Then there was David's retirement plan. He had too much Goliath stock in that plan, especially when considering his Goliath stock options, his employee stock purchase plan and restricted stock holdings, and, perhaps most importantly, the fact that David relied exclusively on Goliath for his annual compensation income. How could he have allowed himself to take so much risk—to bet so much on the success of one company?

David did have some other holdings in his retirement plan. But those holdings were not well coordinated, and only a few of them were working well from an investment perspective.

As we have seen, David and Abby never really bothered with an investment plan—and they paid a steep price for their indifference. In their defense, our experience suggests that many busy executives, like David and Abby, fail to create a thoughtful plan and follow a disciplined savings and investment process. A well-structured investment portfolio requires a planning process of developing and setting realistic goals, identifying return objectives, diversifying risk, and monitoring investment performance (Fig. 7.1). Knowledge of some basic investment concepts can make the time spent planning an investment strategy more productive and help set appropriate investment expectations for a portfolio.

© The Colony Group 2018
M. J. Nathanson et al., *Personal Financial Planning for Executives and Entrepreneurs*, https://doi.org/10.1007/978-3-319-98416-2_7

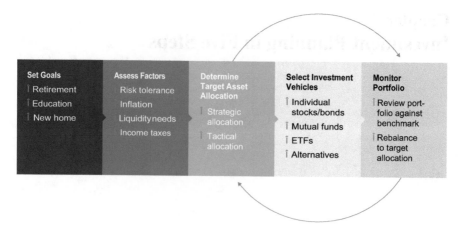

Fig. 7.1 The investment planning process

Step 1: Draft an Investment Policy Statement

Investment goals will differ with the needs and preferences of each investor, and they will probably change in each stage of life. A single person in his or her twenties, for example, may be striving to purchase a first home or pay for higher education costs. A married person in the next stage of life may be buying a vacation home, concentrating on supporting a family, and providing for his or her children's future education. A person close to retirement may be ready to live comfortably from the nest egg he or she has created.

A thoughtful investment policy statement will help achieve personal investment goals by directing a customized asset allocation and investment strategy. We recommend considering the following basic questions at a minimum.

- **Time horizon:** Are you a long-term investor? Do you have 15 or 20 years to invest your money before you will need to access it? Do your investment goals include funding long-term projects such as your children's education or your own retirement savings?
- **Liquidity requirements:** Do you require income from your investments, or are you able to set aside your money for a long period of time?
- **Risk tolerance:** How much variability of return can you tolerate in your investment portfolio? Would a significant drop in value cause you to abandon your investment plan?
- **Asset allocation and investments:** What are the right securities to hold to help you achieve your desired return and risk levels?
- **Tax considerations:** Are your investment accounts taxable or not? What is your marginal federal tax bracket? What state and local taxes may apply? What is your future projected tax situation? Do you hold highly appreciated securities?
- **Legal constraints:** Are you restricted from holding securities of your employer and/or competitors? Are there compliance requirements you must meet?
- **Preferences and restrictions:** Are there any personal preferences or exclusions you wish to express in your investment portfolio, such as environmental or social criteria?

Instead of building those home improvements, David and Abby would have been better off building an investment portfolio after they had set aside sufficient emergency funds. As a general rule, most people should consider setting aside three to six months' worth of living expenses in a highly liquid investment, such as a money-market fund. These savings can provide a buffer against unexpected events, such as a job loss or medical crisis.

David and Abby's lack of an emergency fund exacerbated many of their eventual financial problems. With two young children, a substantial mortgage, two nice cars, and discretionary expenses such as an exclusive country club, they were always "cash poor" and were even borrowing against retirement accounts to complete household projects. Having an emergency fund would have been critical to weather the economic crisis and provide the necessary liquid capital to supplement David's severance.

Step 2: Assess the Applicable Risk Factors

Every investment carries some degree of risk: the risk of losing money, either over short or more extended periods of time; the risk of being able to buy less in the future with the money earned from investments; or the risk of a downturn in the economy or dramatic changes in interest rates. All investments offer a return with an associated level of risk. While there is no way of controlling these risks, understanding them is critical in making appropriate investment choices. An investment strategy should incorporate only risks that the investor is willing, and has the capacity, to take.

Investment Risks

- *Market risk* is the risk that stock, bond, or other markets will decline precipitously or unexpectedly.
- *Business risk* is the risk that an investment in a company will do poorly because that industry or specific company is doing poorly.
- *Inflation risk* is the risk that the rate of return earned from investments will be lower than the rate of inflation, or the rise in the cost of living. This also is called "purchasing power risk" because inflation reduces the amount of goods and services money can buy.
- *Interest-rate risk* is the risk that interest rates will change while an investment has a fixed rate of return (*e.g.*, a bond bought four years ago may earn 4% annually, while a newly issued bond is earning 6% annually).
- *Liquidity risk* is the risk that an investor will not be able to sell an investment at an attractive price when cash is needed.
- *Credit risk* is the risk that a bond or other credit instrument suffers a decline in value due to perceptions (real or otherwise) of its financial security.

- **Default risk** is the risk that principal and interest will not be paid when due and can result in a permanent loss of capital. Default risk is most applicable to corporate debt and, in rarer cases, municipal debt. Debt with the full backing of the U.S. government currently has little to no default risk.
- **Reinvestment risk** is the risk that in a declining interest-rate environment, investors must reinvest income and principal at lower rates, which will lead to lower future cash flows.

Step 3: Determine the Appropriate Asset Allocation

Diversifying Investments

Diversification is the process of combining investments that are sufficiently different from each other such that, in effect, the whole is greater than the sum of the parts. By spreading money out among various types of investments, an investor can avoid becoming dependent upon the performance of any single company, asset class, or sector of the market. This time-tested principle is important because, when appropriately utilized, it not only limits downside risk and volatility but also can enhance total investment returns.

Aside from not having an appropriate emergency fund, David and Abby had an over-concentration of Goliath stock and failed to manage David's equity compensation properly. The company eventually suffered a permanent impairment and was forced to sell itself to a competitor at well below its historic value. This had a detrimental impact on David and Abby's balance sheet, as David's stock options were almost worthless, his retirement account was decimated, and all unvested equity awards were forfeited.

A well-designed portfolio contains a mix of various asset classes, such as equities (stocks), fixed income (bonds), cash-equivalent investments, and non-traditional (low-correlated) assets. When constructing a portfolio, an important goal is to combine asset classes that exhibit low correlation to each other. Each asset class should have a different risk/return profile to achieve portfolio diversification. The proportions of each type of investment an investor chooses depend on his or her investment goals. Generally speaking, equities are for capital appreciation, or growth in the value of the investment. Fixed income is for current income and preservation of capital. Non-traditional assets provide diversification, as their values tend to rise and fall asynchronously from those of traditional assets. Cash equivalents, such as money-market funds, are for stability and liquidity, or easy access to money.

Table 7.1 demonstrates many of the principles of a properly constructed, diversified portfolio.[1] Each column sorts the best performing to worst performing investment type by year. It then annualizes the return of each investment type over the time period in addition to quantifying volatility (risk as measured by the standard deviation of returns). As the table illustrates, each investment type will prosper or weaken at different times, as leadership generally changes year to year. These leadership changes are difficult, if not impossible, to predict ahead of time.

The *Asset Allocation* portfolio represents a common, balanced portfolio of 54% diversified equities, 6% REITs, and 40% fixed income. By design, the portfolio may

Table 7.1 Asset class returns

2012	2013	2014	2015	2016	2017	5-YEAR RETURN 1/1/13 - 12/31/17	5-YEAR VOLATILITY 1/1/13 - 12/31/17
Internat'l 18.7%	Small-cap 39.0%	REITs 31.6%	REITs 4.4%	Small-cap 21.6%	Emerging Mkt 37.6%	Large-cap 15.7%	Emerging Mkt 14.5%
Emerging Mkt 17.6%	Large-cap 32.3%	Large-cap 13.6%	Large-cap 1.3%	Large-cap 11.9%	Internat'l 25.2%	Small-cap 14.4%	Small-cap 13.9%
REITs 17.1%	Internat'l 21.7%	Asset Allocation 7.6%	Fixed Income 0.4%	Emerging Mkt 11.3%	Large-cap 21.7%	REITs 9.0%	REITs 13.8%
Small-cap 16.4%	Asset Allocation 14.7%	Fixed Income 5.9%	Cash 0.1%	Asset Allocation 7.8%	Small-cap 14.9%	Asset Allocation 8.5%	Internat'l 11.2%
Large-cap 15.9%	REITs 1.4%	Small-cap 5.2%	Asset Allocation -0.6%	REITs 6.6%	Asset Allocation 13.4%	Internat'l 7.6%	Large-cap 9.5%
Asset Allocation 11.7%	Cash 0.0%	Emerging Mkt 0.6%	Internat'l -0.9%	Fixed Income 2.5%	REITs 3.7%	Emerging Mkt 4.3%	Asset Allocation 6.0%
Fixed Income 4.1%	Fixed Income -2.4%	Cash 0.0%	Small-cap -4.2%	Internat'l 1.2%	Fixed Income 3.3%	Fixed Income 1.9%	Fixed Income 3.0%

The table uses select Fidelity funds as proxies for asset classes. © FMR LLC. All rights reserved. Used with permission. (Large-cap: Fidelity® 500 Index Investor; Small-cap: Fidelity® Small Cap Index Instl; Emerging Mkt: Fidelity® Emerging Markets Idx Instl; International: Fidelity® International Index Investor; Fixed-Income: Fidelity® US Bond Index Investor; REITs: Fidelity® Real Estate Index Instl; and Cash: Fidelity® Inv MM Fds Prime Money Mkt I.) The "Asset Allocation" portfolio assumes the following weights: 24.6% in the Fidelity® 500 Index Investor; 13.2% in the Fidelity® Small Cap Index Instl; 12.1% in the Fidelity® International Index Investor; 4.1% in the Fidelity® Emerging Markets Idx Instl; 40% in the Fidelity® US Bond Index Investor; and 6% in the Fidelity® Real Estate Index Instl. The Asset Allocation portfolio assumes annual rebalancing. Five-Year annualized (Ann.) return and volatility (Vol.) represents period of 1/1/13–12/31/17. All data represents total return for the stated period. Past performance is not indicative of future returns

not be the best or worst performer in any given year. Over time, however, it has achieved an efficient risk/return profile as a result of combining asset classes that exhibit low correlation to each other. An appropriate asset allocation for any particular investor, regardless of his or her investment personality, will depend on a number of factors, including their specific investment objectives, the length of time they have to invest, their overall financial circumstances, their current tax bracket, and the amount they have to invest. To determine the right mix of assets, it is necessary to consider the characteristics of the major asset classes.

Step 4: Select the Right Investment Vehicles

Once an investor has established an asset allocation, he or she will need to select the appropriate investment vehicles in each asset class.

Stocks

Stocks, or shares of equity ownership in companies, may provide the most capital appreciation over time. In the long-term, stocks have tended to outperform most asset classes in terms of investment return. The average return on stocks over long periods of time also has been well ahead of the average rate of inflation. Keep in mind, however, that the attractive returns that stocks have provided also come at the price of greater fluctuations in value, known as volatility (as measured by the standard deviation of returns). In other words, while stocks have the potential for higher returns, they also come with higher risk. The inherent volatility of stocks tends to even out over time, as the good years offset the bad years. For this reason, stocks should be thought of as a long-term investment.

How Is a Stock Portfolio Constructed?

In most cases, a properly structured equity allocation should have exposure to U.S. domestic large-, mid-, and small-cap stocks. Since over 50% of all equities are non--U.S. stocks, however, it is important to consider having some exposure to international and emerging-market equities as well. Investment depth and breadth is important. A portfolio should also be exposed to a mix of factors that have proven to be persistent return enhancers over time such as value, momentum, and quality.[2]

- **Individual stocks:** Experienced investors frequently construct some or all of their equity allocation by purchasing individual stocks. This comes with a substantial time commitment to research and monitor each company, however, and individual equity strategies may be better implemented by professionals. Owning individual stocks can be tax-friendly, as owners can strategically choose when to realize capital gains or losses.
- **Equity mutual funds:** An equity mutual fund is a pool of money from many investors that typically is managed by a professional investment manager and provides access to a diversified portfolio of stocks. Unlike owning individual stocks, diversification can be achieved with a significantly smaller monetary investment. Many mutual funds are passive index funds designed to track a specific index. When a person buys a mutual fund, he or she buys shares in the investment pool. The price of the mutual fund, known as its net asset value (NAV), is the total value of the underlying investments in the pool divided by the

number of outstanding shares. This price fluctuates based on the value of the investments and is determined at the end of each business day.

- **Exchange traded funds ("ETFs"):** Much like a passive index mutual fund, most exchange traded funds are lower-cost investments designed to track a particular index or segment of the market. Unlike mutual funds, an ETF can be bought and sold throughout the trading day. This feature offers investors flexibility and can be used as a trading tool in certain situations.

Bonds

A bond (fixed-income investment) is a debt obligation issued by a state, local, or federal government, an agency, or a non-governmental entity such as a corporation. The general objectives of a bond allocation are to preserve capital, reduce volatility, and produce income. With most bonds, investors receive predetermined interest payments on specific dates, usually twice a year, during the term of the bond. This is an attractive feature if an investment goal includes current income. For an investor looking to create a source of predictable income from an investment portfolio, bond investments may be a sensible option. If a bond is held to maturity, then the buyer also will receive the principal value of the bond at maturity. Bonds can also offer some tax advantages for those in a higher tax bracket. The interest earned on municipal bonds, for example, is often exempt from federal and state taxation.[3]

Bonds can also reduce the effect of market declines. In the event of significant market changes, bonds tend to fluctuate in price less dramatically than stocks. Generally, bonds tend to outperform equities and other riskier assets when pessimism is prevalent and economic growth is challenged. This does not mean that bond prices always remain steady. Historically, however, they have been less volatile. Just as there is a trade-off between risk and return with stocks, there is a trade-off in connection with bonds. Bonds, for example, due to their stability and lower risk, tend over time to earn lower returns on average than higher-risk investments such as stocks.

When Should an Investor Own Fixed-Income Investments?

Fixed-income investments are not necessarily appropriate for all investors—particularly those with longer time horizons, greater tolerance for risk, and less need for current income. An investor may want to consider fixed-income investments for a portfolio in order to accomplish one or more of the following objectives:

- Produce income
- Preserve capital
- Reduce portfolio volatility
- Maximize return while mitigating risk

How Is a Fixed-Income Portfolio Constructed?

- **Individual bonds:** Investing in individual bonds provides flexibility and control over risk, yield, and taxes. However, investing in individual bonds requires skill, attention, and diligence—in addition to sufficient funds to enable the investor to diversify across several different issuers to ensure a reasonable amount of diversification.
- **Bond mutual funds:** Bond mutual funds, much like equity mutual funds, are professionally managed and provide access to diversified bond portfolios. Bond mutual funds can invest in a variety of strategies, including corporate, municipal, and government bonds.
- **Money market funds:** Money market funds are liquid investment pools generally available through brokerage firms and banks. The underlying investments of these funds often consist of short-term commercial paper, municipal debt, and certificates of deposit. The share price of money market funds historically has been fixed at $1, with a variable interest rate, but the share price generally is not guaranteed.
- **Certificates of deposit:** Most commonly available through retail banks and brokerages, CDs usually are offered for terms of three months to five years. CDs pay a fixed interest rate for the term of the investment and typically levy penalties for early withdrawals of funds.

Investing in bonds and other fixed-income investments requires care, attention, and continuous diligence. Yet, by reducing investment risk, mitigating volatility, generating income, and lowering equity correlation, bonds and other fixed-income investments can play a vital role as part of a well-considered asset allocation plan.

What Are Non-traditional Investments, and Are They Appropriate for All Investors?

In general, "non-traditional investments" include investments in assets other than traditional equity, bond, and cash investments. The following provides a brief description of some popular non-traditional strategies.

- **Real estate:** REITs (real estate investment trusts) are investment vehicles that own income-producing real estate that can include apartments, offices, hospitals, hotels, and shopping malls. REITs are publicly traded on exchanges. Investors can also hold privately-held real estate (either directly as an investment property or through a private partnership or other vehicle).
- **Natural resources:** Companies and other investors in this category are typically involved in the mining, refining, processing, and transportation of natural resources.
- **Commodities:** This category includes investments in precious metals (*e.g.,* gold, silver, or copper) in addition to industrial and agricultural commodities, which can be held physically or through structures such as mutual funds or futures contracts.

- **Hedge funds:** The term "hedge fund" typically refers to lightly regulated investment funds that are set up as private investment partnerships. Many of these strategies combine long positions with short positions and, thus, provide some degree of a "hedge" against downside risk. They can employ a range of investment strategies, including long/short, market neutral, arbitrage, global macro, and distressed securities.

What Role Can Non-traditional Investments Serve in a Diversified Portfolio?

The primary role that non-traditional investments can serve in a diversified portfolio is to reduce volatility and enhance returns. Most strategies provide investments that don't necessarily go up or down with stocks and bonds, with some deliberately moving in the opposite direction. In addition, non-traditional strategies may be able to handle market shocks better than typical stock-only strategies. A variety of studies have demonstrated that introducing non-traditional strategies into a diversified portfolio allowed investors to achieve similar levels of return with materially lower volatility.[4]

How Should a Non-traditional Portfolio Be Constructed?

Investors should consider allocating capital to strategies that historically have had low correlations with traditional stocks and bonds. In addition, investors should consider strategies that have a focus on downside protection. As with stocks and bonds, exposure to non-traditional investments can be made through mutual funds and exchange-traded funds. When appropriate, however, private partnerships are often the more effective vehicle, although they require extensive due diligence and may offer less liquidity and transparency.

Step 5: Monitor and Adjust the Portfolio

Rebalancing

Rebalancing is a systematic process of realigning the assets in a portfolio back to the intended target allocation. For example, let's assume an investor's long-term target asset allocation was 50% stocks and 50% bonds. Over time, the stocks should outperform the slower growing bonds and therefore increase the stock weighting to greater than 50%. Rebalancing would require the investor to sell a portion of their stock allocation and buy bonds to get the portfolio back to the original target allocation of 50/50.

How Often Should an Investor Rebalance His or Her Portfolio, and What Are the Benefits?

While there is no optimal frequency for rebalancing a portfolio, most recommendations are to examine allocations at least once a year, keeping in mind taxes and trading costs. It is possible simply to buy and hold and forego rebalancing, but this generally would be ill-advised. Rebalancing gives investors the opportunity to sell high and buy low by taking the gains from high-performing asset classes and allocating them towards areas that are currently out of favor. Most importantly, rebalancing enforces a level of discipline and should help an investor stay on track with his or her goals-based financial plan.

Principles of Investing (and Common Investor Mistakes)

The investor's chief problem—and even his worst enemy—is likely to be himself.
Benjamin Graham[5]

In our experience, investor behavior is the primary key to successful long-term investing. In reality, there are dozens of behavioral mistakes an investor can make, some worse than others, and many can occur at the same time. Below are some of the more dangerous ones.

No Plan

Along the way, David and Abby made—and spent—plenty of money. They also increasingly attracted the attention of many who sought to "advise" them—in areas that included investments, retirement planning, asset allocation, mortgages, education planning for their children, insurance, and even philanthropy. Sometimes they listened, but usually they didn't...

Like most investors, David and Abby failed to take the time to craft a comprehensive financial plan to meet their numerous goals. They had multiple objectives with varying time horizons and liquidity needs. Successful long-term investing is goals-based and therefore should be driven by a financial plan. Decisions should not be made in a vacuum. However, many investors make the mistake of constructing their investment portfolio on a piecemeal basis. By not having a philosophy or clear strategy in place, over time their portfolio becomes a collection of various stocks, mutual funds, and ETFs. This typically results in lack of diversification, as the portfolio holds assets that are highly correlated. There also tends to be redundancy and overlap of similar strategies, resulting in fee inefficiencies.

As discussed above, it's imperative to start by creating a specific plan by crafting a personal investment policy statement (or "IPS"). Again, a personal IPS should address the following, among other relevant items:

- **Investment goals and objectives:** Are you seeking long-term growth, current income, preservation of capital, or some combination of the three?
- **Risk tolerance:** About what types of risk are you most concerned—losing principal, outliving your assets, or underperforming the market?
- **Income needs and spending plans:** How much income do you need to sustain your desired lifestyle now and in retirement? What is your estimated retirement spending level?
- **Target asset allocation:** How should you divide your assets among stocks, bonds, non-traditional, and cash investments, as well as within those asset classes?

Concentrated Stock Positions

In addition to his base salary and annual incentive bonuses, David had been granted a series of "nonqualified stock options," "incentive stock options," and "restricted stock" at Goliath, which had long been a public company... David did participate in Goliath's "defined contribution" retirement plan; and he did buy Goliath shares as part of the company's employee stock purchase plan.

Having a concentrated stock position is an all-too-common trait for corporate executives like David and Abby. Over the years, executives tend to build up company shares unconsciously through the various equity compensation programs offered. It's not unusual to witness an executive have 30–50%+ of their entire net-worth tied to a single security.[6] Yet, since 1980, over 320 companies were deleted from the S&P 500 for business-distress reasons; and roughly 40% of all stocks have suffered a permanent 70%+ decline from their peak value.[7]

Being in this situation can also have a sinister impact during economic downturns, as David experienced. In times like these, salary and bonus payments are typically reduced, and equity compensation suffers. It is critical for corporate executives to understand their company risks, quantify their single-security exposure, and implement tax-efficient, legally compliant strategies to reduce their concentrated position.[8] Not doing so can have a detrimental impact on their financial lives.

Market Timing

The market timer's Hall of Fame is an empty room.
    Jane Bryant Quinn[9]

It is extremely difficult, if not impossible, to time the top or bottom of the market on a consistent basis—in other words, to know precisely when to exit the market at the peak and buy at the trough. The day-to-day direction and intra-year volatility in the capital markets makes this strategy essentially impossible. Excessive focus on short-term market movements can permanently impair an investor's ability to reach long-term goals. Missing just a handful of the best days in the market can significantly reduce a portfolio's return (Fig. 7.2). On top of this, market timing can trigger taxable events and increase transaction fees. Plan to stay invested. The road to successful investing is to remain disciplined towards a goals-based savings plan and strategic long-term asset allocation.

Fidelity 500 Index Fund (FUSEX) Annualized Returns, 11/30/1988 to 5/31/2018

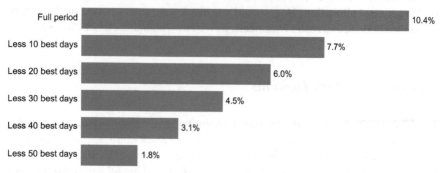

Fig. 7.2 The importance of staying invested
(Based on performance of Fidelity 500 Index Fund (FUSEX). © 2018 FMR LLC. All rights reserved. Used with permission.)

Performance Chasing

"Past performance is not indicative of future results" is one of the most common financial services disclosures, and for good reason. Performance chasing is the act of moving assets from one investment to another that has had a stronger track record over the past few years. An example of this would be swapping a current mutual fund that has lagged the market for another that has significantly outperformed. In order for this strategy to work, past performance needs to be persistent, and substantial research indicates this is not the case.[10] Nevertheless, investors are drawn to the recent "winners," mostly by the financial media outlets. The results of poor investor behavior, performance chasing being one of them, are staggering as quantified by the annual Dalbar report, "Quantitative Analysis of Investor Behavior."[11] The study consistently finds that the average mutual fund investor underperforms the S&P 500 by a significant margin. According to the study, through 2015, the 20-year annualized S&P 500 return was 8.19%, while the 20-year annualized return for the average equity mutual fund investor was only 4.67%, a gap of 3.52%.[12] In dollar terms, this disparity means that an original investment of $100,000 would have resulted in an ending value difference of about $233,000!

Notes

1. For a more detailed illustration based on major indices rather than a limited set of funds, see the "Periodic Table of Investment Returns," Callan, accessed June 14, 2018, https://www.callan.com/periodic-table/. Callan is the creator of the "Periodic Table of Investment Returns," which is the inspiration for the simpler illustration in this book.

2. See Michael J. Nathanson, "How can factor-based investing better position a portfolio for success?" *Worth Magazine*, 2017.

3. The taxation of fixed-income investments is discussed in greater detail in Chap. 8.

4. See, *e.g.*, Craig M. Lewis, *Liquid Alternative Mutual Funds: An Asset Class that Expands Opportunities for Diversification* (Vanderbilt University, 2016).

5. See Benjamin Graham, Warren Buffett and Jason Zweig, *The Intelligent Investor: a Book of Practical Counsel*, rev. ed. (New York: Harper Collins, 2003).

6. See Michael Cembalest et al., "The Agony & the Ecstasy: The Risks and Rewards of a Concentrated Stock Position" (J.P. Morgan, 2014).

7. See Michael Cembalest et al., "The Agony & the Ecstasy: The Risks and Rewards of a Concentrated Stock Position" (J.P. Morgan, 2014), 1–4.

8. A discussion of how to address concentrated positions from a tax and legal perspective appears elsewhere in this book.

9. Jane Bryant Quinn, *Making the Most of Your Money Now* (New York: Simon & Schuster, 2009).

10. See, *e.g.*, "Quantifying the impact of chasing fund performance," Vanguard, published 2014, https://pressroom.vanguard.com/nonindexed/Quantifying_the_impact_of_chasing_fund_performance_July_2014.pdf.

11. See DALBAR, Inc., "Quantitative Analysis of Investor Behavior," Rep. 21st ed. (Boston: DALBAR, Inc., 2015).

12. See DALBAR, Inc., "Quantitative Analysis of Investor Behavior," Rep. 21st ed. (Boston: DALBAR, Inc., 2015).

Chapter 8
Tax Planning and the Ten Commandments

And continuing with the theme of taxes, David and Abby's misery only gets worse from there. They had to pay taxes not only on their "deemed distribution" of the outstanding retirement plan loan balance but also on the vested stock options that David had accumulated and not exercised. During Goliath's distressed sale, the acquiring company had agreed to pay out cash to all holders of vested, "in-the-money" stock options. While most of the stock options were underwater and therefore worthless, some of David's options had been valuable enough to earn him a cash payout. David was of course grateful to have the cash, though it was a small fraction of what he had dreamed it would be one day. Yet, he now learned that he would have to pay ordinary income taxes plus employment taxes on the full amount of the payments. This was a great disappointment, as David had understood that, at least for his incentive stock options, he would one day have the benefit of capital-gain taxation at lower rates—if he had followed the rules for ensuring that favorable result.

David did get favorable tax treatment when the outright shares of Goliath stock he owned outside of his retirement plan were acquired by Goliath's competitor, but he was distraught when he finally figured out why. It seemed that David, on the advice of one of his friends at work, made a Section 83(b) election when he had received his restricted stock awards. He remembered that this election had caused him to pay substantial taxes when he received the stock—even though it was still subject to vesting—but he always thought he would have to pay less tax in the future when he finally sold the stock at a gain after it vested.

Unfortunately, he was now selling his vested stock for dramatically less than the value on which he had paid taxes. Even worse, when David was terminated by Goliath, all of his unvested options and restricted stock were forfeited. Even though David had paid ordinary income taxes on the receipt of his unvested restricted stock, he never actually got the very stock on which he paid those taxes. That's right: David had paid taxes on the value of something that he never got! His only consolation now was a large capital loss that could be used to offset his paltry capital gain.

© The Colony Group 2018
M. J. Nathanson et al., *Personal Financial Planning for Executives and Entrepreneurs*, https://doi.org/10.1007/978-3-319-98416-2_8

As David and Abby learned—too late—failing to plan thoroughly for taxes can have catastrophic consequences for anyone, but especially for corporate executives. Through careful, advance planning, however, taxes can be minimized, and the burden of taxation can be satisfied.

When done right, tax planning is a broad-based, continuous, and dynamic process. In this chapter, we will discuss the basics of tax planning for corporate executives. It is important to remember that some of the most effective tax planning that can be done is quite simple! We'll also get into some of the more complex planning that only the best-advised executives undertake.

We know what you're thinking at this point. Taxes are boring. Taxes are bad. Taxes are complicated. All true! But tax planning is critical—and expected—nonetheless. Even the courts say so:

> *Over and over again courts have said that there is nothing sinister in so arranging one's affairs as to keep taxes as low as possible. Everybody does so, rich or poor; and all do right, for nobody owes any public duty to pay more taxes than the law demands: taxes are forced exactions, not voluntary contributions. To demand more in the name of morals is mere cant.*
>
> Judge Learned Hand, Second Circuit Court of Appeals[1]

Now, had David and Abby read this book, they would have known about—and followed—what we consider to be the Ten Commandments of Tax Planning (Fig. 8.1), on which we will base the rest of this chapter. Before we do that, however, we want to point out that our discussion will, of necessity, be general in nature, as each executive will have different circumstances to consider. It isn't practicable to address all of the specific tax implications of those specific circumstances. It's also impractical to address all of the potential state, local, and foreign tax variations that may be applicable, so we will continue to focus our discussion on federal income taxes, as we have done throughout this book.

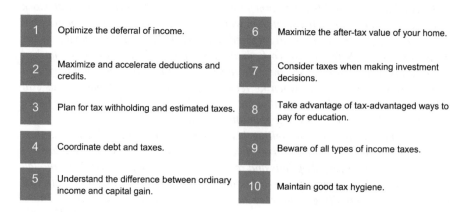

1 Optimize the deferral of income.	6 Maximize the after-tax value of your home.
2 Maximize and accelerate deductions and credits.	7 Consider taxes when making investment decisions.
3 Plan for tax withholding and estimated taxes.	8 Take advantage of tax-advantaged ways to pay for education.
4 Coordinate debt and taxes.	9 Beware of all types of income taxes.
5 Understand the difference between ordinary income and capital gain.	10 Maintain good tax hygiene.

Fig. 8.1 The ten commandments (of tax planning)

Optimize the Deferral of Income

Perhaps the simplest form of tax planning is to follow the general rule of deferring taxable income whenever possible. Of course, there are exceptions to this rule, such as when tax rates are expected to rise in the future; however, in most cases, an executive will benefit from deferring the obligation to pay taxes.

Why? Consider this basic example (Fig. 8.2).

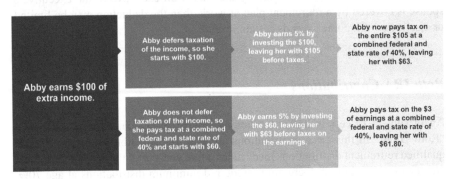

Fig. 8.2 Abby defers the taxation of $100

This example is oversimplified and overly general in many respects, but it illustrates a very important principle regarding the deferral of taxes: all else being equal, untaxed dollars grow faster than taxed dollars. Unfortunately, many corporate executives may find it difficult to defer their receipt of taxable income and avail themselves of this advantage because a good portion of their income comes from regularly scheduled salary payments. Yet, even salaried executives can defer income by participating in tax-deferred retirement plans or deferred compensation plans. They can even ask (or be required) to delay their receipt of bonuses when appropriate. Equity-based compensation offers additional tax deferral opportunities, though planning around these awards is complex enough to have its own chapter in this book.[2]

To be sure, David did participate in Goliath's tax-deferred retirement plan, but his overall approach to deferring income was lacking. Abby, too, missed some special opportunities. A comprehensive deferral strategy can include a variety of common and traditional deferral techniques. In fact, it can be advantageous to use multiple techniques, especially if doing so creates more flexibility when the time ultimately comes to take income distributions.

IRA Contributions

A well-established and common way to put money away in a tax-deferred account is by making a contribution to a traditional individual retirement account (or "IRA"). Earnings on the account eventually will be taxed as ordinary income at distribution, but distributions currently are not required to begin until age 70½. There is, however, a 10% penalty for early withdrawals before age 59½, with certain exceptions. Exceptions include cases of death, disability, the payment of qualified higher education expenses, and the first-time purchase of a home.[3]

If an executive is not covered by a retirement plan at work, IRA contributions (which are subject to annual dollar limitations)[4] generally are deductible, offering a tax-deferral opportunity not only on earnings but also on the principal amount of the contributions. Keep in mind, however, that distributions from a deductible IRA will be taxable in their entirety as ordinary income. If an executive or the executive's spouse is covered by a retirement plan at work, then the deduction may be limited or disallowed if income exceeds certain levels.[5]

Roth IRA Contributions

Again subject to certain dollar limitations, contributions can also be made to a "Roth" IRA.[6] In this case, contributions are not tax-deductible, but earnings and qualified retirement distributions made at least five years after the account is opened are tax-free. In addition, there are no required minimum distributions at age 70½, and holders can take a withdrawal up to the amount of their contributions at any time, tax- and penalty-free.[7]

Roth IRAs can make sense for executives who believe that they will be in a higher tax bracket in retirement, so they are ideal for younger executives who can benefit from decades of tax-free growth. They also can be ideal for an older, wealthy executive to leave to an heir, as discussed in the next chapter.[8] Contributions to a Roth IRA are not allowed if income exceeds certain levels, but it may be possible to convert a traditional IRA to a Roth IRA.[9]

Roth Conversions

Deciding whether or not to convert all or a portion of a traditional IRA into a Roth IRA depends on the executive's age, projected tax rates now and later, and estate plan. Generally, a Roth conversion is treated as a taxable distribution unless there are non-taxable assets in the converted IRA. Potential benefits include the elimination of income tax on future withdrawals and no required minimum distributions in the future, as well as the option to leave the account behind as a tax-free bequest to an heir.

Qualified Retirement Plans

In a traditional qualified retirement plan such as a 401(k) plan, an executive is afforded the opportunity to defer certain amounts of taxable income by electing to make deductible contributions to the plan. As is the case with a traditional IRA, the account eventually will be taxed as ordinary income at distribution, but distributions currently are not required to begin until age 70½. There is a 10% penalty for early withdrawals before age 59½, but exceptions again are available in cases of death, disability, the payment of qualified higher education expenses, and the first-time purchase of a home.[10]

While a current deduction is helpful in reducing taxable income, an executive on the younger side who expects to be in a higher tax bracket later in life may wish to enroll in a Roth 401(k) plan, assuming the company offers one. Under a Roth 401(k) plan, the executive will forego a current deduction but will enjoy tax-free growth and retirement withdrawals.[11] Since it can be hard to predict future tax rates, some executives hedge their bets and divide their contributions between traditional and Roth 401(k) contributions.

Nonqualified Deferred Compensation Plans

Even if an executive maximizes his or her company retirement plan contributions, the company may also offer a supplemental deferred compensation plan. Contributions to these plans are made on a pre-tax basis, deferring taxation until payments ultimately are received from the plan. Importantly, however, participants in a nonqualified deferred compensation plan must be aware that these deferred compensation accounts do not have the same ERISA protections as traditional retirement plans such as 401(k) plans.[12] In general, if the sponsoring company were to fail, the account holder would need to stand in line with other creditors in an effort to recover the funds. Also, under Section 409A of the Internal Revenue Code, a participant generally should make a specific distribution election at the same time that the decision to contribute is made. When making this distribution election, it is once again important to consider taxation. For example, having all distributions occur in a lump-sum at retirement could result in a large tax bill. It may be better to consider spreading distributions over several years. In any event, the distribution plan cannot be changed, except to delay the distribution by at least five years. Failure to follow these additional requirements can result in the imposition of penalties and interest, as well as a loss of deferral. [13]

SEP-IRAs

A simplified employee pension individual retirement account, or "SEP-IRA," is available for use by self-employed individuals or companies of any size. Under a SEP-IRA, an executive currently can make a contribution of up to 25% of compensation, subject to certain limitations.[14] There are several important advantages in using a SEP-IRA structure, including that it can be established easily, with lower costs, and that it allows for flexibility in determining annual contributions. Importantly, however, when a SEP-IRA is used by an employer with employees, the employer generally will need to make equal contributions for all eligible employees.[15]

SIMPLE IRAs

A "savings incentive match plan for employee individual retirement account," or "SIMPLE IRA," is available for use by companies with 100 or fewer employees. Under a SIMPLE IRA, an employee may make limited contributions, and the employer is then required either to match the employee's contribution up to a certain percentage or make a non-elective contribution for the employee.[16] Like a SEP-IRA, a SIMPLE IRA is easy and inexpensive to establish, but it offers less flexibility on the part of the employer relative to annual contributions for employees. Again, all eligible employees must be allowed to participate, though the rules regarding eligibility are slightly different than those for a SEP-IRA.[17]

Abby could have utilized a SEP-IRA or SIMPLE IRA structure at Slingshot. She also could have established a qualified retirement plan. Any of these structures would have offered deferral opportunities that could have supplemented the deferral opportunities available to David through Goliath's qualified plan and its other deferral offerings.

Traditional Business Planning

Of course, even without utilizing the above opportunities, there are common-sense business-planning techniques that can be equally impactful in deferring income. We are not suggesting that an executive allow "the tax tail to wag the dog." Current income, especially in the form of cash, is a good thing! In instances where deferring that income is helpful, however, an executive with some flexibility—like Abby— can take deferral measures such as simply controlling the timing of salary and dividend payments. Depending on accounting methods, an executive like Abby also can delay issuing invoices for services by, for instance, billing for December services in the following January. Common-sense, simple measures such as these can often be effective methods of deferral, especially when a corporate executive is self-employed or otherwise in control of a smaller company.

Maximize and Accelerate Deductions and Credits

The other side of deferring income is, of course, maximizing and accelerating deductions and credits. Again, this strategy generally makes sense for corporate executives; though, in some cases, such as when tax rates are expected to rise in the future or the executive expects income to increase significantly, it can be beneficial to defer deductions and credits if possible.

Virtually every corporate executive has ample opportunities to accelerate deductible expenses, but it is important not only to accelerate these expenses but also to ensure that they are properly identified in the first place. Many executives have no idea that they are incurring expenses for which they are entitled to a tax deduction!

Common expenses for which corporate executives claim deductions include the following (Table 8.1):

Table 8.1 Expenses for corporate executives

Deduction	Description	Planning tips
Business expenses	Can deduct ordinary and necessary business expenses.[a] Self-employed executives have greater flexibility than employees to deduct business expenses.[b]	Pay business-related expenses from the business, not personal accounts. Consider the deductibility of equipment and auto use or purchases. Consider the possibility of home-office deductions. Consider prepaying business expenses in years in which income and tax rates are high.
Charitable contributions	Can deduct charitable contributions of cash or property to qualified organizations. Generally can deduct up to 60% of AGI, but 20% and 30% limitations apply to certain contributions of property. For example, there is a 30% limitation on the donation of long-term capital gain property to public charities.[c] Deduction for the contribution of short-term capital gain property is limited to cost basis. Unreimbursed expenses and mileage related to donation of services may also be deductible.	The deduction generally is equal to the fair market value of the property on the date of contribution. It can be better to donate long-term appreciated securities to a charity rather than selling the securities and donating the proceeds, thereby avoiding tax on the appreciation. If, however, a security is trading at a loss, it can be better to sell the security to realize the loss and then donate the proceeds. Consider accelerating charitable contributions in years in which income and tax rates are higher. Qualified donor-advised funds can offer a convenient vehicle for doing so.
Health insurance	Self-employed executives generally can deduct 100% of health insurance premiums for medical, dental, and long-term care coverage for themselves, spouses, and dependents. This deduction may not be available if eligible for group insurance from an employer or spouse's employer.[d]	Amounts are similarly excluded from income for executives who are employees. Consider Health Savings Accounts when available. An HSA is a tax-advantaged medical savings account available to those enrolled in a high-deductible health plan (HDHP). Money in an HSA generally can be invested, and withdrawals for qualified medical expenses are tax-free.
Medical & dependent care expenses	Can claim an itemized deduction for unreimbursed medical expenses to the extent that they exceed a certain percentage of AGI.[e]	Consider Flexible Spending Accounts when available. An FSA is a tax-advantaged way for employees to save for unreimbursed medical or dependent-care expenses. Contributions are pre-tax. Money in a healthcare FSA can be used for certain expenses such as deductibles, copays, and other expenses not covered by insurance.

(continued)

Table 8.1 (continued)

Deduction	Description	Planning tips
State and local taxes[f]	Can claim an itemized deduction for state and local taxes paid during the year, subject to limits.[g]	These taxes may be state and local income taxes, or they may be state sales taxes, but not both.[h] Typically deduct the higher of the two. The sales tax deduction is generally only used by those who pay little or no state income taxes, such as those living in states that have no income tax. Consider prepaying deductible taxes in years in which income and tax rates are higher. For example, in some years, it may be advisable to make a fourth-quarter state estimated tax payment in December rather than waiting for the January deadline.
Real estate taxes[f]	Can claim an itemized deduction for real estate taxes paid on personal residences, subject to limits.[i]	In general, do not claim an itemized deduction for real estate taxes on rental properties. Instead, it may be better to treat those real estate taxes as an expense against rental income.
Personal property taxes[f]	Can claim an itemized deduction for personal property taxes paid during the year, subject to limits.[j]	These taxes typically are imposed on personal property, such as automobiles, based on the assessed value of the property.
Interest	Can claim an itemized deduction for interest paid on a loan secured by main home or a second home if the loan is used to buy, build, or improve the home. Interest paid is deductible on outstanding mortgage debt up to certain limits. If total debt exceeds these limits, the interest deduction may be limited.[k] "Points" paid on a loan can be deducted ratably over the life of the loan, and in certain circumstances can be deducted in full in the year paid.[l]	Interest paid on a loan secured by a rental property generally should be deducted against rental income. Consider prepaying mortgage interest in years in which income and tax rates are higher. For example, in some years, it may make sense to accelerate a January mortgage payment into the prior December.

[a]See I.R.C. § 162

[b]See I.R.S. Publication 529. Note that the availability of itemized deductions was limited by the Tax Cuts and Jobs Act of 2017

[c]See I.R.C. § 170

[d]See I.R.C. § 162(l)

[e]See I.R.C. § 213. For 2018, unreimbursed medical expenses generally can be deducted to the extent that they exceed 7.5% of AGI, but under the Tax Cuts and Jobs Act of 2017, the AGI limitation is set to jump to 10% in 2019

[f]These deductions are not available in the Alternative Minimum Tax calculation, which is discussed below

Table 8.1 (continued)

[g]See I.R.C. § 164. Note that under the Tax Cuts and Jobs Act of 2017, there is a cap of $10,000 on deductions for aggregate state and local income and property taxes

[h]See I.R.C. § 164(b)(5)

[i]See I.R.C. § 164. Note that under the Tax Cuts and Jobs Act of 2017, there is a cap of $10,000 on deductions for aggregate state and local income and property taxes

[j]See I.R.C. § 164. Note that under the Tax Cuts and Jobs Act of 2017, there is a cap of $10,000 on deductions for aggregate state and local income and property taxes

[k]See I.R.C. § 163. Note that under the Tax Cuts and Jobs Act of 2017, qualified residence interest is deductible on debt of up to $750,000 ($375,000 if married filing separately) for mortgages incurred after December 15, 2017. For earlier mortgages, the limit is $1,000,000 ($500,000 if married filing separately)

[l]See I.R.C. § 163

Now, we have been limiting our discussion thus far to deductions. Keep in mind that tax *deductions* are different from tax *credits*, as tax *credits* provide a dollar-for-dollar reduction in income tax liability. By contrast, tax *deductions* lower taxable income and therefore provide a savings that is equal to the deduction multiplied by your marginal tax rate. For example, if you are in the 37% federal tax bracket, a fully usable $1,000 charitable contribution deduction generally will save you $370 in tax.

Tax credits are less common than deductions. Nevertheless, they may be available on a limited basis and under certain conditions for such items as:

- Adopting a child[18]
- Child and dependent care expenses[19]
- Education expenses[20]
- Retirement plan contributions[21]
- Foreign taxes[22]
- Energy-efficient improvements to a home[23]

It is important to undertake an annual exercise to determine which credits, if any, may be available.

Plan for Tax Withholding and Estimated Taxes

It seems like a simple concept, but many executives fail to plan properly to pay their taxes throughout the year. As a basic rule, be sure to withhold enough tax from your compensation, and, if necessary, make estimated federal tax payments, so that you pay in at least 90% of your current year's tax or 100% of your prior year's tax, whichever amount is smaller. If you come up short, you'll have to pay interest or penalties. Moreover, executives who have a higher AGI may be required to pay even more throughout the year, as they must pay 90% of the current year's tax or *110%* of the prior year's tax, whichever amount is smaller.[24]

Similar rules apply in many state and local jurisdictions, which may also require withholding and estimated tax payments. Unfortunately, however, the rules can vary from jurisdiction to jurisdiction, often requiring a multi-jurisdictional assessment and planning exercise.

For self-employed executives, withholding may be impractical, leading to the need to make greater estimated tax payments. The calculation process for estimated taxes can be complicated and can change from quarter to quarter, but estimated taxes generally are due for federal and state tax purposes in January, April, June, and September of each year.[25]

Coordinate Debt and Taxes

As mentioned above, qualified mortgage interest generally is eligible for an itemized deduction. Other types of interest also are deductible. Subject to certain limits, investment interest is deductible, as is business-related interest, including interest on business debts and debts incurred to buy a stake in a business.[26]

From a tax perspective, it therefore can be said that mortgage interest, investment interest, and business interest are favorable relative to interest paid on personal and other non-deduction-bearing debt such as credit card or auto loan debt. In this sense, it is often better to restructure deductible debt and pay off personal, non-deductible debt, depending on interest rates.

Of course, it's typically a good idea to keep high-interest, non-deductible credit card debt to a minimum in any event. Paying off a credit card that charges 15% is like getting a 15% return on your money!

Because mortgage and investment interest deductions are subject to specific limitations, while business-related interest is subject to far fewer limitations, there is a general hierarchy of what type of interest is often best from a tax perspective. It looks something like this (Fig. 8.3).

Fig. 8.3 The interest hierarchy

Understand the Difference Between Ordinary Income and Capital Gains

Most types of income are taxable as "ordinary income." Ordinary income includes compensation, business profits, royalties, rental income, and most other forms of income.[27]

In contrast, "capital gain" is income earned on the sale or exchange of a capital asset such as stock or another type of investment property.[28] The amount of this gain is limited to the amount realized over the holder's tax basis in the asset—generally the total investment amount plus certain adjustments. "Long-term capital gain" includes gain recognized on the sale or exchange of an asset held for more than one year, while "short-term capital gain" includes gain recognized on the sale or exchange of an asset held for exactly one year or less.[29]

Ordinary income and short-term capital gain are usually taxable at higher rates than long-term capital gain, generally making long-term capital gain more attractive than ordinary income and short-term capital gain. For this reason, though all income is good, long-term capital gain income is usually most valuable on an after-tax basis, especially when the executive is in a higher tax bracket. In turn, to the extent that an executive can control the nature of the income he or she receives, it will be optimal to produce as much long-term capital gain as possible. Some examples of opportunities for producing long-term capital gain are:

- Investing for long-term appreciation in non-income or low-income producing securities such as growth stocks
- Re-investing business profits with the intent of building equity value for eventual sale of the equity
- Making a Section 83(b) election on restricted stock when appropriate
- Not engaging in disqualifying dispositions of shares acquired under an incentive stock option if circumstances warrant holding the shares

It's best to offset capital gain whenever possible with any capital losses realized in the current or prior years. Realized capital losses can be used to offset realized capital gains, plus an additional $3,000 against ordinary income.[30] Excess capital losses can be carried forward by an individual until actually used.[31]

Maximize the After-Tax Value of Your Home

Home ownership remains a tax-favored concept in the United States. We spoke above about the rules for deducting qualified residence interest and real property taxes, but the tax benefits don't end there. Married couples may be eligible to exclude up to $500,000 ($250,000 for singles) of capital gain when they sell their main home. To qualify, they must have owned and used the property as their main home for at least two out of the previous five years prior to the date of sale. They are not eligible for the exclusion, however, if they excluded the gain from another home sale in the previous two years.[32]

We also referenced the potential availability of home-office deductions, especially for self-employed executives. Anyone who works out of their home, whether an owner or a renter, and who segregates space exclusively and regularly for trade or business purposes may be eligible to deduct the expenses attributable to this space.[33] While we recommend that anyone entitled to this deduction actually claim it, we also caution that our experience suggests that it is a highly audited deduction. Be ready to defend it, or beware of claiming it!

Consider Taxes When Making Investment Decisions

Before we begin to discuss the basics of incorporating tax considerations into your investment strategy, we must first begin with some advice that's going to sound a bit contradictory: don't let taxes get in the way of good investing! To express this sentiment, we often use the old expression "don't let the tax tail wag the dog."

Now, we're not saying that taxes shouldn't be considered. They should, and that's the key point here. They just shouldn't replace core investment fundamentals. Tax considerations should be balanced with investment fundamentals to arrive at the right balance of investment and tax planning.

So what are the core tax considerations?

Defer and Reduce Taxable Events When Optimal (See the First Commandment)

Again, we are not saying that an investment that should be sold from an investment perspective should continue to be held just for tax purposes. We are saying, however, that if an investment can comfortably be held for long enough to achieve long-term capital gain status (*i.e.*, more than one year), then it will be beneficial to have the investment gain subjected to tax at a lower rate. Similarly, there may be circumstances in which it is advantageous to sell a position in January rather than the prior December (*e.g.*, if tax rates will be lower starting in January).

A variation on this theme is to invest in securities and portfolios that do not generate unnecessarily excessive amounts of tax liability. This goal can be accomplished, for example, by investing in portfolio strategies that minimize turnover, thus minimizing the realization of unnecessary taxable gains.

Look for Opportunities Within Your Portfolio to Realize Losses to Offset Gains

This may seem like another simple concept, but our experience is that poorly advised executives often fail to go through an annual exercise of assessing realized gains and determining whether there are loss positions that can be realized to offset those gains and reduce net tax liabilities.

But Remember the 30-Day "Wash Sale" Rule

Yes, look annually for opportunities to realize losses to offset gains, but note that in order to make those losses stick for tax purposes, it will not be possible to buy the same or substantially identical position within 30 days before or after the sale, or the losses will be disallowed![34]

Also Remember That Special Tax Rules—Some Favorable and Some Unfavorable—Apply to the Sale of Certain Investments

The sale of collectibles, including most forms of gold and art, is subject to a higher rate of capital gain taxation.[35] Depreciable assets also can attract a higher rate of capital gain taxation.[36] These are examples of important considerations when investing in different asset classes, as projected net returns must be reduced to reflect these higher tax rates.

In contrast, gain from the sale of "qualified small business stock" held for more than five years is eligible for an exclusion of 50% to 100%, depending on the date of acquisition and certain limitations. In general, to qualify, the stock in question must meet several requirements, including the following:

- It must have been issued by a domestic C corporation with less than $50 million in gross assets
- It must have been acquired after August 10, 1993, at original issuance, meaning that it must have been acquired directly from the issuing corporation
- It must have been issued by a corporation that satisfies certain tests for being involved in an active, qualified business[37]

Qualified small business stock may also be eligible for a tax-free rollover if the investor holds the original stock for more than six months and acquires replacement qualified small business stock within 60 days of the sale of the original stock.[38]

Favorable tax treatment is also available for the sale of certain small-business stock sold at a loss. Among the requirements that must be satisfied are that:

- At the time the stock was issued, the corporation was a small-business corporation that received no more than $1 million for its stock, as capital contributions, and as paid-in surplus
- The stock was issued by the corporation for money or property other than stock or securities
- For the five most recent years, more than 50% of the corporation's gross receipts came from sources other than royalties, rents, dividends, interest, annuities, and sales of stock or securities[39]

Eligible stock that is sold at a loss will generate an ordinary loss—as opposed to a less-valuable capital loss—up to certain limits.[40]

There's also a little known tax break that applies to company stock held within a retirement plan, referred to as Net Unrealized Appreciation ("NUA"). Upon qualifying, NUA treatment makes it possible to convert the gain on the sale from ordinary income to long-term capital gain, which is typically taxed at a lower rate. The NUA rules are discussed in greater detail in Chap. 4.

Consider the Taxability of Any Income to Be Produced by the Investments

Many investments are acquired with a view to producing income other than capital gain. Stocks that pay dividends or bonds that pay interest are typical examples of investments that produce regular income (sometimes in addition to capital gain). The taxability of this distributable income must be considered in advance.

For example, the interest payable on bonds, which generally is taxable as ordinary income, can be subject to wildly different tax regimes, depending on the nature of the bond (Table 8.2).

These rules can become even more complex in the cases, for example, of "private activity bonds" or bonds that do not pay interest regularly and instead pay interest upon maturity. All of these factors must be considered at length when making investments in bonds and similar investments.[41]

Like interest, dividends also are generally taxable as ordinary income; but there are exceptions and nuances to that rule too. Dividends that are "qualified dividends" are taxable at the same lower rates as capital gain. Subject to certain exceptions, to qualify for this special treatment, the following requirements must be satisfied:

Table 8.2 Interest on bonds

Interest on corporate bonds	• Taxable federally • Taxable by states
Interest on U.S. Treasury bonds	• Taxable federally • Not taxable by states
Interest on municipal bonds	• Not taxable federally • Not taxable by resident state if issued by same state

- The dividends must have been paid by a U.S. corporation or a qualified foreign corporation
- The recipient must meet certain holding-period requirements
- The dividends cannot be certain types of special dividends that are explicitly excluded from qualified-dividend status[42]

Naturally, when making investment-related decisions regarding dividend-paying stocks, projected net returns should account for whether the dividends will be qualified dividends. All else being equal, the investment will be more attractive if they will.

Use the Right Type of Account to Hold an Investment

As important as it is to gauge the tax consequences of making a particular investment, it is equally important to think about the type of account in which the investment will be held. Referring back to our brief discussion of bonds, for example, it probably will not make sense to own municipal bonds in a non-taxable account such as a qualified retirement account. A tax-advantaged account is not necessary for a tax-free investment and, depending on the type of account, may even make the tax-free interest taxable upon distribution from the account. In contrast, when thinking about a taxable investment, it may make sense to have that investment held in a tax-deferred account or a child's account if the child is subject to a lower tax rate. Furthermore, depending on the situation, it may make sense to hold investments that produce mostly qualified dividends and long-term capital gain in a taxable account in order to take advantage of the lower tax rate on this type of income. This concept can broadly be referred to as "asset location" and, though often ignored, is critical in making investment-related decisions!

Take Advantage of Tax-Advantaged Ways to Pay for Education

As education costs have risen more quickly than most other expenses, education planning has become a more critical component of the financial planning process. And as with other expenses, gaining a tax advantage in preparing to pay, and ultimately paying, those expenses has gained corresponding importance. We have offered a broader discussion of this topic in our chapter on achieving financial independence, but it's nevertheless worth emphasizing some of the key tax considerations at this time.

Unfortunately, most of the tax-advantaged methods of saving for and ultimately paying education expenses are available only to people who are at lower levels of annual income. As mentioned below, however, one major technique—the use of "529 plans"—is more broadly available.[43]

Table 8.3 Some tax-favored tools for paying for education

529 plans	• Contributions not deductible for federal income tax purposes • Earnings grow free of federal income tax and are not taxed when money is taken out to pay for qualified primary and secondary education expenses • Some states offer a full or partial tax deduction or credit for 529 plan contributions • No income limits, but may include contribution limits • Gift tax rules may apply
Coverdell education savings accounts	• Contributions not deductible • Earnings grow free of federal income tax and are not taxed when money is taken out to pay for qualified expenses for both primary and secondary education • Income limits apply
Student loan interest deduction	• Limited federal income tax deduction for interest paid on qualified student loans • Income limits apply
Federal education tax credits	• Limited annual American opportunity credit available for the first four years of post-secondary education • Limited lifetime learning credit available for amounts spent on undergraduate, graduate, or professional-degree courses • Income limits apply

The above table provides a snapshot of the way that we think about the basic education-related landscape from a tax perspective (Table 8.3).[44]

There's more, but those are some of the most important and broadly available tax-favored vehicles to understand. It's also worth noting that if your child or dependent is fortunate enough to earn a scholarship, then, under most circumstances, the scholarship will not be subject to federal income tax to the extent that the scholarship is used for qualified tuition and related expenses.[45]

On a related but different topic, what about *employee* education expenses? What if an executive incurs reimbursed or unreimbursed expenses related to his or her own education?

Let's start with employer-reimbursed education expenses. Many employers offer educational assistance programs, and, as long as they are properly structured (in writing), amounts received (subject to limits) under those plans for use by the executive are not subject to income taxation.[46] Unreimbursed employee education expenses generally are not deductible under current tax law.

Beware of All Types of Income Taxes

By now you probably can see that the concept of an "income tax" is far broader than some may mistakenly believe. Income taxes can include federal income taxes, state income taxes, local income taxes, and foreign income taxes. They also can include taxes on different types of income, like "ordinary income" and "capital gain."

But it's even more complicated than that! A corporate executive needs to be aware of several specific forms of income-based taxation, in addition to the ones we just mentioned.

The Alternative Minimum Tax

The Alternative Minimum Tax, or "AMT," was established in the 1960s to ensure that high-income taxpayers with large amounts of itemized deductions paid at least a minimum amount of federal income tax. Under the AMT, individuals are required to calculate their tax using two separate calculations—the regular tax and the AMT—and pay whichever is higher.

The two calculations have very different rules. For example, various itemized deductions such as real estate taxes and state income taxes paid, while limited under the regular tax calculation, are not allowed at all in the AMT calculation. Especially important for corporate executives is that the exercise of incentive stock options (as opposed to the sale of the underlying stock) is not taxable for regular federal income tax purposes, but the spread of the fair market value over the exercise price at exercise is includible in the AMT calculation.[47]

Strategies to minimize AMT exposure include reducing income through pre-tax retirement plan contributions or flexible spending accounts. It also is important to plan for the optimal timing of payments of real estate and state estimated taxes. While these payments may be deductible for regular federal income tax purposes, they may not help you if you are subject to the AMT in a particular year. For executives who may or may not be subject to the AMT in any particular year, it often can be beneficial to accelerate or defer these payments to mitigate the effects of the AMT.[48]

Employment Taxes

Employment taxes (also known as payroll taxes) apply to earned income such as wages or self-employment income. "Old-Age, Survivors, and Disability Insurance" or "OASDI" taxes, commonly referred to as Social Security taxes, and Hospital Insurance or "HI" taxes, commonly referred to as Medicare taxes, make up the bulk of these employment taxes.

The employee is responsible for half of these taxes, while the employer pays the other half.[49] Self-employed individuals must pay the entire amount.[50] Under the 2010 Affordable Care Act, higher earners owe an additional 0.9% Medicare tax on earned income above certain thresholds.[51]

Employment taxes can be substantial, thus necessitating planning around them whenever possible. While both employed and self-employed executives have opportunities to minimize these taxes, the strategies for doing so are likely to differ.

Net Investment Income Tax

If an executive has net income from investments, then, under the Affordable Care Act, he or she may be subject to a net investment income tax of 3.8% on the lesser of net investment income or the amount by which modified AGI exceeds a statutory threshold amount. In general, net investment income for this purpose includes, but is not limited to, interest, dividends, capital gains, rental and royalty income, and non-qualified annuities. It generally does not include wages and most self-employment income; and, with certain exceptions, it does not include income derived in the ordinary course of a trade or business.[52]

Our experience is that many executives do not fully understand the applicability of this additional tax on net investment income. They often mistakenly believe, for example, that capital gain attributable to the sale of a business in which they are actively involved is subject to the tax. Again, careful planning is essential.

Kiddie Tax

The federal "Kiddie Tax" was designed to discourage parents who hoped to reduce their taxes by shifting their investments over to their children. In general terms, the Kiddie Tax is applied to the amount of a child's unearned income that exceeds certain thresholds and is imposed at the ordinary and capital gains rates applicable to trusts and estates. Trusts and estates reach the highest tax brackets at much lower incomes than do individuals.

At one time, the Kiddie Tax only applied to children under age 14. Now, however, children are affected by the Kiddie Tax if their unearned income exceeds certain low thresholds and, at the end of the year, they are:

- Under age 18;
- Age 18 and didn't have earned income that was more than half of their support; or
- A full-time student that is at least age 19 and under age 24 and didn't have earned income that was more than half of their support.[53]

Nevertheless, executives who are aware of these rules can still do some marginal planning within the above-mentioned thresholds. While the annual impact of this planning may be small, it certainly can be substantial over longer periods of time.

Other Taxes

There are other types of income-based taxes that should be considered, such as, for example, the additional golden-parachute taxes or deferred-compensation taxes we described above.[54] The list of these taxes is long, and some are less likely to be relevant for corporate executives, but most of these taxes can be mitigated with proper planning.

Maintain Good Tax Hygiene

Well that's an odd expression, isn't it? What we really mean is that, just as we take care of our personal hygiene by following certain patterns and rituals, so it is important to do so with taxes!

Here are some of the essential rules for proper tax hygiene:

Work with a Tax Advisor

Even if you are a devout do-it-yourselfer, there is no substitute for at least allowing a tax professional to review your return. Tax software these days is quite good, but, in our view, it has not yet replaced human intuition. Experienced and qualified tax professionals can almost always earn their fees by ensuring that the Ten Commandments of Tax Planning are followed, while also ensuring that no aggressive or improper tax positions are being taken, potentially leading to audits or worse.

Run Tax Projections Over the Course of the Year to Maximize Tax Efficiency, Eliminate Surprises, and Avoid Paying Interest and Penalties

Taxes are a dynamic matter. As long as it's impossible to predict the future, it remains impossible to predict with certainty the exact tax consequences attributable to any future period. For this reason, it is important to recalibrate—constantly.

Keep Good Records

Statutes of limitations for audits vary, but, in most cases, we recommend keeping complete records—copies of receipts, checks, tax forms, and everything else—for a period of at least six years after filing a return for each year. Keep copies of the returns too. It's best to be prepared to substantiate and defend any tax position, and electronic storage capabilities—as long as they are secure—now make that easier than ever.

From a tax perspective, David and Abby could have avoided many of their problems had they simply maintained better tax hygiene. Most importantly, a professional tax advisor could have helped them mitigate the many tax-related mistakes that cost them so much in the end.

Notes

1. <u>Commissioner v. Newman</u>, 159 F.2d 848 (2d Cir. 1947). Learned Hand also said: "Any one may arrange his affairs that his taxes shall be as low as possible; he is not bound to choose that pattern which will best pay the Treasury; there is not even a patriotic duty to increase one's taxes." See <u>Helvering v. Gregory</u>, 69 F.2d 809, 810–811 (2d Cir. 1934).
2. See Chap. 4.
3. See I.R.C. § 408.
4. As we discuss tax planning around concepts such as IRAs, we must constantly refer to the legal limits for participating in these opportunities. As these limits are subject to constant change, we have decided to focus instead on the general concepts rather than on the specific limits in effect at the time of publication. For 2018, the annual traditional IRA contribution limit is the smaller of (1) $5,500 ($6,500 for individuals over 50) or (2) the individual's taxable compensation for the year, subject to certain limited reductions. See I.R.S. Publication 590-A.
5. See I.R.C. § 408.
6. For 2018, the annual Roth IRA contribution limit is the smaller of (1) $5,500 ($6,500 for individuals over 50) or (2) the individual's taxable compensation for the year, subject to reduction for higher-earning individuals. See I.R.S. Publication 590-A.
7. See I.R.C. § 408A.
8. See Chap. 9.
9. See I.R.S. Publication 590-A.
10. See I.R.C. § 401.
11. See I.R.C. § 402A.
12. See I.R.C. § 457.
13. See I.R.C. § 409A and Treas. Reg. § 1.409A-2.
14. See I.R.C. § 408.
15. See I.R.S. Publications 560 and 3998.
16. See I.R.C. § 408.
17. See I.R.S. Publications 560 and 3998. Publication 3998 offers a helpful comparison of the key structures for deferral-based retirement planning.
18. See I.R.S. Publication 972.
19. See I.R.S. Publication 503.
20. See I.R.S. Publication 970.
21. See I.R.S. Publication 590-A.
22. See I.R.S. Publication 514.
23. See I.R.C. §§ 25C and 25D.
24. See I.R.S. Publication 505.
25. See I.R.S. Publication 505.
26. See I.R.C. § 163.
27. See I.R.C. § 61.
28. See I.R.C. § 1222.
29. See I.R.C. § 1222.
30. See I.R.C. § 1211.
31. See I.R.C. § 1212.
32. See I.R.C. § 121.
33. See I.R.S. Publication 587.
34. See I.R.C. § 1091.
35. See I.R.C. § 1(h).
36. See I.R.C. § 1245.
37. See I.R.C. § 1202. The exclusion is available only for investors that are not corporations.
38. See I.R.C. §§ 1045 and 1202.
39. See I.R.C. § 1244.

40. See I.R.C. § 1244. As of 2018, the amount of loss that can be treated as an ordinary loss is limited to $50,000 (or $100,000 for married couples filing jointly).
41. See I.R.C. § 103 and I.R.S. Publication 550. Interest can also be taxable when it is earned, even if it has not yet been received; and debt instruments that do not pay annual interest can be treated as paying annual interest for tax purposes. See I.R.S. Publication 550 and I.R.S. Publication 1212.
42. See I.R.S. Publication 550.
43. See I.R.C. § 529. I.R.S. Publication 970 offers a helpful guide to the various tax-favored mechanisms related to education.
44. See I.R.S. Publication 970.
45. See I.R.C. § 117.
46. See I.R.S. Publication 970.
47. See I.R.C. § 56.
48. Note that under the Tax Cuts and Jobs Act of 2017, the exemption amounts for avoiding the AMT were increased, limiting the future applicability of the AMT.
49. See I.R.S. Publication 15.
50. See I.R.C. §§ 1401 and 1402.
51. See I.R.C. § 1401.
52. See I.R.C. § 1411.
53. See I.R.C. § 1(g) and I.R.S. Publication 929. These rules, along with all tax-related rules, are subject to further change in the future.
54. See I.R.C. §§ 280G, 409A, and 4999.

Chapter 9
Estate Planning and Why It's Really So Important

In the ambulance, he felt the chaos around him. He heard the technicians working on him. But he was not thinking about himself. He was thinking about his family. How would they live without him? Would he miss seeing his children grow up? How would they remember him? He heard Abby crying …

David recovered—physically at least. Alone in a hospital bed, he barely slept.

He reflected on all of the opportunities he had at Goliath to plan for his family. He never did. "No," he thought at the time, "there's no need to think about estate planning right now. I'm going to live for many more years. Besides, estate planning is all about taxes, and it's possible the estate tax will be repealed by the time I die."

But in that bed, tortured and terrified, he wondered: "What if I *had* died?" He hesitated.

"What if I die tomorrow?"

That night in the hospital, David rethought everything.

Lessons from David and Abby

People often overlook estate planning—as David and Abby did—because they tend to believe in a couple of old myths.

- Myth #1: "Estate planning is all about taxes, specifically the estate tax."

Yes, planning for taxes, such as the estate tax, the gift tax, and the generation-skipping-transfer ("GST") tax, is part of estate planning, but there is so much more! Who will oversee your estate? Who will represent you medically, financially, and legally in the event you are incapacitated? Who will take care of your children? How will your family live without your income? Your stewardship?

- Myth #2: "Estate planning is only for older or sick people."

© The Colony Group 2018
M. J. Nathanson et al., *Personal Financial Planning for Executives and Entrepreneurs*, https://doi.org/10.1007/978-3-319-98416-2_9

David had been an athlete in high school and in good shape for most of his life. He thought that estate planning would be pointless for him, especially since the laws were always changing. Consequently, he never prepared for something like a heart attack, and as we have seen, he could have paid a substantial price by leaving his family unprepared to go on without him.

Much of estate planning is planning for the unknown—and sometimes the unlikely. Throughout this chapter, we will explain some of the most important parts of estate planning. In keeping with the theme of the book, we will outline the estate process for David and Abby without a plan at the beginning of the chapter and with a plan at the end of the chapter.

The Purposes of Estate Planning

Each element of estate planning is more important for some than for others, but for most, the main objectives of estate planning are:

Welfare Planning

The top priority of estate planning is to ensure the ongoing welfare and care of family members, dependents, and even the person doing the planning, who may become disabled or otherwise incapacitated prior to death.

Income Continuity

When there is a sudden loss of income due to a death, survivors may need to sell property, adjust spending, search for new or different employment, and/or apply for loans in the absence of immediately available liquidity. Proper estate planning seeks to avoid or mitigate this necessity.

Orderly Distribution of Estate

If there is no will or a poorly written will, members of a family may be embroiled in probate for years administering the decedent's estate.

Tax Mitigation

If property is left to others without an effective plan, state and federal estate taxes may dramatically reduce the amount remaining and available for family and other beneficiaries.

Asset Protection

Thoughtful estate planning can provide asset protection against claims of personal liability, estranged partners, spendthrifts, and creditors both during life and at or after death.

Beneficiary Security

A well-conceived estate plan will provide not only for income replacement but also for long-term security of heirs, especially with respect to their health, education, maintenance, and ongoing support.

Philanthropy

Many people see their estate plan as an opportunity to leave assets to support their favorite charitable causes, leading to an opportunity for longer-term legacy building and impact.

The Estate Planning Process for David and Abby (Without a Plan)

David and Abby never planned for their family in the event of an untimely death. Suppose David had died from his heart attack. What would have happened?

David would have died "intestate," meaning that the state of Connecticut would have appointed an administrator, paid for by David's estate, to dispose of his property according to the laws of Connecticut through a complicated, expensive, lengthy, and sometimes contentious legal process known as probate. Much of his property— but not all of it—would have passed to Abby but only after undue effort and expense.

In fact, as part of the probate process, the court would have contacted all of David's creditors. Remember that David and Abby were "cash poor," arguably living outside of their means. Abby might have had to battle with creditors in court while simultaneously working hard not only to sustain and increase her income from Slingshot but also to raise the children.

And speaking of the children, Abby probably would have had a will written shortly after David died. Having now experienced the difficult and seemingly unfair nature of the probate process, she would have realized that, if she died without a will, it would be up to Connecticut law and a court to choose a guardian for her children—a fate that could have befallen the family had she and David died together in an accident or other unfortunate event.

So, how should David and Abby have planned so that their family could avoid these potentially disastrous consequences?

The Essentials of Effective Estate Planning

Estate planning is complex, primarily because of tax considerations. That said, much of estate planning is completely separate from taxes. Accordingly, we will first consider the essentials of estate planning independent of taxes and then return to taxes in the sections that follow.

Let's start with some basics that don't even involve death. There are some basic "advance directives," for example, which should be addressed as part of any basic estate planning process. Insurance, titling of assets, beneficiary designations, lifetime gifting, wills, and trusts are also fundamental to the process.

Power of Attorney

By executing a Power of Attorney ("POA"), a person (the "principal") can designate another person (the "agent") to act on his or her behalf legally and financially in the event that the principal becomes incapacitated—either temporarily or permanently.[1] It is advisable to appoint both an agent and a contingent agent in the event that the agent cannot serve if called upon.

There are generally two ways in which power can be granted to an agent: immediately upon execution, under a "durable" POA, or only upon the occurrence of a specific event, under a "springing" POA. Neither is necessarily right or wrong, and both come with risks. For example, under a durable financial power of attorney, your agent will possess a current ability to access and transact in your financial accounts on your behalf. This level of authority opens the door for a level of access with which you might not be comfortable, at least while you are of sound mind.

A springing power might seem to address this issue by limiting the ability of your agent to act only in certain circumstances. However, it gives rise to the possibility that your agent would experience a delay in gaining the ability to act on your behalf if, for example, the document requires verification of your incapacity by a medical professional. With these points in mind, the decisions of whom to appoint as your agent and how to grant authority to that individual should not be taken lightly.

One additional note: after children attain the age of majority pursuant to state law, it becomes necessary to treat them as separate adults for most estate-planning purposes. Therefore, it is advisable that adult children execute their own POAs too.

Living Will and Healthcare Proxy

Executing a "living will" is more important than ever, if only because people are living longer and have access to increasingly complex medical options. A living will, sometimes referred to as a healthcare directive, specifies the wishes of the person executing it with respect to the medical treatments that he or she would find acceptable (or unacceptable) in the event of a serious medical condition.

Along with a living will, a person can authorize an agent to make important medical decisions if the person cannot make them personally because of a medical incapacity. The instrument used for this purpose is a medical power of attorney also known as a "healthcare proxy." The agent appointed by a principal is sometimes known as "an attorney-in-fact." In the absence of a medical power of attorney, a doctor may designate a healthcare surrogate to make medical decisions on a person's behalf.

As in the case of a POA, it is advisable to appoint a contingent healthcare agent. Also, as is the case with POA, adult children should execute their own healthcare proxy documents, and parents should not assume that they automatically will be able to serve as healthcare agents without a legal document in place.

HIPAA Authorization

The Health Insurance Portability and Accountability Act of 1996, commonly referred to as "HIPAA," had the effect of establishing broad policies and procedures for ensuring the privacy and the security of individually identifiable health information. As a result, in the event of a serious medical event, a healthcare agent or other family member may have difficulty accessing information held by medical providers during a time of need. For this reason, many people now execute an advance HIPAA authorization—in addition to a living will and healthcare proxy—affording access to medical records and other information in the event of a serious medical condition.

Insurance

Insurance often plays a critical role in the estate planning process. Life insurance is an obvious consideration, but long-term-care, disability, and other types of insurance may also be relevant. Because of the importance of insurance, we have separately dedicated an entire chapter to the subject.

Titling of Assets

Some of the simplest estate planning involves the thoughtful consideration of how and by whom assets should be owned. In some cases, it is appropriate to transfer or retitle assets so that they are owned jointly with a spouse or other person as "joint tenants with right of survivorship." As the name suggests, this registration ensures that, upon the death of one of the joint owners, the surviving owner automatically acquires full title, typically outside probate.

A similar result can be achieved when property is owned by spouses as "tenants by the entirety." In this case, state law may allow property to be treated as if it were effectively owned by a single unit comprised of both spouses.

Yet, the titling of assets requires careful consideration of matters outside probate. For example, holding property as joint tenants with rights of survivorship can expose assets to the creditors of both joint tenants. Holding assets as tenants by the entirety may provide somewhat better protection against such claims, but state law must be considered as part of an overall analysis of how best to own the assets.

Similarly, there are potential gift tax considerations in holding property as joint tenants with rights of survivorship with non-spouses. Consultation with a trusted advisor is strongly advised.

Beneficiary Designations

The ability to designate a beneficiary or multiple beneficiaries for specific assets is a simple, yet critical estate planning tool. Perhaps due to the simplicity of the process, this tool is often overlooked or neglected. Regular review of the beneficiary designations attached to a person's retirement accounts, life insurance policies, and other assets that allow for a beneficiary designation should be a part of any financial and estate planning engagement. This discipline is critical because life is dynamic. Marriages, divorces, deaths, births, and other life events frequently precipitate the need for changes to these designations. Failure to make them can be awkward at best and financially disastrous at worst.

Lifetime Gifts

Lifetime gifting is another helpful tool in the estate planning process. One-time and/ or periodic transfers of assets to others during life can be far more effective than postponing those transfers until death. Gifting can be complicated, however, particularly given the potential tax consequences, which will be described later in this chapter.

Last Will

A will is a legal document by which a person (the "testator") provides for the disposition of property upon his or her death and, if necessary, appoints a guardian for minor children and possibly others. A will may also provide for the funding of one or more trusts designed to distribute assets over time and subject to certain conditions. At the death of the testator, the executor of the will (the person appointed to be in charge of executing the will) administers the estate and, if necessary, petitions for probate, presenting the will to a court and the public.

When someone dies without a will (or "intestate"), the courts are more involved in the process. In most cases, someone petitions the appropriate court for appointment of an administrator (the person in charge of the estate in the absence of a will). Typically, someone close to the decedent, such as a spouse or a child, will be appointed. From that point, without guidance from a will, state law will govern the distribution of all property. Consider the potential consequences. If most of your family were no longer alive, an estranged sibling with significant debt could claim all of your property instead of a lifelong friend. Alternatively, and perhaps more likely, a child in college could suddenly inherit a substantial sum of money, without the maturity to manage such a fortune. To avoid these or other unfortunate-but-possible scenarios, a will is imperative.

Of course, a will is even more critical if you have minor children. In the event that both of a child's parents die without a will, a court will intervene to appoint that child's future guardian. Importantly, anyone can petition for appointment. While the court generally will endeavor to act in the child's best interest, the court, not you, will make the determination of exactly what constitutes "best interest."

Simple Will

Under a simple will, a.k.a. an "I love you will," a person passes all of his or her property to another person (or persons), typically a spouse and/or children. This type of will is a basic form of estate planning and can be effective for estates that are not expected to exceed the federal estate tax exemption and, importantly, where state estate taxes are not a consideration. For estates that are expected to exceed the federal estate tax exemption and in circumstances where state estate taxes are a consideration, more involved estate planning may be required.

Testamentary Trust Will

A testamentary trust will is a will that, upon the death of the testator, creates a trust to hold at least a portion of the testator's assets for the benefit of his or her beneficiary(ies). The will serves to provide direction to the personal representative and the probate court as to how the trust should be funded. Critically, the terms of the trust are also embedded in the will.

Pour-Over Will

A pour-over will is a document that effectively transfers all remaining assets in a decedent's estate to a specified trust. A pour-over will can be used in conjunction with a testamentary trust, as described above, but in most cases, a pour-over will is used as a complement to an inter-vivos trust (a.k.a. a "living trust"). When used in this manner, a pour-over will effectively serves the same purpose of transferring all remaining property in a decedent's estate to a specified trust, but it does not actually create the trust. The inter-vivos trust is already in existence at the time of death, and presumably, if the proper steps are taken, most of the decedent's estate has already been transferred to that trust during his or her lifetime. The purpose of the pour-over will typically is to serve as a "catch-all," simply directing the transfer of any assets that remain outside the trust through probate to that trust.

Trusts

A trust is a legal document by which a person (the "grantor") transfers property to a trustee for the benefit of certain individuals and/or entities ("beneficiaries"). Property held in trust generally will be distributed outside the probate process and may be better protected than property disposed of by a will.

Testamentary Trusts

A will, upon the death of the testator, can create a testamentary trust to hold at least a portion of the testator's assets for the benefit of his or her beneficiary(ies). The will serves to provide direction to the personal representative and the probate court as to how the trust should be funded and managed by a trustee named in the will. Critically, the terms of the trust are also embedded in the will.

Living Trusts

Also known as inter-vivos trusts, living trusts are created during the grantor's lifetime. Generally speaking, living trusts are most effective when estate planning objectives include flexible lifetime planning, easing the burden of estate administration, privacy, and minimizing exposure to probate. The living trust is a useful tool, particularly for larger estates and in instances where the grantor owns property in multiple states. While the cost to draft a living trust is generally higher than that associated with drafting a testamentary trust, when used appropriately, the savings realized later can easily exceed that up-front expense by a wide margin.

Irrevocable Vs. Revocable Trusts

If a trust is irrevocable, then it generally cannot be unwound or changed by the grantor after it has been created. A completed gift to an irrevocable trust generally will remove the gifted asset from the grantor's estate for estate tax purposes, and therefore, the grantor must not exercise control of or influence over assets within the trust. For this reason, a potential grantor must give careful consideration to future liquidity needs before executing a gift to an irrevocable trust. That said, irrevocable trusts offer substantial opportunities for asset protection, tax-efficient transfers of wealth, and philanthropic planning when used properly.

In contrast, if a trust is revocable, the grantor retains control of the trust and the assets owned by the trust. A revocable trust offers fewer opportunities for asset protection, tax reduction, and philanthropic planning, but such a trust can be useful for other important purposes, such as preservation of access to and control over trust assets, as well as probate avoidance.

Revocable Living Trusts

Many people choose to place property in a revocable living trust, mostly because property held in trust upon the death of the grantor will pass to the trust beneficiary(ies) outside of probate. Because the trust assets avoid probate, the property in such a trust generally can be made available to beneficiaries shortly after the death of the grantor.

The Essentials of Taxes in Relation to Estate Planning

Now, we'll introduce the impact of taxes.

Estate Tax

The federal estate tax applies to transfers of property at death. If a taxable estate (defined later) is valued at more than the current estate tax exemption amount ($11.18 million as of January 1, 2018), the difference between the full value of the taxable estate and the exemption amount will be subject to the estate tax. Although the estate tax is a graduated tax, all transfers in excess of the exemption amount are taxed at the top rate (40% in 2018) because the exemption amount exceeds the threshold at which the top rate applies.

The impact of state estate tax laws also must be considered. A number of states do not impose estate taxes, and for those that do, they have varying exemption amounts.

Gift Tax

The federal gift tax applies to transfers of property during life. Similar to the estate tax, which provides an exemption amount at death, the federal gift tax provides an exemption amount for transfers during life. The lifetime gift-tax exemption is currently the same as the estate-tax exemption, and any usage of the gift-tax exemption depletes your estate tax exemption on a dollar-for-dollar basis. In other words, if you make an otherwise taxable gift during your lifetime of $100,000 to your niece to help her pay for a home purchase, the estate tax exemption available at your death is permanently reduced by $100,000.

Generation-Skipping-Transfer ("GST") Tax

In addition to the estate tax and the gift tax, another federal tax is applied to transfers of property to individuals two or more generations removed from the transferor. A separate exemption of equivalent value to the estate tax is available for this specific type of transfer for gifts and bequests. Transfers subject to the GST tax are taxed at the top rate under the gift and estate tax.

The Equation for a Taxable Estate

In determining the extent, if any, to which an estate is potentially taxable federally, a simple formula would be as follows:

Gross Estate − Liabilities − Allowable Deductions = Taxable Estate

Once the amount of the taxable estate is determined, any available exemption amounts can be applied in the form of a credit to reduce the actual estate tax due, potentially to zero.

Gross Estate

The concept of "gross estate" is perhaps the easiest place to start. In general, for any decedent, it is the fair market value on the date of death or the alternate valuation date of all property, real or personal, tangible or intangible, wherever situated.[2]

Using the Gift-Tax Exclusion to Remove Property from the Gross Estate

Annually, all gifts valued at $15,000 (in 2018) or less given by one individual to a non-spousal recipient are excluded from gift-tax reporting. A married couple can elect to "split" a gift to an individual, thereby effectively doubling the amount they can give on their own without gift-tax consequences. While there is a limit to the excludable value of a gift given to one individual in a given year, there is no limit to the number of recipients to whom a person can make these annual exclusion gifts. In addition to the annual exclusion, there are exclusions available for spousal gifts (full marital deduction) as well as medical and educational exclusions.[3]

With regard to gifts made to spouses, except in the case of a gift to a non-U.S.-citizen spouse, the gift tax does not apply, no matter the amount gifted. If a spouse is not a U.S. citizen, the IRS sets a limit on the amount that may be gifted annually. In 2018, that limit is $152,000.[4]

To be eligible for the gift-tax exclusion for medical expenses paid, a gift must be given to a medical institution or an insurance corporation for a qualified expense or expenses. Specifically, all medical expenses that are deductible in the calculation of income taxes are excludable in the calculation of gift taxes. To be eligible for the educational exclusion, the amount must be paid directly to a qualified institution on behalf of an individual as payment for tuition only.[5]

From a tax-reduction perspective, lifetime gifting can be very powerful. To the extent that assets above a certain amount will not be required to fund your future living expenses, gifting assets out of your estate in a coordinated and continuous manner could significantly reduce the potential value of your taxable estate. The benefit is twofold: one, you can mitigate your exposure to the estate tax; and two, you can glean enjoyment from the positive impact your generosity has on the lives of the recipients.

Liabilities

Liabilities that can be deducted from a gross estate include liabilities for mortgages, medical bills, funeral expenses, unpaid taxes, and other debts.[6]

Estate Tax Deductions

There are two primary deductions available when adjusting the value of a gross estate for purposes of calculating the value of a taxable estate. The first is the unlimited marital deduction. Similar to the gift-tax exclusion discussed above for lifetime transfers, the unlimited marital deduction allows a decedent spouse to transfer an unlimited amount to a surviving spouse at death, free of estate-tax consequences. Also similar to the gift-tax exclusion, the rule is different if a spouse is not a U.S. citizen. In this case, the transfer will be treated as if it were made to a non-spousal recipient, subject to estate tax to the extent the value of all such transfers exceeds the current estate-tax exemption amount.[7]

The second important deduction is the deduction available for charitable contributions. If a decedent leaves property to a qualifying charity, the value of that property is deductible from the gross estate.[8] Other available deductions include estate-related administrative expenses and casualty and theft losses during the estate administration process.

Select Estate-Planning Strategies

In this section, we'll review some fundamental concepts, structures, and strategies. As a part of the discussion, we'll identify ways in which taxes can be mitigated.

Portability

With the passage of the American Taxpayer Relief Act ("ATRA") on January 2, 2013, the concept of a "portable" estate-tax exemption became law. Under ATRA, subject to certain requirements and limitations, when a married individual dies and does not utilize his or her entire estate-tax exemption, an election can be made to "port" the unused exemption amount to the surviving spouse. If (and only if) this election is made on a timely-filed estate-tax return for the decedent spouse, the decedent spouse's unused exemption amount can then be added to the surviving spouse's own estate-tax exemption for use when making taxable gifts or upon his or her death. Note that the unused estate-tax exemption of the decedent spouse is not adjusted for inflation. For example, if a married individual died in 2015, when the estate-tax exemption was $5,430,000, and the surviving spouse died in 2017, when the estate tax exemption was $5,490,000, the total exemption available to the estate of the second spouse to die would be equal to $10,920,000 ($5,430,000 + $5,490,000).

Portability is a useful tool, but it does not negate the need for thoughtful, ongoing estate planning. For example, with a young couple having a combined taxable estate of less than the effective exemption amount, the by-pass trust structure described below permits estate-tax mitigation on all of the growth in the assets of the by-pass trust. In addition, portability is not automatic. Be sure to seek legal counsel if you plan to utilize portability.

Step-Up (or Step-Down) in Basis

Generally speaking, under current law, the basis of an asset includable in the estate of a decedent is readjusted to equal the fair market value of that asset on the date of death (or the alternate valuation date).[9] The rules for applying basis adjustments are complex and beyond the scope of this discussion. For our purposes, it is sufficient to be aware of the opportunity for tax savings presented by this point of law. The ability to adjust cost basis up to the fair market value of a particular asset on the date of death effectively eliminates all embedded, unrealized capital gain as the asset is transferred to the beneficiary. As a result, the asset can subsequently be sold by the beneficiary with little to no income tax consequences. With this point in mind, due consideration should be given to asset ownership and gifting strategies at all times, but particularly later in life and for terminally-ill individuals.

Two-Share Trust Arrangement

In a two-share arrangement, the estate of the first spouse to pass is divided into marital and non-marital shares. The assets that are set aside to fund the marital share might transfer outright to the surviving spouse, or they might be directed to a marital trust, established for the exclusive lifetime benefit of the surviving spouse. In either case, the transfer is exempt from federal estate tax as a result of the unlimited marital deduction. When the surviving spouse dies, the assets in the marital share are included in his or her gross estate and will be eligible to be sheltered from tax by the his or her available estate-tax exemption.

Any assets not transferred to the surviving spouse are set aside as the non-marital share and transferred to a non-marital trust, also known as a credit-shelter trust or a bypass trust. Typically, the surviving spouse will be granted limited access to the assets in the bypass trust. The limited nature of the surviving spouse's access is intentional and necessary, as it severs the link between the assets in this trust and the estate of the surviving spouse. By this arrangement, assets that comprise the non-marital share can be subjected to estate tax upon the death of the first spouse. As long as the aggregate value of the assets in the non-marital share is less than the current estate-tax exemption (less the value of any lifetime gifts made by the decedent spouse), the non-marital share will pass to the bypass trust unreduced by federal estate tax.

Again, state law may impact the structure and amounts that fund these trust shares, but the general objective is to avoid estate tax at the first death and, to the maximum extent possible, mitigate estate tax at the second death.

While the recent addition of portability to the tax code provides another planning tool, it does not necessarily negate the utility of the classic two-share arrangement. For example, if appreciable property is subjected to estate tax at the first death and transferred to the bypass trust, any post-mortem investment income and capital appreciation will be subject only to income tax. Importantly, it will not compound as part of the surviving spouse's estate. Additionally, the lifetime exemption may be portable at the federal level but not at the state level, which could add an additional level of administrative and reporting complexity at the second death. Further still, if the surviving spouse remarries, only the lifetime exemption from the most recent spouse is effective. This dynamic could create complications, especially if there are children from both marriages.

Marital Trusts

As noted earlier, by virtue of the unlimited marital deduction, all property transferred to the marital trust is exempt from estate tax until the death of the surviving spouse. In order to qualify trust-owned assets for the marital deduction, the surviving spouse must be the sole beneficiary during his or her lifetime and must have the right to receive all trust income over that period of time. In many cases, the surviving spouse will have unfettered access to trust principal as well. With these points in mind, the primary purpose of a marital trust is to provide financial support for the surviving spouse. Depending upon the structure of the marital trust, it may also afford a level of asset protection for a particular class of future beneficiaries, such as the decedent spouse's children in the event that the surviving spouse remarries.

The three most common types of marital trusts are as follows:

1. **General power-of-appointment ("GPA") marital trust.** A GPA marital trust is a trust that provides the beneficiary spouse with an unlimited power to appoint trust assets. Critically, the beneficiary spouse may exercise a GPA to appoint assets to himself or herself, to his or her estate, to his or her creditors, and/or to the creditors of his or her estate.
2. **Limited power-of-appointment ("LPA") marital trust.** An LPA marital trust is similar to a GPA marital trust, except that the beneficiary spouse's power to appoint trust assets is limited to a specific group of named beneficiaries or a specific class of beneficiaries defined within the trust document.
3. **Qualified terminable interest property ("QTIP") trust.** A QTIP trust is a more restrictive form of marital trust. Under a QTIP trust, the beneficiary spouse must receive all trust income during his or her lifetime. With regard to trust principal, the surviving spouse may have limited access or no access at all. Furthermore, the grantor spouse identifies the ultimate beneficiaries that will receive the trust assets after the death of the surviving spouse. QTIP trusts can be very useful in certain circumstances, most commonly when one or both spouses have children from another marriage.

Non-marital Trusts (Bypass Trusts)

A bypass trust is funded with assets that intentionally were included in the taxable estate of the first spouse to die. From a mechanical standpoint, there are different ways to direct the funding of a bypass trust, but the primary objective is the same: to maximize the utility of the estate-tax deduction upon the first death in order to minimize future estate-tax obligations.

As discussed earlier, the tax basis of assets owned by the decedent at the time of death is adjusted to reflect the date-of-death value of those assets. This applies to property owned directly by the decedent or owned in his or her revocable trust.

Transferring assets to which a step-up in tax basis has been applied into a bypass trust is potentially favorable both for estate-tax and income-tax purposes. As a practical example, consider the following scenario. First, assume that David owned

Goliath stock worth $1,000,000, with a total tax basis of $250,000 at the time of his heart attack. Next, assume that David unfortunately died as a result of his heart attack. In this scenario, the tax basis of that stock would have been adjusted up to $1,000,000 as a part of the estate-administration process. Finally, assume that the stock subsequently was transferred, unreduced by estate taxes, to a bypass trust by operation of David's will; and while in trust, the value of the stock increased to $5,000,000. Upon disposition, the capital gain would be figured using $1,000,000 as the tax basis, effectively wiping away $750,000 of embedded gain over David's original cost. Additionally, the $4,000,000 of appreciation that accumulated while the stock was held in the bypass trust should avoid estate tax entirely upon Abby's death. Applying the maximum federal tax rate on long-term capital gains and accounting for the 3.8% Medicare surtax on net investment income, the income tax savings created by the initial step-up in basis calculates to about $178,500 ($750,000 × 23.8%). From an estate tax perspective, assuming a 40% tax rate, the savings calculates to $2,000,000 ($5,000,000 × 40%).

By contrast, if the stock passed directly to Abby or to a marital trust for Abby's benefit, the shares would be eligible for a second step-up in basis from $1,000,000 to $5,000,000 if she held them until her death. In the aggregate, the double step-up in tax basis would wipe away $4,750,000 worth of unrealized capital gain, which, using the rates above, would result in total federal income tax savings of $1,130,500. Of course, the full value of the stock would then be subject to estate tax as a part of Abby's estate, since it was not taxed as a part of David's estate. If the value of Abby's taxable estate exceeds her available estate-tax exemption by the full value of the stock, the 40% estate-tax levy on $5,000,000 worth of stock would more than eliminate the income-tax savings generated by the double step-up in basis.

The following Table 9.1 provides a more complete example:

Table 9.1 Appreciation and bypass trusts

	W/out bypass trust	W/ bypass trust
David's estate at death (1/1/2014)	$6,000,000	$6,000,000
Abby's estate at David's death (1/1/2014)	$5,000,000	$5,000,000
Bypass trust funding at David's death (Goliath stock only)	$0	$1,000,000
Abby's taxable estate at death (1/1/2017)	$15,000,000	$10,000,000
Available estate-tax exemption at Abby's death (David's unused exemption included, if applicable)	$10,830,000	$9,830,000
Value of property taxed as part of Abby's estate	$4,170,000	$170,000
Amount owed in federal estate taxes (40%)	$1,668,000	$68,000
Unrealized gain subject to capital-gain tax at disposition	$0	$4,000,000
Investment income tax upon disposition[a]	$0	$952,000
Total federal tax exposure	$1,668,000	$1,020,000

[a]Assumes 20% long-term capital gain tax plus 3.8% Medicare surtax on net investment income

Of course, this scenario is a significant departure from the story of David and Abby with which we have become familiar. In that story, Goliath's stock plummets in value, which hardly mattered because David and Abby had accumulated very little in the way of non-retirement savings, company stock, or otherwise. At the time of David's heart attack, we know they were more concerned about maintaining the roof over their heads than funding a bypass trust. Building on that point, we know they weren't worried about funding a bypass trust simply because they had done so little planning that there is no conceivable way they would have even known what the term meant. All of that said, this alternative scenario should clearly illustrate the utility of the bypass trust as a tax-mitigation technique for taxable estates.

Life Insurance and Irrevocable Life Insurance Trusts

An irrevocable life insurance trust ("ILIT") is generally employed to support the wealth-transfer objectives of a grantor. The leverage inherent in life insurance, especially in the early years of a policy, makes it a useful tool for many estate-planning objectives. When properly executed and appropriately funded, an ILIT can create a pool of money outside the estate of the grantor that can be used to replace funds lost to estate taxes; to serve as a source of liquidity to pay estate taxes while preserving other, less liquid assets owned by the estate; to pair with and serve as a hedge against a negative outcome for a complementary estate planning strategy; or even to fund a post-mortem philanthropic objective.

Had David and Abby planned for their future, saved more diligently, and created substantial wealth, the large whole-life policy that David had purchased for all of the wrong reasons ultimately may have been transferred to an ILIT at some point in the future. The transfer of an existing policy is considered a gift, and it does require a special valuation of the policy for gift-tax reporting purposes. Once the gift is executed, the donor must survive at least three years in order to avoid a "clawback" of the policy (and, critically, the death benefit) into the donor's estate. Assuming the donor survives the clawback period, the policy is then safely outside of the donor's estate, and the entire death benefit, when paid, is not only exempt from income tax but also not subject to estate tax. With those points in mind, there are few, if any, other solutions that offer the same combination of tax efficiency, potentially significant investment leverage, and a contractually guaranteed payout offered by a properly executed ILIT strategy.

Spousal Lifetime Access Trust

A spousal lifetime access trust ("SLAT") is a lifetime gifting strategy that can serve the dual purpose of reducing future exposure to the estate tax and retaining lifetime access to the gifted property. With that point in mind, a SLAT can serve as a solution for married individuals who would like to gift assets during their lifetime but are reticent to permanently part with a sizeable portion of their combined estate. To execute a SLAT, one spouse (the grantor-spouse) gifts assets to an irrevocable trust established for the benefit of the other spouse (the beneficiary-spouse) using all or some portion of the grantor-spouse's lifetime exemption to shelter the gift from gift taxes. This structure allows the trustee to make distributions to the beneficiary-spouse during the beneficiary-spouse's lifetime, if necessary. Ideally, however, SLAT assets would be not be withdrawn by the beneficiary-spouse and, instead, allowed to grow outside of both spouses' estates.

Aside from providing income protection for the beneficiary-spouse and potential future estate-tax reduction, a SLAT can be a useful estate planning strategy for a number of other reasons, including:

- Probate avoidance and asset protection
- The ability of a terminally-ill grantor-spouse to replace low-basis assets in the SLAT with high-basis assets owned personally prior to death, to allow the grantor's estate to avail itself of the step-up in basis upon the grantor's death.
- The ability to allocate generation-skipping-transfer tax exemption amounts to the initial transfer, which can be particularly powerful when a SLAT is funded, at least in part, with a life insurance policy.

As with all of these strategies, there are a number of important planning points and potential pitfalls that should be considered when implementing a SLAT strategy. Therefore, it is critical that you review all aspects of your financial landscape with a trusted advisor prior to drafting and executing the formal trust document.

Grantor Retained Annuity Trust

A grantor retained annuity trust ("GRAT") is a lifetime gifting strategy that involves an agreement between a grantor and a trustee to exchange an asset for a stream of income (principal plus a specified rate of interest) over a specified term of years. The objective of the strategy is to capture excess value within the GRAT, after all payments have been made back to the grantor. Initially, the grantor identifies and transfers to the trust an asset that is expected to appreciate significantly during that term. The trustee makes payments back to the grantor, typically annually, for the term of the GRAT. After all payments have been made, any excess value remaining in the trust can be distributed to the GRAT beneficiaries free of gift tax.

Aside from the realized appreciation of the gifted asset, the most critical component of a GRAT is the interest rate used to determine the total amount of the payments that must be made back to the grantor. That reference rate, known as the Section 7520 rate, is updated and published by the IRS on a monthly basis. While a more involved discussion of the mechanics of a GRAT is beyond the scope of this discussion, it is important to understand that the strategy is best employed in a low interest-rate environment.

Finally, we should note that the initial transfer is considered a gift by the grantor for gift tax purposes and that a GRAT can be drafted in such a way as to effectively reduce the value of any gift to $0. With that point in mind, a truly successful GRAT is one that shifts significant value while expending little-to-no lifetime exemption.

The Estate Process for David and Abby (with a Plan):
The Resurrection

David and Abby properly planned for their family's welfare. David survived his heart attack, but the following paragraphs provide a snapshot of what things would have looked like had he died.

Income Continuity

In addition to a well-funded GPA marital trust, the ILIT David had funded with his life insurance policy would provide plenty of income for Abby, the children, and hopefully generations to come.

Orderly Distribution of Estate

Most of David's property had been in trusts, so Abby spent little time on probate. Abby also kept most of her property in trusts, so the property ultimately would pass to her children stress-free.

Tax Reduction

Subsequent to David's death, under the guidance of the family advisor, Abby sold much of David's stock, paying only a pittance in long-term capital gains tax. By virtue of properly executed beneficiary designations, Abby was able to transfer assets in David's retirement plans to retirement plans in her own name, thereby delaying IRS-mandated required minimum distributions well into the future.

Asset Protection

Using the proceeds from the stock sale, Abby was able to retire the mortgage and other minor debts. Not only was the elimination of this debt emotionally comforting, it also eliminated the possibility that her personal representative would have to contend with creditors if she were to pass away prematurely. Furthermore, since all assets that would ultimately benefit the children were held in trust, she was comfortable that she had done what she could to protect the assets against future misuse and/or misappropriation.

Philanthropic Planning

Abby also drafted a new ILIT, which subsequently purchased insurance on her life. Knowing, however, that the children would be financially secure during their lifetimes, she established this ILIT for the benefit of David's and her favorite charity.

David thought about this morbid scenario but breathed a sigh of relief. That night in the hospital, as nervous as he was about his own health, David had peace of mind.

Notes

1. See Michael J. Nathanson, Ian D. Barclay, and Cary P. Geller, "Estate Planning: It's Not Over," *Financial Advisor*, April 3, 2017.
2. See I.R.C. § 2031. In some cases, the value of a gross estate can be determined after the date of death—on an alternate valuation date. See I.R.C. § 2032.
3. See I.R.C. § 2503 and I.R.S. Publication 559.
4. See I.R.C. § 2523.
5. See Treas. Reg. § 25.2503-6.
6. See I.R.C. § 2053.
7. See I.R.C. § 2056.
8. See I.R.C. § 2055.
9. See I.R.C. § 1014.

Chapter 10
Planning for Philanthropy and What It Can Do for Everyone

David and Abby's lack of planning limited their ability to use their income and assets to support their community and contribute to causes they cared about. In addition to maximizing the amount of wealth that can be used for, or transferred to, others, careful and thorough planning will involve a strategy to ensure the future welfare of family members, non-family dependents, and charities or similar institutions that an executive may wish to support.

One of the often-neglected aspects of financial planning is giving money to charity or supporting cultural institutions or medical research that is important to the executive and his or her family members. It is both a delight and responsibility to use wealth to support the public good and specific causes or charities in local communities and beyond. But doing charitable giving right involves far more than just donating money when asked. There are tax, legal, and personal considerations that all need to be assessed. This takes time, dedication, and often expert advice.

Making philanthropy part of the financial planning exercise doesn't just maximize the impact of making financial gifts. Done properly, it can have a major impact on tax bills, freeing up money for other purposes—or for more philanthropy!

An executive might make charitable gifts for many different reasons, including:

- The executive wants to contribute to causes or communities about which he or she cares.
- The executive wants to support the charitable endeavors of family, friends, or colleagues.
- It can reduce income taxes.
- It can facilitate smart estate planning.
- It visibly demonstrates values the executive is trying to instill in the next generation.

David and Abby didn't have a formal plan for their charitable giving, and they never managed to generate enough spare cash to make major gifts; but, to continue our story, their tax returns showed a pattern of regular giving via check to their house of worship and a couple of health and welfare charities whose causes meant something to them. What was a bit of a surprise to David and Abby in reviewing

© The Colony Group 2018

M. J. Nathanson et al., *Personal Financial Planning for Executives and Entrepreneurs*, https://doi.org/10.1007/978-3-319-98416-2_10

their hastily prepared tax returns was that the majority of their charitable giving was associated with attending functions for the causes of friends and colleagues, rather than anything particularly close to their hearts. While much charitable giving is driven by a desire to support good causes and effect change, many corporate executives find that they are also asked to fund the causes of others around them.

The key to getting the biggest impact—financially and emotionally—out of charitable giving is to establish a charitable gifting plan, something not all executives do. David and Abby never bothered with this, but they should have. It's another example of how a little thought and planning, under the right guidance, can help an executive, their family, and countless others.

Elements of a Charitable Gifting Plan

There are five key elements to charitable gifting for every donor:

1. Establishing a budget
2. Becoming familiar with the basic income tax rules
3. Selecting the most tax-efficient assets to give
4. Choosing how to make the gift
5. Making an impact

We could write an entire book on each one, with the entire collection possibly being called "The Five Books of Charitable Gifting," but we will just summarize the key points here. Individuals with concentrated stock positions or business interests, as well as those with substantial wealth, have a sixth element—advanced planning.

Establishing a Budget

An executive and his or her family should establish a charitable gift budget each year that's appropriate for their particular financial circumstances. Most people set aside a percentage of income, often as much as 10% to 20% of income, or a set dollar amount. The important thing is to set a budget and consciously allocate to the causes that are important, while leaving room for other charitable responsibilities, including the likelihood of wanting to contribute to causes that are important to colleagues and friends.

Basic Income Tax Rules

The tax rules for deducting charitable gifts are stringent and can be quite complex. This section is meant to provide a brief overview, not to replace the very detailed tax laws and regulations or the advice of qualified tax counsel. Most executives won't need to understand all of these rules in great detail, but it's useful to explore the available deductions. Had David and Abby done so, their giving could have been much more effective.

An individual generally can deduct contributions of money or "qualified property" subject to the following[1]:

1. The gift must be made to a qualified organization, which can include churches, domestic governmental units, and nonprofit charitable organizations that have received approval from the U.S. Treasury to be exempt entities. The IRS provides an excellent resource to check the status of recipients via the "Exempt Organizations Select Check Tool" at https://www.irs.gov/charities-non-profits/exempt-organizations-select-check.

2. Contributions must be made to, or for the use of, a qualified organization and cannot be set aside for a specific person. Also, an individual generally is not entitled to a deduction to the extent the individual receives a personal benefit, such as valuable merchandise or food and entertainment, in return for a gift.

3. Charitable gift deductions are limited to a percentage of income. Cash gifts are deductible up to 60% of adjusted gross income, and gifts of "qualified property" are generally limited to 30% of AGI. A 20% limit applies to gifts to private, non-operating foundations. Carryforward provisions may be available on a limited basis when these limitations cause a disallowance in any year.

4. Gifts of property are often only deductible up to what the property cost when purchased. There are, however, many valuable exceptions. For example, publicly traded marketable securities, including stocks, bonds, ETFs, and mutual funds held for more than one year are deductible at fair market value at the time of the gift. The deduction for property held for one year or less generally cannot exceed its cost. Contributions of tangible property such as art and collectibles that are held for more than one year are deductible at fair market value only if given to a charity that uses it in fulfilling its exempt purpose. If given to a charity that does not use it in its exempt purpose, the deduction is limited to cost. For example, art given to an art museum should qualify for deductibility at fair market value, while the same gift given to a medical research facility may be limited to original cost.

5. Other property held for more than one year may be deductible at fair market value if given to public charities or operating foundations. Many special rules govern gifts of real estate, property encumbered by debt, operating businesses, and other complex assets. Unvested stock options and restricted property are generally not eligible for lifetime charitable gifting, both by their contractual limitations and by the ensuing income-tax ramifications. However, they can be an efficient asset for charitable giving by an estate.

6. In addition to proof of payment, a donor is required to keep a contemporaneous written acknowledgement from the charitable organization for any contribution over certain amounts. The written acknowledgment must state whether the donor received any goods or services in consideration for the contribution, and, if so, include an estimate of their value. Noncash contributions are subject to additional requirements, including a receipt from the charity showing the name of the

organization, the date and location of the gift, and a description of the property. Note that clothing or household items must be in good condition to be eligible for deductibility. Noncash gifts over certain amounts also require that donors keep records that show how and when they got the property (*e.g.*, purchase, gift, etc.) and the cost or other tax basis. Noncash gifts over $5,000 generally require a qualified appraisal and a completed Section B of Form 8283 with the tax return. However, gifts of publicly traded securities, including open-end mutual funds, do not need a qualified appraisal and are reported on Section A of the Form 8283.

7. Again, gifts of property held for one year or less are only deductible in an amount equal to the lesser of cost or fair market value. Gifts of ordinary income property, including inventory and self-created work, are also deductible only to the extent of their cost. Property that is subject to mortgages or liens is subject to special rules that, in effect, create a partial sale.

8. Generally, a donor cannot deduct the gift of a partial interest in property. However, there are a number of exceptions that can be very valuable in financial planning, including for qualified charitable remainder trusts, charitable lead trusts, fractional interests of tangible property, conservation easements, and remainder interests in a home or farm. An advisor can help with any or all of these specialty areas.

Selecting the Most Tax-Efficient Gift

Appreciated Assets

Writing a check or setting up automatic contributions on a credit card might work for some basic contributions, but it's almost never the best way to make major gifts. The most efficient assets to give to charity generally are highly appreciated assets held for more than one year. For most executives, this means identifying stock, mutual fund, and ETF holdings with the largest built-in long-term capital gains as the primary source of charitable gifts. By gifting qualified highly appreciated assets, the executive not only can be eligible for a charitable deduction at fair market value but also can eliminate the potential capital gain tax on the appreciation.[2]

In the case of David and Abby, they might have been in the habit of making charitable gifts using cash of about $10,000 a year, which might have saved them about $3,500 in taxes. If, instead of cash, they gave qualified, highly appreciated securities with very low tax basis, they still would have saved almost $3,500 in taxes from the charitable deduction, but they also would have saved themselves eventually paying capital gain taxes on the nearly $10,000 of gains.

Once these asset positions have been identified as a potential candidate for gifting, an executive should then consider which positions should be sold by asking several additional questions. Is this an opportune time to reduce an overweight to company stock or other concentrated positions? Which positions are so insignificant that they are just noise in the portfolio? The best decisions involve a consideration of both tax and non-tax factors.

Other Sources for Charitable Gifts

If a privately held business is facing a near-term liquidity event, an executive of that business may wish to consider gifting a portion of their holdings prior to the transaction. A properly executed gift to a donor-advised fund or community foundation should result in a charitable deduction for the fair market value and serve to eliminate the potential capital gain. The gift of non-marketable securities is subject to many complexities, however, which may include the requirement for a full appraisal.[3]

Executives over 70½ currently can make qualified charitable distributions ("QCDs") from their IRAs of up to $100,000 per year.[4] These distributions directly to public charities can satisfy requirements for minimum distributions. The advantage of a QCD versus taking the distribution and deducting the charitable gift largely has to do with the effect on lowering income for other tax-related calculations and add backs.

In the case of shares acquired through ESPPs and ISOs, the employee must own the shares for at least one year and also hold the shares for two years from the date of grant to avoid recognizing compensation.[5] We generally advise against using stock options and unvested restricted stock for lifetime gifts, as the income upon exercise or lapse of restriction will be included in income. However, gifting options can be a strategy for testamentary charitable giving.

How to Make Gifts

There are a host of vehicles that can be used to optimize gifts to charity. Here is a brief rundown of some of the more popular vehicles for executives.

Donor-Advised Fund[6]

A donor-advised fund ("DAF") or community foundation account is a powerful tool to simplify the management of an executive's charitable giving. It lets the executive receive an immediate tax deduction, invest the principal free of taxes, and distribute amounts to qualified charities as the executive and his or her successors recommend.

A DAF offers many of the benefits of a private foundation—but with fewer headaches—and can be arranged at most major brokerage firms. Other than for gifts into the fund, the detailed substantiation paperwork for gifts to charities is eliminated. The executive can fund it in a year in which the executive has higher income, and, as of the writing of this book, there is no minimum charitable distribution from a legal perspective. Still, it is important to note that the DAF cannot be used to provide the donor with any personal benefit, such as a charity dinner or ticket. As explicitly stated in a recent IRS notice, the IRS will disqualify (and subject to excise taxes) transactions in which the DAF pays only the deductible portion and the taxpayer pays the nondeductible portion of a donation involving a benefit.[7] However, the same ruling indicates that the IRS is taking a softer stance in the case of using the DAF to discharge a personal pledge obligation as long as certain basic rules are met. In particular, there can be no reference to the existence of the pledge in any paperwork between the DAF and the charitable recipient.

DAFs may also make an ideal recipient for complex assets that wouldn't normally qualify for charitable deductions at fair market value. For instance, if Abby's business became a success, she might consider giving a small piece of her business to a DAF in advance of a liquidity event. Such a gift could serve to create a charitable deduction, avoid future capital gain, and create a source of funds for future charitable donations.[8]

Gift Annuities[9]

Gift annuities are vehicles set up by charities for donors to make a charitable gift while returning a fixed stream of cash flow for life. They offer an immediate tax deduction for a portion of the gift, and the annuity received will be partly ordinary income and partly a return of principal. But these vehicles don't pay much in a low-interest rate environment. At the time of writing, a 70-year-old couple making a gift would be eligible for a fixed payout of less than 5% per year. Still, this sort of arrangement might make sense for those wishing to support their favorite art museum, orchestra, or church.

Charitable Remainder Trusts[10]

A charitable remainder trust ("CRT") is a sophisticated wealth management tool established by a donor, generally during life, to shelter appreciated property from immediate capital gain taxation in exchange for a lifetime percentage of asset payouts measured each year. The remainder goes to the designated charities, including foundations selected by the donor.

Under this arrangement, the donor receives an income-tax deduction for a percentage of the fair market value of the contributed property when the trust is established. Lifetime payments are taxable based on the type of income realized by the trust. The tax rules look at undistributed income over the lifetime of the trust and deem distributions first to carry out ordinary income, followed by capital gains, followed by nontaxable income.

These trusts are perhaps best suited to corporate executives with large, highly concentrated, low-cost basis positions who may wish to consider implementing a charitable remainder trust as a diversification tool. They are particularly helpful for managing shares received with substantial net unrealized appreciation ("NUA") from qualified retirement plans.

Charitable Lead Trusts[11]

A charitable lead trust ("CLT") strategy typically pairs a commitment to philanthropy with minimizing gift or estate taxes to the donor's family. A CLT can be established during life or at death. During the "lead period," usually a term of years, a percentage of assets or annuity is paid to charity. The remainder is paid to the donor's heirs.

This strategy is appropriate for wealthy executives with taxable estates who have an interest in philanthropy. Though ultimately governed by the Internal Revenue Code and Treasury Regulations, there is planning and creativity involved in drafting an effective CLT. The income, gift, and estate tax consequences are complex and can vary, depending on how the CLT is structured.

Private Foundations[12]

A private foundation is a private charitable organization formed to receive donations, manage its assets, and make grants (usually to charitable organizations) to fulfill its exempt purpose. Private foundations are subject to stringent regulation and reporting by the Treasury Departments and the Attorneys General of states in which they operate.

This option is most appropriate for wealthy donors who want to make large charitable gifts yet retain significant control over the reinvestment and ultimate distribution of the funds. They're favored by donors who want to create a multi-generational legacy of purpose and family communication, for example to maintain support of a medical or cultural institution.

Making an Impact

Finally, in addition to maximizing their gifts, we note that donors also want to ensure that their dollars are going to organizations that will use their gifts effectively. Donors can do so in a number of ways, including:

- Being selective as to the charities they fund
- Learning from online and other charitable research tools, including GuideStar, a database of over 1.8 million non-profit organizations that summarizes each one's mission, programs, and financials, and Charity Navigator, for which a team of analysts rates charities on a numbers-based system to help donors easily compare charities
- Spending time and volunteering with their selected charitable organizations to understand needs and strengths
- Choosing to fund a specific endeavor or project

- Leading or participating in collective giving efforts to amass larger funds for transformational gifts
- Creating a family legacy by involving children and grandchildren in philanthropic decision-making

In the end, planning for charitable giving is far more than just a feel-good exercise. It's to the benefit of both the givers and the recipients to know the rules, seek advice, do the research, and search their hearts for the best fits between need and charity. Had David and Abby spent just a little effort on this aspect of their finances, they—and those around them—would all have been better off.

Notes

1. See I.R.C. § 170. See also I.R.S. Publication 526.
2. See I.R.S. Publication 526.
3. See I.R.S. Publication 561.
4. See I.R.C. § 408(d)(8).
5. See I.R.C. §§ 421 and 422.
6. See I.R.C. § 2055.
7. See I.R.S. Notice 2017-73.
8. Note the importance of consulting with a tax advisor prior to making a charitable contribution in advance of a future liquidity event. Under certain circumstances, a deduction may not be available under a legal theory known as the "step-transaction doctrine."
9. See I.R.C. § 501.
10. See I.R.C. § 664.
11. See I.R.C. §§ 170, 2055, and 2522.
12. See I.R.C. § 509.

Chapter 11
Managing Some of Life's Great Risks Through Insurance

They just didn't have much in the way of discretionary income, and, on their fixed salaries—which increased on occasion to account for the effects of inflation—they couldn't afford to worry about the future, including saving money for ... buying insurance for seemingly abstract concepts like long-term care, disability, or untimely death.

David had known that he needed to buy some life insurance, but he didn't really know how much or what type he needed. His friend told him that he needed a $5 million whole-life policy, which would cost him about $50,000 per year. David knew that he could have purchased less expensive term insurance, but his friend had said something about whole-life insurance being partly for investment purposes. David didn't take the time to evaluate his choices and bought the policy from his friend, having never investigated his real needs for insurance and how he could have obtained more efficient policies for his family's particular circumstances. Now he and Abby had to face the real prospect of having to cash out the policy, which had a value of about $35,000, or else have to continue paying premiums they could no longer afford.

Yet, if they cashed out the policy, could David ever get life insurance again? He had just had a heart attack, and his insurability was now very much in question. In short, David had bought himself into an insurance trap—keep his expensive policy that he could no longer afford or risk having no life insurance at all. David felt especially guilty when he remembered that there had been an optional "disability rider" on the policy that would have paid the premiums in the event of David's disability; but remember—David hadn't believed that he could become disabled.

In broad terms, insurance is a form of risk management, employable both by individuals and entities. The specific nature or source of risk does not necessarily need to be purely financial, but in order to make that risk insurable, it must be reducible to financial terms. While there are myriad types of insurable risks, we'll focus primarily on those personal risks that most commonly disrupt or devastate individual and, by extension, family financial planning. Those risks can be categorized accordingly (Fig. 11.1):

© The Colony Group 2018
M. J. Nathanson et al., *Personal Financial Planning for Executives and Entrepreneurs*, https://doi.org/10.1007/978-3-319-98416-2_11

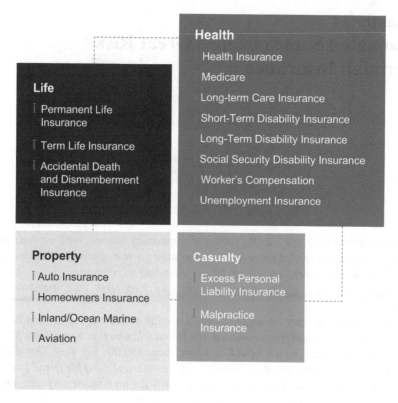

Fig. 11.1 Basic categories of insurance

1. Risk to health
2. Risk to life
3. Risk to property
4. Risk of personal liability for negligent acts or omissions

The cautionary tale of David and Abby introduces us to the each of these risks, at least indirectly, and it forces us to consider the potentially catastrophic consequences of inadequate protection. Before we move forward in our discussion, however, we should highlight several fundamental terms for future reference.

- **Policy.** Generally speaking, an insurance policy is a contract between an insurer and a policy owner that sets the scope, duration, cost, and financial benefit(s) of the insurance coverage.
- **Insurer.** The insurer, for our purposes, is the company (or "carrier") that agrees to pay compensation to the policy owner in the event that the insured suffers a covered loss.
- **Insured.** The insured, for our purposes, is the "at-risk" individual(s) or property.

- **Policy owner.** Most of the time, the policy owner will be the same as the insured individual or the owner of the insured property. Nevertheless, the policy owner can be a related third party as long as the policy owner has an insurable interest in the risk borne by the insured. There are exceptions to the insurable interest rule of thumb, but those are beyond the scope of this discussion.
- **Insurable interest.** An insurable interest in property may be established by ownership, possession, or preexisting relationship and defined by the expectation of financial loss if that property is damaged or lost. Similarly, an insurable interest in the health, life, and bodily safety of an individual may be defined by the expectation of financial loss by reason of that individual's illness, death, or injury.
- **Premium.** The premium is the price of insurance protection for a specified risk for a specified period of time.
- **Claim.** A claim is a demand made by the policy owner, or the beneficiary of the policy, for payment of the benefits as provided by the policy.
- **Benefit.** For our purposes, an insurance benefit is the nature and amount of compensation an insurer is obligated to pay to the policy owner if the insured suffers a covered loss.
- **Beneficiary.** The named recipient(s) of any benefit paid by the insurer as a result of a covered loss is a beneficiary.

There are many other insurance-related terms that could be added to this list, but those included here provide a solid foundation for our discussion.

As described above, insurance is designed to provide financial protection against specific, but uncertain risks. Uncertain as those risks may be, in a goals-based planning process, we can and should project the impact that any one of those risks, if realized, would have on future financial viability. Once the potential impact is understood in dollar terms, it becomes a relatively easy process to source and evaluate options for insurance protection, if the projection is executed and reviewed in a timely manner. For most healthy, financially secure individuals, insurance may be an important issue, but it rarely rises to the level of urgent. An appropriate level of urgency, as in David and Abby's case, may only be ignited when it is too late and insurance is no longer an option.

Health Insurance

Before focusing on the many ill-informed insurance-related decisions David and Abby made, we will focus our attention on one good decision. David should receive some credit for accepting a temporary extension of benefits under the group health insurance plan offered by Goliath after he was terminated. This option was made available under the Consolidated Omnibus Budget Reconciliation Act of 1985, now commonly referred to as "COBRA."[1] Under COBRA, certain employers must offer qualified individuals and their families the opportunity for a temporary extension of health insurance coverage (called continuation coverage) in certain instances where coverage under the plan would otherwise end. Importantly, the employer is relieved of extending premium subsidies to the terminated individual. Although the cost was much higher (David's cost was the maximum allowable amount of 102% of the cost to the plan), David accepted it without much thought. As a result, when he fell victim to a heart attack soon after he left Goliath, the vast majority of the immediate medical expenses he incurred were paid for by his insurance company. Total expenses for treatment, which included administration of life-saving procedures by emergency medical technicians, transportation by ambulance to the local hospital, usage of the hospital's emergency room and associated medical equipment, care administered by the attending physician, administration of prescription drugs, and follow-up visits with his cardiologist, ran into the hundreds of thousands of dollars. Fortunately for David, Goliath's group health insurance plan, known as a Preferred Provider Organization, or "PPO," was a relatively generous one.

A PPO is a type of health insurance plan that contracts with medical professionals and facilities to create a network of participating providers.[2] As a participant in a PPO plan, an individual usually pays a lower cost when using "in-network" providers and facilities. Other "out-of-network" providers and facilities may be used by a participant, but the participant generally will be responsible for the additional cost. David didn't realize it at the time he elected coverage under the PPO, but the PPO offered by Goliath had an expansive network, especially in the area around his home.

The previous November, during open enrollment, David had the option of selecting another type of plan know as a Health Maintenance Organization, or "HMO." An HMO differs from a PPO in that an HMO generally limits coverage to care from doctors who work or contract with the HMO.[3] An HMO generally won't cover "out-of-network" care except in an emergency. In David's case, he liked his primary care physician, and he knew that his physician wasn't a part of the HMO offered by Goliath. For this reason (and this reason alone), David selected the PPO.

Because all of his care was performed by in-network providers at in-network facilities, David was responsible for co-pay, deductible, and co-insurance amounts up to the annual individual out-of-pocket maximum of $3,000. Even considering the increased cost of coverage under COBRA, the savings afforded to him by his health insurance plan for this singular event was easily equivalent to decades of premium payments. By maintaining access to benefits through COBRA continuation coverage, David ensured that costs related to medical care would not disrupt his family's financial future.

When evaluating options for health insurance at open enrollment, an executive must be mindful of the fact that the health-insurance and medical-services industries are in a perpetual state of flux. Premium costs for coverage are just the proverbial tip of the iceberg when it comes to potential plan changes each year. For example, you should never assume that just because your doctor has accepted your insurance in prior years that your doctor will accept your insurance the following year. You should never assume that the hospital closest in proximity to your home is an in-network facility. You should never assume that your co-pay for certain prescription drugs will remain the same from one year to the next. Each year, prior to open enrollment, you should assess your family's expected healthcare needs and carefully review your options for health insurance with that information in mind.

Keep in mind, your ability to change health insurance between open enrollment windows is limited.

As noted above, COBRA is a transitional benefit, offering only a temporary extension of benefits. Depending upon the circumstances and the covered beneficiaries, COBRA requires that continuation coverage extend for a period of 18 or 36 months. Continuation coverage can be terminated early for a number of reasons, including the following[4]:

- The employer ceases to maintain any group health plan
- A qualified beneficiary begins coverage under another group health plan after electing continuation coverage
- A qualified beneficiary becomes entitled to Medicare benefits after electing continuation coverage
- A qualified beneficiary engages in conduct that would justify the plan in terminating coverage of a similarly situated participant or beneficiary not receiving continuation coverage (such as fraud)

Additionally, and perhaps obviously, continuation coverage may be terminated for non-payment of premiums. This point is particularly important because not only is the (former) employee responsible for up to 102% of the premium expense but also the premium expense will now be paid for on an after-tax basis. Consider the difference in David's case (Table 11.1):

Table 11.1 The relative cost of COBRA

	Employer/employee share (%)	Monthly expense (David)	Tax-adjusted cost[a]
Pre-tax benefit	80/20	$292.50	$163.80
COBRA continuation	0/102	$1,491.75	$1,491.75

[a]Assumes 37% federal and 7% state income tax rates

David and Abby actually might have had an alternative to continuation coverage under COBRA. It's certainly possible that Slingshot would have had an employer plan available. Under the Affordable Care Act, as of January 1, 2016, employers with 50 or more full-time employees must offer health insurance to at least 95% of their full-time employees or be subject to a fine.[5] For purposes of this discussion, however, we assume that Slingshot had fewer than 50 employees, was exempt from that requirement, and did not offer health insurance to its employees.

One other point bears mention as part of this discussion. If David recovered to the point where he could consult on a part-time basis as a self-employed individual, he could take advantage of a special tax deduction to help lower the out-of-pocket cost of health insurance. By way of background, unemployed individuals and individuals who work as employees but do not purchase health insurance under an employer-sponsored plan can only purchase health insurance on an after-tax basis (similar to the discussion of COBRA premiums, above). However, self-employed individuals are allowed to deduct the cost of health insurance, as well as dental insurance and qualifying long-term care insurance, for themselves, their spouses, their dependents, and their children who are under age 27 at the end of the calendar year (even if that child is not otherwise considered a dependent).[6] Importantly, the total value of this deduction cannot exceed earned income from the business in a given year. Depending upon the self-employed individual's marginal tax bracket, using the 2018 tax rates, this deduction could reduce the net cost of health insurance by up to 37%.

Disability Insurance

For David, his health insurance provided critical financial support for immediate, lifesaving medical care. Unfortunately, as we know, David's long-term physical well-being had been impaired by his heart attack.

As a direct result, David and his family faced a devastating long-term financial outlook. David was now (1) out of work with only a few short weeks of severance pay remaining, (2) physically unable to look for work, (3) physically unable to take on additional household responsibilities to free up Abby's time, (4) responsible for monthly committed expenses that far exceeded monthly household income, and (5) in possession of total assets that barely exceeded total liabilities, especially on an after-tax basis. As sad as it might be to consider, his family would have been in a better financial position had David died. His decision to forego long-term disability coverage under the Goliath group plan was an egregious financial mistake.

Before we consider exactly what he gave up by eschewing that benefit, we should acknowledge that, as a result of his termination, David might not have been covered under the group disability income plan at the time of his heart attack even if he had enrolled in that plan as an employee. Similar to the way in which he elected health-insurance continuation coverage under COBRA, he would have had to make an election to convert his employer-sponsored group disability income benefit to an individual policy within a specified period of time after his termination. Also similar to the health-insurance continuation coverage, the cost for individual disability income coverage likely would have been higher. That said, the increase might not have been as dramatic because Goliath was not subsidizing the premium expenses for employees under the disability income plan.

We know that the employer-sponsored disability income plan provided a benefit equal to 60% of his annual pay, and because premiums were collected by the plan on an after-tax basis, we know that any benefit received would have been exempt from income tax.[7] To measure the magnitude of the foregone benefit, we need to fill in a few details. First, a typical employer-sponsored disability income policy will pay a percentage of income up to a specified maximum monthly amount. Let's assume that (1) the maximum monthly benefit under the Goliath plan was $15,000 per month, and (2) David earned at least $300,000 in annual compensation. Next, to qualify for a long-term disability income benefit, the duration of the insured's disability must exceed an "elimination period." Let's assume that the Goliath plan had an elimination period of 90 days, which is a typical elimination period, particularly for employer-sponsored plans. Third, it is important to understand how a policy defines a "disability" because benefit payments generally cease at the earlier of age 65 or the point at which the insured is no longer considered disabled. Some policies define "disability" as the inability to perform the substantial duties of *your specific occupation* (a.k.a., "own occupation" or "own occ" policies), whereas other policies define it as an inability to work in *any occupation* that may be reasonably suitable for you based on certain criteria, including education, experience, and age.

Let's assume that (1) the Goliath plan used the "own-occupation" definition of disability, (2) David was 40 years old when he suffered the heart attack, and (3) David never recovered to the point at which he could have returned to his previous job. Following this fact pattern, he would have qualified for a tax-free monthly benefit of $15,000 on the 91st consecutive day of his disability, which would have paid him until age 65. Even if there was no annual cost-of-living adjustment built into the plan, David would have received $4,500,000 in tax-free benefits over the course of 25 years.

Of course, it's possible that David earned significantly more than $300,000 on an annual basis. As such, any benefit received under the employer-sponsored group plan would have helped replace his income, but it wouldn't have covered all of it. Depending upon factors such as age, accumulated savings, other sources of income, and anticipated future expenses and goal-specific liquidity needs, many highly compensated executives might be willing and able to self-insure against a future loss of income to a certain point. Obviously, David and Abby, with limited savings and break-even cash flow with two incomes, were not in a position to self-insure. Had they explored the magnitude of this insurance gap with a trusted financial counselor, David may not only have purchased coverage under the group plan, but also he may have purchased an individual disability income policy as a supplement to the group coverage.

The basic components of an individual policy are essentially the same as described above. One key distinction, however, is that an individual policy is not tied to your employment. As long as you pay the premium, an individual policy will remain in-force no matter whether you accept a job with another company, change careers, become self-employed, or even become unemployed (as long as you are actively looking for work). With this point in mind, an individual policy might be purchased initially as a supplement to employer-based group coverage, but it can stand on its own if coverage under a group policy is lost. David could have enrolled in the Goliath plan and purchased an individual policy sometime thereafter. Had he done so, he could have opted not to maintain the Goliath policy on an individual basis after he was terminated but still maintained coverage under his individual policy while he was unemployed.

To analyze what David and Abby gave up by not exploring disability protection further, let's first adjust our annual income assumption for David to $450,000. Let's then assume that he did purchase an individual policy, which provided a monthly tax-free benefit of $11,500, while also enrolled in the group plan at Goliath. Finally, let's assume that he elected to maintain both policies after he was laid off. Under this scenario, with all other assumptions remaining the same, he would have received

$26,500 per month (or $318,000 per year) until age 65. On a tax-adjusted basis, the cumulative benefit would be close to his after-tax employment income. If he continued to receive benefits to age 65, he would have received cumulative benefits of $7,950,000, again without any cost-of-living adjustment built into the benefit structure of either policy.

It is important to note that benefits payable under an individual disability income policy will generally layer on top of any available group plan benefits. As a part of the underwriting process, insurers will collect information about other disability income protection policies, including employer-sponsored group coverage. Considering that it could actually incentivize individuals against returning to work, insurers are careful to limit aggregate benefits to an amount less than 100% of current income. In fact, that combined benefit limit might be as low as 65–75% of total compensation income. For very highly compensated executives and individuals with non-traditional sources of income, the percentage of total income that can be protected through mainstream insurance channels could be even lower and might not be nearly sufficient. For such cases, personal high-limit disability insurance could be an option.

Additionally, depending upon employment history as well as the severity and expected duration of the disability, the disabled individual might be eligible for benefits under the Social Security Disability Income program.[8] In David's case, because he was not rendered completely incapable of working in the future and because he did not meet the strict definition of disability under the SSA guidelines, that benefit was not available.

Only after it was too late did David realize the value of disability income insurance. David's plight serves as an excellent illustration of precisely why this type of insurance is *especially* important for younger executives whose peak-earning years (and peak-expense years) are still ahead of them.

Life Insurance

Life insurance, in its most basic form, is a simple product. Unlike many other forms of insurance that provide financial protection against multiple, related risks, life insurance generally protects a named beneficiary against a single risk: the death of the insured. Somewhat surprisingly, David did own a life-insurance policy. It becomes much less surprising, however, when we learn that the policy was wholly unsuitable for his family's needs and circumstances. To understand why the policy was unsuitable, we should first understand the coverage options he would have had available to him.

Life insurance is most commonly segregated into two categories:

1. Term life insurance
2. Permanent life insurance

Term life insurance, as the name suggests, is designed to pay a death benefit to the policy owner if the insured dies within a specific period of time, such as 15 or 20 years. For that period of time, the policy premium is fixed. After the initial term expires, coverage under the policy is still available. However, the policy becomes annually renewable on the anniversary date, and the policy premium is subject to scheduled increases each new policy year. Generally, the premium increases are substantial, particularly in the first year after the expiration of the initial term. If a policy owner chooses not to renew coverage at the increased rate, then the policy will lapse. With these points in mind, term insurance is best utilized as protection against lost income due to an unexpected death during working years or to ensure funding for a specific goal, such as paying for college or retiring a mortgage.

Permanent insurance is designed to provide lifetime coverage, and although there are many different variations of permanent insurance, it is generally more expensive than term insurance. Because these products provide lifetime coverage, they are useful when planning objectives require financial protection regardless of age and/or accumulated wealth. For example, permanent insurance is particularly useful when applied toward wealth-transfer objectives in the estate-planning process.

In addition to providing lifetime coverage, permanent life insurance products offer another distinguishing characteristic when compared to term life insurance: "cash value." Cash value is a savings component that is funded, at least in part, by premium payments. Depending upon the type of permanent insurance, contributions to the cash value may be augmented by interest, dividends, and even price appreciation from investments made within the cash value. Importantly, the Internal Revenue Code allows cash value within a life insurance product to grow on a tax-deferred basis.[9]

It was the cash-value feature that convinced David to buy a type of permanent insurance product known as level-premium whole life (or ordinary life) insurance. There are several variations of whole-life insurance, but the most common form is known as a participating policy, in which the cash value grows based on annual dividends paid by the insurance company. In this type of policy, the death benefit and the annual premium are fixed.

Other primary forms of permanent life insurance include universal life ("UL") and variable universal life ("VUL"). Relative to whole life, these forms of permanent insurance provide much more flexibility. A UL policy provides flexible premiums, requiring only that a minimum premium be paid to keep the policy in force. Subject to certain limitations, a UL policy will even allow you to "skip" premium payments by allowing the cost of insurance to be deducted from the cash-value balance. UL policies also offer an adjustable death benefit. Again, subject to certain limitations spelled out in the contract, a policy owner could increase (usually subject to new underwriting) or decrease the death benefit to adjust for a change in insurable need. Regarding the cash value, premium amounts in excess of the actual cost of insurance and internal policy expenses are credited to the policy owner along with interest. The crediting rate for the interest payments, subject to a contractual minimum, is determined by the insurer. As a result, UL policies are interest-rate sensitive vehicles. Generally speaking, crediting rates have declined with interest rates over the past several decades.

Building upon the UL concept, VUL policies allow for even more flexibility by offering policy owners the opportunity to control the investment of their cash value. In a VUL policy, a policy owner can invest cash value much like a 401(k) plan participant would invest plan contributions in one or more investment options offered by the plan. This structure allows a policy owner to create a custom portfolio of investments and offers the opportunity to participate in equity-market returns. Of course, higher equity exposure in a given allocation will give rise to higher levels of volatility in the cash value, which may or may not be tolerable, depending upon the policy owner's objectives.

Before shifting our attention back to David and Abby, we should note that all permanent life insurance products should be evaluated on a regular basis. Ongoing monitoring is particularly important for UL and VUL policies, which offer few to no guarantees regarding future viability. Policy owners can request an exhibit known as an in-force illustration from the insurance agent of record or directly from the insurance company itself. These illustrations will generally include projections based on:

1. Relevant guaranteed policy minimum funding and maximum expenses
2. Current funding rates and expenses
3. Estimated future funding (if provided) and current expenses

Based on these scenarios, a policy owner can determine well in advance the point at which a policy might become vulnerable and then plan accordingly.

We know that David purchased a whole-life policy with a fixed death benefit of $5,000,000 and a fixed annual premium of $50,000. We also know that, at the time of his heart attack, the total accumulated cash value, including dividends, in David's policy was $35,000. Finally, we know that, after David's heart attack, David and Abby could not afford to pay future premiums on this policy out of pocket. They were essentially trapped because the policy structure offered no recourse (other than the disability rider that David had declined when he applied for the policy).

They could have let the policy lapse naturally by ceasing premium payments and allowing the cash value to carry the cost of insurance for as long as possible. But their financial circumstances were so dire that surrendering the policy in order to recoup the minimal cash value was their only viable option. Not only would they have to accept a significant financial loss in the surrender transaction, especially after accounting for surrender charges, but they would also now have to bear the financial risk associated with David's death on their own.

Accounting for all that we've reviewed, the magnitude of this insurance trap is hard to overstate. Having done no research on his own and, instead, relying on the advice of an inherently conflicted insurance agent, David wildly overpaid for his life insurance. Had David and Abby worked with an objective advisor, they would have explored their insurable need, reviewed their options for coverage, and identified the most cost-effective approach. That process might have led them to the conclusion that, for the amount of life insurance they needed, term insurance would have been the more appropriate solution. This conclusion would have saved David and Abby thousands of dollars annually. Ironically, just a small portion of that cost savings would have been enough to purchase the disability income insurance policy that he was statistically far more likely to need anyway![10]

Long-Term-Care Insurance

Long-term-care insurance, while not an immediate consideration for David and Abby, is still an important insurance topic that deserves mention here. In fact, many people in David and Abby's generation will probably first hear of long-term-care insurance from or explore it as an option for aging parents. Generally speaking, this type of insurance will protect the insured and/or the beneficiaries of the insured's estate from depletion of assets over time due to the cost of long-term healthcare. The types of covered care are myriad, but they generally arise from the inability of the insured to do one or more of six specific activities of daily living: bathing, dressing, eating, transferring, toileting, and continence.

The need for long-term care insurance is understandable when you consider that current research suggests that about 50% of current 65 year-olds will need long-term care at some point[11] and that the national monthly median cost of nursing-home care in a semi-private room was $7,148, while, for a private room, the monthly cost of care jumps to $8,121.[12] Long-term-care insurance was first offered in the 1960s, and by the 2000s, policies were offered by more than 100 companies. Since then, the marketplace has undergone significant contraction, with only about 12 companies writing new policies in 2017.[13] Additionally, premiums have increased on existing policy holders, and coverage options have been reduced on new policies. All of these results can be sourced to the fact that policies were mispriced by insurers as the market developed over the course of the first few decades. Even as state regulators and insurers work to address historical problems in the marketplace, trends (demographic, mortality, etc.) suggest that demand for long-term-care insurance products will grow.

There are many factors that should be considered when exploring your potential need for long-term-care insurance, including current age and life expectancy, health status, assets, local cost of care, cost of coverage, and the financial stability of the insurer. Additionally, the unique and intimate nature of long-term-care services should be taken into consideration when determining whether you would prefer to pay a professional for services rendered or rely on a willing family member to provide the necessary care. If the former is desired or the latter is not an option, long-term-care insurance should at least be a consideration, along with self-insurance (asset depletion) and/or Medicaid (after assets have been depleted). A long-term-care policy will provide a pool of money, expressed as a daily benefit amount, to an insured for purposes of buying long-term-care services. The daily benefit amount is the maximum amount the insurer will pay for services in any single day. Referring back to the national median cost for a private room in a nursing home, the daily cost calculates to $266. You could design a policy to cover that cost for a period of years, or you could opt for a lower daily benefit amount if, for example, you plan to self-insure for a portion of the cost. With long-term-care insurance, the potential needs are so varied and so personal that further discussion is beyond the scope of this chapter. Suffice it to say that independent, unbiased research and analysis are critical to the decision-making process with respect to these products.

Property and Casualty Insurance

Before we leave the topic of insurance, we should address the risks to real property, financial assets, and income. These risks, although not a focal point in the tale of David and Abby, can be significant, and the very act of reading this book is an indication of your potential exposure. For example, owning a car, a home, a boat, valuable jewelry, and/or valuable collectibles exposes you to these risks. Letting another person operate your vehicle exposes you to these risks. Having a household employee exposes you to these risks. Serving as a fiduciary to another individual and/or entity exposes you to these risks. Protecting your property against damage or total loss and protecting your assets and income against claims of liability are the roles of property and casualty insurance.

As with the other forms of insurance discussed in this chapter, there are a multitude of coverage sub-categories that nest under the property and casualty insurance canopy. Most readers will be familiar with auto insurance and homeowners insurance. Each form of insurance covers multiple types of risk associated with owning/operating an automobile and owning a home, respectively. Auto insurance, specifically, is required coverage in almost every state. Although state-mandated minimum coverage varies, the covered risks generally include limited financial protection for medical expenses and property damage incurred by others if the driver of your vehicle (not necessarily you) is determined to be at fault in an accident. Policies also generally include some level of uninsured/under-insured motorist coverage, which provides protection in an instance where the other party is at-fault but does not have adequate insurance to cover the cost of damages. Policies will also offer collision coverage and comprehensive coverage, which protects against damages incurred as a result of something other than a collision, such as fire or theft. Other, less critical but still helpful features such as substitute transportation and towing may be included as a part of an auto policy as well. Limits of coverage for each risk are outlined in the declarations statement. Regardless of which party is determined to be at-fault in an accident, or even if no fault is assigned, having adequate insurance in force at the time of an auto accident can potentially save thousands, if not hundreds of thousands, of dollars.

Similar to auto insurance, homeowners insurance is designed to provide financial protection against property damage and medical expenses. In the case of homeowners insurance, covered property generally will include the dwelling, other structures, and personal property. It may also include limited coverage for valuable articles such as jewelry, art, rugs, and collectibles. Again, the limits of coverage for each risk will be outlined in the declarations statement. For both auto and homeowners insurance, there are important exclusions that will be explained in the actual policy documents. For example, damage to your home as a result of flooding, unless the cause is sudden and accidental, such as a burst pipe, is specifically excluded from coverage under most standard homeowners insurance policies. You should review these exclusions carefully to determine whether supplemental coverage, such as a flood insurance policy, is appropriate.

Personal excess liability insurance and umbrella insurance are almost always linked directly with specific homeowners and auto insurance policies. An excess liability insurance policy layers on top of the personal liability coverage provided by the auto and homeowners insurance policies, increasing total personal liability protection for holders of such policies. A true umbrella insurance policy will generally do the same, but it will also provide additional coverage not included in the underlying policies. The excess liability protection is important because, generally speaking, limits of liability protection on the underlying policies are relatively low. An umbrella or excess liability policy can provide several million dollars of additional liability protection for a relatively small premium. For those with assets in excess of their underlying policy limits, a judgment in excess of that limit will leave them exposed to claims against their personal assets. As with almost all insurance products, the hope is to never file a claim on an excess liability policy, but the premium expense can prove to be well worth it.

As noted above, umbrella insurance coverage can provide other important types of liability protection as well. Usually offered via specific endorsement, a policy owner can secure employment-practices liability coverage, which provides financial protection against claims of discrimination, wrongful termination, and harassment made by employees. This coverage may not seem like it would be applicable to most people, but a family that employs an individual to provide a service in their home, such as a nanny, a housekeeper, or a personal assistant, is vulnerable to employment-related lawsuits. Under an umbrella insurance policy, a policy holder can also secure not-for-profit board liability coverage via endorsement. Most people who serve on not-for-profit boards assume they have coverage under the organization's directors-and-officers liability policy. While they may have some level of protection, they are likely still personally exposed to claims of financial loss due to, for example, pending and prior litigation.[14] With all of these points in mind, the value of excess liability insurance as a part of your risk-management portfolio is clear. In a worst-case scenario, a properly designed umbrella policy can be the difference between financial security and financial ruin.

It should be clear from your experience and this review that there are many different risks that must be considered when building a plan to achieve financial peace of mind. Statistically speaking, some of these risks may be very remote, and others may be more likely. Your personal circumstances, which are not accounted for in the statistics, should be weighed heavily in determining whether it is worth insuring against a particular risk.

Notes

1. See "Health Plans & Benefits: Continuation of Health Coverage—COBRA," The United States Department of Labor, accessed June 4, 2018, https://www.dol.gov/general/topic/health-plans/cobra.
2. See "Preferred Provider Organization (PPO)," U.S. Centers for Medicare & Medicaid Services, accessed June 4, 2018, https://www.healthcare.gov/glossary/preferred-provider-organization-PPO/.

3. See "Health Maintenance Organization (HMO)," U.S. Centers for Medicare & Medicaid Services, accessed June 4, 2018, https://www.healthcare.gov/glossary/health-maintenance-organization-HMO/.

4. See "FAQs on COBRA Continuation Health Coverage," The United States Department of Labor, accessed June 4, 2018, https://www.dol.gov/sites/default/files/ebsa/about-ebsa/our-activities/resource-center/faqs/cobra-continuation-health-coverage-consumer.pdf.

5. See "Employer Shared Responsibility Provisions," Internal Revenue Service, accessed June 4, 2018, https://www.irs.gov/affordable-care-act/employers/employer-shared-responsibility-provisions.

6. See "Don't Miss the Health Insurance Deduction if You're Self-Employed," Internal Revenue Service, accessed June 4, 2018, https://www.irs.gov/newsroom/dont-miss-the-health-insurance-deduction-if-youre-self-employed.

7. See I.R.C. §§ 104 and 105.

8. See "Benefits for People with Disabilities," Social Security Association, accessed June 4, 2018, https://www.ssa.gov/disability.

9. See I.R.C. § 7702.

10. According to the Social Security Administration, in 2017, the probability of an individual worker experiencing a disability before normal retirement age is 26.8%. The probability of death while never disabled before normal retirement age is only 6.1%. See https://www.ssa.gov/oact/NOTES/ran6/an2017-6.pdf.

11. See Ellen Stark, "Long-Term-Care Insurance Gets a Makeover," Consumer Reports, published August 31, 2017, https://www.consumerreports.org/long-term-care-insurance/long-term-care-insurance-gets-a-makeover/.

12. See "Cost of Care," Genworth, accessed June 4, 2018, https://www.genworth.com/services/servlets/pdf/CostofCare_2017.

13. See Stark.

14. See "Directors and Officers Insurance," Insurance Information Institute, accessed June 4, 2018, https://www.iii.org/article/directors-and-officers-insurance.

Chapter 12
Finding the Right Advisors

Along the way, David and Abby made—and spent—plenty of money. They also increasingly attracted the attention of many who sought to "advise" them—in areas that included investments, taxes, retirement planning, asset allocation, mortgages, education planning for their children, insurance, and even philanthropy. Sometimes they listened, but usually they didn't, especially when they felt that the "advisor" was really just trying to sell them something. They used tax software that they found online to do their own tax returns—usually right before the deadline.

The story of David and Abby thus far makes us wonder how things might have played out differently had they identified and worked with some qualified advisors along the way. Like many families, they were impacted by events that were simply beyond their control. Some of these events were significant and would have an enduring, adverse impact on their lives. Could they have prepared themselves better to emerge successfully from these dark days?

They had been offered financial advice from time to time, but they were often skeptical of that advice. Yet, instead of forging ahead alone, they could have worked toward identifying advisors that they could trust and the right advice model for their personal circumstances.

Getting Started

Understandably, David and Abby did not want to entrust their finances to an advisor solely on the basis of advertising or sales tactics. A 2016 Spectrem Group study found that 29% of ultra-high-net-worth individuals and 31% of millionaires selected honesty and trustworthiness as the most important factors when choosing an advisor. Only 10% of those same groups considered an association with a well-known brand to be most important.[1] Unfortunately, David and Abby kept putting off the effort it would require to find an advisor they could trust.

© The Colony Group 2018

M. J. Nathanson et al., *Personal Financial Planning for Executives and Entrepreneurs*, https://doi.org/10.1007/978-3-319-98416-2_12

Studies have been conducted to gain a better understanding of how satisfied millionaires are with their current wealth managers. The 2016 Fidelity Millionaire Outlook Study analyzed such clients using the Net Promoter System[®2] developed by Bain & Company, which identifies three types of clients:

Promoters: loyal enthusiasts who keep buying from a company and urge their friends to do the same

Passives: satisfied but unenthusiastic clients who can be easily wooed by the competition

Detractors: unhappy clients, with high rates of defection

The study results show that 55% of millionaires surveyed are Promoters, 25% Passives, and 20% Detractors, with over two-thirds of Promoters having referred their advisor at least once in the past year.[3] A PricewaterhouseCoopers study calculated that 39% of millionaire investors are likely to recommend their current wealth manager.[4] All this means that using family, friends, and colleagues can be a great resource to find an advisor.

For David, another logical place to start an advisor search might have been speaking to Goliath's human resources department. It is possible that Goliath had a company-sponsored financial planning benefit, through which the company would pay a stipend for executives to receive financial planning services. Even if Goliath did not pay for financial planning as an executive benefit, it might have maintained a list of professional advisors that were aware of the company compensation and benefits packages and adept at working with company executives. Using such a list, David could further have benefited from speaking with other executives about their experiences in working with these advisors as part of his diligence process.

Of course, great advisors can also be found through advertising or online searching. Whatever the source of a referral to an advisor—whether a friend, colleague, company, or independent search—corporate executives should perform due diligence to ensure at a minimum:

1. That the advisor is qualified and trustworthy
2. That the service offering is appropriate for their own circumstances
3. That they understand the exact nature of the advisor's compensation structure

If David and Abby had known what questions to ask, they would have been able to sort through the offers of advice they received or find the right advisor for their circumstances after gathering leads from trusted sources. Once David and Abby had gathered some leads for a potential advisory team, they could have interviewed each advisor and team using a set of prepared questions to make sure they were comfortable prior to signing an advisory agreement. The following questions are ones we generally recommend asking a potential advisor, and we will explore each topic in more depth throughout the rest of this chapter.

Interview Questions for a Potential Advisor

- What financial advisory services do you offer?
- Are you a fiduciary?
- How do you get compensated for the advice you recommend?

- What professional credentials do you hold?
- Where will you custody my assets, and how can I feel confident that they are secure?
- Whom will I be interacting with in addition to you? What are their roles?
- What is your investment philosophy? How are investment decisions made?
- Describe the types of clients you work with most often. Would you be able to provide references?
- How often should I expect to hear from you if we work together?
- What is your succession solution should something unforeseen happen to you?

What Financial Advisory Services Do You Offer?

As we can see from David and Abby's story, a typical corporate executive will need expert advice on much more than investments. The Fidelity study mentioned above found that Promoters (those most satisfied with their advisor) used a broad array of services (Fig. 12.1). The Spectrem Study found the top three services to be sought in the future by ultra-high-net-worth and millionaire investors were: planning for long-term care (14% UHNW, 22% M); establishing an estate plan (14% UHNW, 21% M); and implementing tax-advantaged strategies (12% UHNW; 16% M).[5]

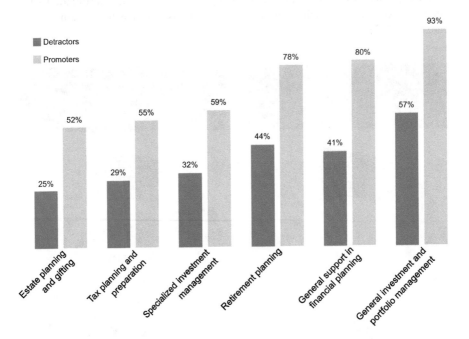

Fig. 12.1 Services to consider
*Promoters use a broader array of services than detractors. See "The 2016 Millionaire Outlook Study," Fidelity, published 2016, https://clearingcustody.fidelity.com/app/literature/item/9870983. html?sapl=go. © 2018 FMR LLC. All rights reserved. Used with permission

In addition, advisors who focus on goals-based planning seem to fare better, with 94% of Promoters agreeing that "my advisor helps me achieve my financial goals" and 89% that the advisor "considers my unique needs/goals/preferences," compared to 47% and 42%, respectively, of Detractors.[6]

Advisors who are preferred by Promoters also seem to be more proactive in reaching out to clients, with 82% of Promoters "interacting with [their] advisor 3+ times a year," compared to 57% of Detractors. Similarly, 74% of Promotors agreed that the "advisor made contact during market volatility," compared to just 49% of Detractors.[7]

Thus, when searching for an advisor, a corporate executive should make sure not only that the range of services provided is appropriate for his or her circumstances but also that the advisor will take the time to understand fully his or her situation and provide customized advice. Corporate executives should ask potential advisors to explain their financial planning processes and ask how often they can expect to hear from those advisors each year.

Finally, David and Abby should have been seeking a financial advisor who would be a true personal advocate, coordinating strategies with a team both within the advisory firm as well as externally. A talented advisory team will be adept at identifying or coordinating with other trusted professionals, including estate planning attorneys, accountants, mortgage and insurance brokers, and others, to ensure that agreed-upon strategies are properly executed. The chart below illustrates the traditional approach, where the client is challenged to take on the coordination role, versus a proactive approach where the financial advisor acts as the personal advocate (Fig. 12.2).

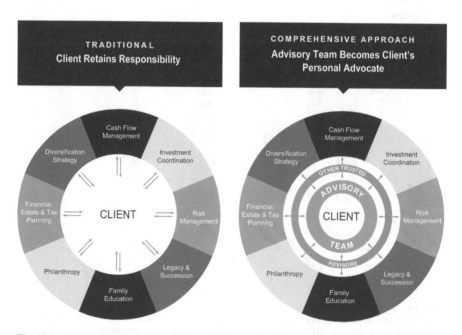

Fig. 12.2 Coordination and implementation of advice

Are You a Fiduciary?

When searching for an advisor, it is important to understand the two principal, competing legal standards of advice to which most advisors currently are bound. The "fiduciary standard"—which we consider to be the gold standard of investment advice—requires one simple thing above all others: that the interests of clients always come first. In contrast, the "suitability standard" allows advisors to recommend any investment that is suitable for their client, even if the investment is not necessarily in their client's *best* interests.[8]

In our view, while conflicts between the interests of advisors and their clients can arise under either legal standard, they are more likely to arise with respect to advisors operating under the suitability standard. Such advisors might defend these conflicts of interest by arguing that the conflicts are always disclosed to their clients. While this may be true, our experience is that clients do not always fully understand (or, in some cases, even read) these disclosures. In all cases, and regardless of the legal standard to which their financial advisors are subject, clients should seek out advisory models that minimize conflicts of interest (Table 12.1).

Table 12.1 Types of advisors and what they do

Company type	Standard of advice and service model
"Wirehouses" (broker-dealers)	Advisors generally are held to the suitability standard.[a] Often compensated via commissions and may be incented to sell other products such as insurance, annuities, and mortgages. Often more investment-oriented, with lower emphasis on comprehensive financial planning.
Independent broker-dealer platforms	Advisors generally are held to the suitability standard.[a] Model is similar to the wirehouse model, but teams operate as smaller groups within the umbrella of a larger platform. Have some range of investment choices.
Independent Registered Investment Advisors (RIAs)	Advisors generally are held to the fiduciary standard. Often planning oriented, sometimes with tax and estate planning solutions. Advisors have flexibility to choose from a wide range of investment solutions.
Robo advisors	Allow investors to input basic information and come up with a low-cost investment solution executed via computer algorithms. Solutions currently are somewhat limited, and there is little planning and tax advice.

[a]But see SEC Release No. 34-83,062 (proposing a new "regulation best-interest" standard). Note also that the U.S. Department of Labor promulgated rules that impose a fiduciary standard on all financial professionals when they provide advice on retirement plans or accounts. See 81 FR 20945 (April 8, 2016). This rule, however, has been challenged judicially and otherwise, and, as of the writing of this book, its future is in doubt

How Can I Feel Confident That My Assets Are Secure?

Regardless of the type of advisory firm that David and Abby might have engaged, one of the most basic and important considerations would be gaining an understanding of the security of their assets. Many will recall the Madoff investment scandal of 2008 or various other Ponzi schemes reported over the years. Often, these criminal practices are the result of an advisor taking custody of assets and then distributing inaccurate reports to investors. Investors are led to believe that their assets are growing when in fact the assets are being drawn down by the "advisor" to fund his or her personal lifestyle.

In order to mitigate the risks of fraud, David and Abby ideally would have wanted to have their assets:

- Held by an established, third-party custodian that is subject to rigorous regulation and audit
- Managed by an advisor subject to strict regulation and audits by a governmental agency

For example, RIAs are regulated by the Securities and Exchange Commission ("SEC") or state securities authorities and are subject to audits at any time. RIAs typically engage third-party custodians to hold their clients' assets.[9] These custodial institutions allow the advisors to manage and allocate the assets independently but generally without the ability to withdraw assets except as directed by the client. They carry insurance in case of unanticipated problems and allow the investor direct access to instantaneous reporting, so the advisor does not have sole control over when and how the investor can view the status of their assets.

In addition, a corporate executive should also ask about an advisor's internal security policies, safeguards, and procedures. An executive can use FINRA's Broker Check website or the SEC's Investment Adviser Public Disclosure website to see whether an advisor at the firm has been found to have committed a felony, misdemeanor, or other unethical act in the past ten years.

How Do You Get Compensated for the Advice You Recommend?

David and Abby were uncomfortable with previous interactions they had had with advisors. They felt as if they were being sold something, rather than getting true advice. They may have been correct!

Historically, advisors were compensated largely based on commissions, meaning they typically were paid based on a percentage of the transactions generated by their clients. Since the amount paid out to the advisors differed by product, the advisors may have been influenced to sell the higher-priced products to their clients. They also may have been influenced to engage in as many transactions as possible, as their compensation typically was based on these transactions.

Over the years, additional pricing models have been introduced into the market, from hourly and fee-based models to the popular assets under management ("AUM") model. Under the AUM model, clients are charged a percentage of the assets the advisor is managing. Typically, although not always, that percentage graduates downward as the magnitude of assets managed increases.

Many believe that the AUM model is fairer to the client than a commission-based model, as the advisor is financially incented to increase the value of the client's portfolio, rather than engage in transactions. Under the AUM model, additional services, such as tax return preparation or trustee services, may or may not be priced separately.

Given the wide variability in compensation models, it is not surprising that some investors are confused. When asked "how do you compensate your primary advisor for the services you receive," 24% of investors admitted "I am not sure how my provider is compensated," and an amazing 14% believe—incorrectly—that "I do not compensate my advisor."[10] In finalizing any agreement with an advisory firm, David and Abby would have wanted to understand clearly the services and fees covered in the agreement to make sure the advisor's interests were aligned with theirs.

What Professional Credentials Do You Hold?

Advisory companies that are investing in attracting, developing, engaging, and retaining top talent typically will have team members with a range of advanced degrees and professional designations. The management team of the firm, for example, may include C-suite executives with MBA, JD, and other advanced degrees, indicating they studied topics that could assist in successfully running a growing enterprise for years to come.

As for the advisory talent counseling clients on a day-to-day basis, it can also be comforting to see an ample list of team members with professional degrees. An attorney that has transitioned to a financial advisory practice, for example, can bring additional value to clients, including the ability to work adeptly with estate planning attorneys on strategy and documentation. An attorney now acting as a financial advisor also might have been equipped to advise David on his employment agreement, as previously discussed.

In addition to advanced degrees, the financial advisory profession has its own set of certifications that advisors may earn over time. Almost all require studying and sitting for a certification exam, continuing education, and meeting ethical standards. Many also require a certain level of experience in a financial advisory role. Some of the most relevant professional designations are listed below (Table 12.2).

Table 12.2 Certifications

Title & Acronym	Description
Accredited Estate Planner (AEP®)	The AEP® designation is awarded by the National Association of Estate Planners and Councils to recognize estate planning professionals who meet special requirements of education, experience, knowledge, professional reputation, and character.[a]
Accredited Investment Fiduciary (AIF®)	The AIF® designation certifies that the recipient has knowledge of fiduciary standards of care and their application to the investment management process.[b]
Certified Financial Planner (CFP®)	The CFP® certification is recognized in the United States and a number of other countries for its: (1) high standard of professional education; (2) stringent code of conduct and standards of practice; and (3) ethical requirements that govern professional engagements with clients. The CFP® Board's financial planning subject areas include insurance planning and risk management, employee benefits planning, investment planning, income tax planning, retirement planning, and estate planning.[c]
Certified Investment Management Analyst (CIMA®)	The CIMA® certification signifies that an individual has met initial and on-going experience, ethical, education, and examination requirements for investment management consulting, including advanced investment management theory and application.[d]
Certified Private Wealth Advisor (CPWA®)	The CPWA® designation signifies that an individual has met initial and on-going experience, ethical, education, and examination requirements for the professional designation, which is centered on private wealth management topics and strategies for high-net-worth clients.[e]
Certified Public Accountant (CPA)	CPAs are licensed and regulated by their state boards of accountancy. While state laws and regulations vary, the education, experience, and testing requirements for licensure as a CPA generally include minimum college education (typically 150 credit hours with at least a baccalaureate degree and a concentration in accounting), minimum experience levels, and successful passage of the uniform CPA examination. In order to maintain a CPA license, states generally require the completion of 40 hours of continuing professional education (CPE) each year (or 80 hours over a two-year period or 120 hours over a three-year period).[f]
Chartered Alternative Investment Analyst (CAIA®)	The CAIA® charter is awarded by the Chartered Alternative Investment Analyst Association, which offers an education program designed for individuals specializing in alternative investments.[g]
Chartered Financial Analyst (CFA®)	The CFA® charter is a globally respected, graduate-level investment credential established in 1962 and awarded by the CFA Institute—the largest global association of investment professionals. The three levels of the CFA program test a proficiency with a wide range of fundamental and advanced investment topics, including ethical and professional standards, fixed-income and equity analysis, alternative and derivative investments, economics, financial reporting standards, portfolio management, and wealth planning.[h]
Chartered Life Underwriter (CLU®)	CLU® is a professional designation for individuals who wish to specialize in life insurance and estate planning.[i]
Chartered Market Technician (CMT®)	CMT® is a professional designation that confirms proficiency in technical analysis of the financial markets.[j]

(continued)

Table 12.2 (continued)

Title & Acronym	Description
Personal Finance Specialist (PFS™)	PFS™ is a designation granted by the American Institute of Certified Public Accountants (AICPA) to individuals who are CPAs and meet its examination and work experience requirements. The designation signifies CPAs who specialize in various areas of financial planning.[k]

[a]See "AEP Introduction—NAEPC." National Association of Estate Planners and Councils, accessed June 5, 2018, http://www.naepc.org/designations/estate-planners

[b]See "Centre for Fiduciary Excellence," Centre for Fiduciary Excellence, accessed June 5, 2018, https://www.cefex.org/steward/training-accredited.shtml

[c]See "CFP Board," The Certified Financial Planner Board, accessed June 5, 2018, https://www.cfp.net

[d]See "Investments & Wealth Institute," Investments & Wealth Institute, accessed June 5, 2018, http://investmentsandwealth.org/cima

[e]See "Investments & Wealth Institute," Investments & Wealth Institute, accessed June 5, 2018, http://investmentsandwealth.org/cpwa

[f]See "AICPA," Association of International Certified Professional Accountants, accessed June 5, 2018, https://www.aicpa.org/becomeacpa.html

[g]See "CAIA Association," Chartered Alternative Investment Analyst Association, accessed June 5, 2018, https://caia.org

[h]See "CFA Institute," The Chartered Financial Analyst Institute, accessed June 5, 2018, https://www.cfainstitute.org/programs/cfaprogram/Pages/index.aspx/

[i]See "The American College of Financial Services," The American College of Financial Services®, accessed June 5, 2018, https://www2.theamericancollege.edu/ads/clu

[j]See "CMT® Association," The Chartered Market Technician® Association, accessed June 5, 2018, https://cmtassociation.org

[k]See "AICPA," The American Institute of Certified Public Accountants, accessed June 5, 2018, https://www.aicpa.org

Who Will I Be Interacting With in Addition to You, and What Are Their Roles?

It is not adequate simply to feel confident that a firm has professionals with advanced degrees and designations. A firm may have strong professionals but may merely assign a single advisor to support each client relationship. Clients like David and Abby should expect to be working with a talented team that is touching various aspects of the planning, investment, and tax work. Clients should feel comfortable interacting with these professionals on a regular basis, whether they are discussing aspects of their retirement plans, choosing an asset allocation, or planning for taxes.

What Is Your Investment Philosophy? How Are Investment Decisions Made?

Chapter 7 outlines some of the investment-related mistakes David and Abby could have avoided, as well as the opportunities that they could have taken advantage of along the way. When choosing an advisory team, it is important to understand not only the investment solutions available to the team and its clients but also the underlying philosophy. Does the firm favor active or passive strategies or integrate a combination of the two? How does the firm view macroeconomic events and risk? Does the firm believe in market timing?

Most importantly, how are investment decisions made? Is an individual advisor making all of the decisions? Or is an investment committee or other structure in place to maintain discipline during volatile markets and expertise in various asset classes? Clients like David and Abby should ask enough questions to feel confident in both the philosophy and decision-making structure around strategic and tactical investment decisions.

Describe the Types of Clients You Work With Most Often. Would You Be Able to Provide References?

Just as David and Abby would seek out physicians who specialize in specific areas to address their needs or their children's ailments, they should have done the same in seeking out an advisory solution. Ideally, they would have interviewed firms that have a track record of experience and success in working with companies and executives. Finally, before making a definitive choice on an advisory team, David and Abby should have spoken with multiple references, running through a similar list of questions to hear what actual clients were experiencing on a day-to-day basis. With some effort and references, David and Abby would have been able to find a team well equipped to address proactively David's circumstances as an executive at a larger corporation and Abby's as a business owner.

How Often Should I Expect to Hear from You Should We Work Together?

Busy executives like David and Abby might have very specific preferences around how they would like to interact with their advisory team on an ongoing basis. They may prefer to handle many tasks via conference calls with fewer in-person meetings. They may also expect the advisor to take a key role in coordinating the professionals surrounding them, including attorneys, insurance agents, and others, so that they can attend to their busy careers.

Most importantly, David and Abby would have benefitted from an advisory team that was proactive in communicating with them on important items in advance of issues arising. Whether it be business, health, or any other foreseen or unforeseen event, a strong advisory team should be available to clients at all times, often reaching out to their clients in anticipation of problems and proactively offering potential solutions.

What Is Your Succession Solution Should Something Unforeseen Happen to You?

As previously discussed, advisors should be available to assist clients through planned and unplanned life events. But what happens if something unforeseen happens to the advisor? The SEC and state regulators have increased pressure on firms to outline a succession solution so that clients are protected. The fact remains, however, that many firms simply may not have the resources or the depth of talent to continue to take adequate care of clients should something happen to the primary advisor.

When interviewing advisors, it is important to have the courage to ask them what would happen should they no longer be able to serve you. Do you feel confident in the team supporting the advisor? Do others at the firm have an adequate skill set to serve you? Is there a dedicated management team in place with the leadership required to support the firm? A strong firm will have a dedicated leadership team and deep talent so that, even in the most tragic of circumstances, the firm can continue to serve clients for many years to come.

Notes

1. In "The Affluent Investor" study by The Spectrem Group (2016), an ultra-high-net-worth individual is placed at $5–25 million, not including primary residence, and millionaires at $1–5 million, not including primary residence. Spectrem Group. Used with permission.
2. See Reichheld, "The One Number You Need to Grow," *Harvard Business Review* (December 2003).
3. "Creating Advisor Advocates to Help Boost Referrals," The 2016 Fidelity® Millionaire Outlook Study. © 2018 FMR LLC. All rights reserved. Used with permission.
4. See "Sink or Swim: Why Wealth Management Can't Afford to Miss the Digital Wave," PricewaterhouseCoopers LLP, 2016, https://www.pwc.com/sg/en/publications/wealth-20.html (survey of more than 1000 individuals in Europe, North America, and Asia).
5. See "The Affluent Investor," Spectrem Group, published 2016, https://spectrem.com/Content_Product/mass-affluent-series-2016.aspx.
6. See "The 2016 Millionaire Outlook Study," Fidelity, published 2016, https://clearingcustody.fidelity.com/app/literature/item/9870983.html?sapl=go.
7. See "The 2016 Millionaire Outlook Study," Fidelity, published 2016, https://clearingcustody.fidelity.com/app/literature/item/9870983.html?sapl=go.
8. We note that, as of the writing of this book, the SEC has proposed a new "best interest" standard under which broker-dealers and others associated with broker-dealers would be required "to act in the best interest" of retail customers "at the time a recommendation is made without placing the financial or other interest of the broker-dealer … ahead of the interest of the retail customer." See SEC Release No. 34-83,062 (April 18, 2018). The proposal offers little guidance as to the exact parameters of this standard, but it is seen by some as potentially more rigorous than the suitability standard and less rigorous than the fiduciary standard.
9. Examples include Fidelity Investments, Pershing, Charles Schwab, and TD Ameritrade.
10. Emily Zulz, "Higher Fees Won't Spook Most Advisory Clients: SEI," Think Advisor, published February 4, 2016, https://www.thinkadvisor.com/2016/02/04/higher-fees-wont-spook-most-advisory-clients-sei/?slreturn=20180505093857.

Chapter 13
The Alternative Story of Delilah, Redemption, and the Promised Land

Over the next several years, David and Abby welcomed two children (a boy and a girl) and acquired an oversized home (and an oversized mortgage to go with it), two nice cars, and a membership at an exclusive country club. They also built a successful business for Abby while working for David's eventual ascendancy to corporate executive at Goliath.

Along the way, David and Abby made—and spent—plenty of money. They also increasingly attracted the attention of many who sought to "advise" them—in areas that included investments, taxes, retirement planning, asset allocation, mortgages, education planning for their children, insurance, and even philanthropy. Sometimes they listened, but usually they didn't, especially when they felt that the "advisor" was really just trying to sell them something. They used tax software that they found online to do their own tax returns—usually right before the deadline.

Let's imagine what could have happened had Abby reconnected with her old friend, Delilah. She hadn't seen Delilah since college, but when they saw each other at their college reunion, the conversation was almost instantly comfortable and familiar. Abby and Delilah had lost touch with each other a short time after graduation, but the memory of their friendship was strong, and they soon found themselves laughing at the frenetic pace of their conversation as they rushed to update each other with the important—and not so important—events of their lives since college.

Then, as it often does, the laughter itself shifted the tone of the conversation to a more reflective one. They reminisced about the infinitely simpler lives of their past, and, at some unidentifiable point during the course of the conversation, Abby had a realization. For the first time in her life, she was burdened with real worry—and not the normal kind of worry that comes with the experiences of everyday life. She was deeply worried about the increasing complexities of the world and the reactive, almost random ways that she and David lived in that world. Were she and David in control of their futures, or were they instead subject to the whims of the world around them? How had things gotten so complicated for the power couple?

© The Colony Group 2018
M. J. Nathanson et al., *Personal Financial Planning for Executives and Entrepreneurs*, https://doi.org/10.1007/978-3-319-98416-2_13

Earlier, Delilah had told Abby about her career as a financial planner at an independent wealth management firm called Redemption Wealth Management. She talked about having earned certain professional designations and how she was now one of several owners of Redemption who acted as a team of "trusted experts" providing "comprehensive" financial planning services for their clients. She also had spoken of "objectivity" and "customized advice" centered on the specific needs of her clients.

"Delilah, I was thinking about what you said about the work you're doing at Redemption," Abby said.

And that was the beginning of a new journey for Abby, David, and their family. The following week, Abby and David visited Delilah at her office, where they learned about how Redemption worked with its clients. They learned that Redemption offered not only investment management services for its clients but also tax planning, estate planning, cash-flow planning, risk-management advice, and many other types of financial planning services alongside their investment offering. They also learned that Redemption followed what Delilah called the "fiduciary standard," which required Delilah and her company to place the interests of their clients above all others, including their own.

Within a month of hiring Redemption, Abby and David understood just how precarious their situation had been and how they needed to change the way they thought about their finances before it was too late for them and their family. After a thorough process of investigating what seemed to be every aspect of their financial, business, and sometimes family lives, Delilah presented the couple with a detailed, written financial plan and, along with that plan, a timetable for implementing it.

The Plan

The plan for Abby and David was extensive, but it essentially called for the following coordinated measures (Fig. 13.1):

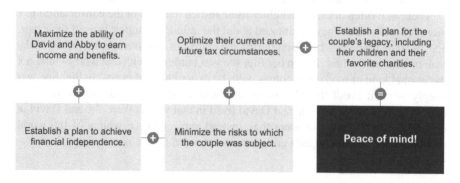

Fig. 13.1 The plan for Abby and David

Maximize the Ability of David and Abby to Earn Income and Benefits from Their Companies

At about the time that they hired Redemption, David had just become an officer of Goliath and had been presented with a formal employment agreement. Prior to that time, David had received an "offer letter" to become an "employee at will" and a series of letters that updated the original offer letter, but he had never received anything so formal until now. The employment agreement was about 15 pages long and addressed base and variable compensation, corporate benefit plans, equity opportunities, termination and severance scenarios, changes of control, and "restrictive covenants." David did not feel comfortable negotiating the agreement, as it seemed fair, if not generous, and he also did not feel that it would send the right message to his employer if he hired a lawyer or other advisor to evaluate it—even though the agreement explicitly made David represent that he had been afforded the opportunity to do exactly that.

But Delilah had other ideas. She reviewed the agreement for David and, with the help of an experienced employment lawyer that Delilah recommended, made several important suggestions that she and the lawyer believed were fair for both David and Goliath:

- Clarify that any future changes to his title or roles and responsibilities would need to be mutually agreeable, with the understanding that any disagreements he had with future changes would need to be reasonable in nature
- Add a "good reason clause," allowing David to be treated as though he were terminated without cause if he left because the company materially diminished his position or compensation (unless all comparable executives experienced the same diminution) or if he were required to move more than 75 miles in connection with his job
- Add a provision affording him the right to a pro-rata bonus in the event that he was terminated without cause during the year
- Change the severance provisions to afford David with severance in the event of any termination without cause equal to two weeks per year of employment—not one—at the rate of his current base salary, *increased as though it included a proportionate amount of any short-term incentive payments he received during the prior year*
- Change the definition of "change of control" to provide for a 50% threshold
- Provide for immediate vesting of any unvested equity awards in the event of a change of control, regardless of whether David was terminated in connection with the change of control
- Change the "cutback" provision applicable to golden-parachute payments to a "best-net-result" provision, allowing for a cutback of severance payments only to the extent it leads to the best result net of taxes
- Supplement the dispute-resolution clause with a clause stating that the loser of any claim would pay the winner's legal expenses and that mediation would be required before going to court

Delilah also asked David to do two more things:

- Ask Goliath for an allowance to pay for his professional fees to have the employment agreement reviewed and negotiated
- Request a copy of Goliath's insurance policies applicable to its officers so that she could ensure that he was sufficiently protected from any shareholder or other claims that might be brought against him personally in his capacity as an officer

To David's surprise and relief, Goliath accepted many of Delilah's suggestions. In some cases, Goliath used different wording than Delilah and the lawyer would have preferred, but the substance of what they wanted was really all that mattered. In any event, David certainly hoped that the protective provisions in question would never be needed.

Delilah also reviewed Goliath's entire benefits structure to ensure that David was maximizing the value of each of those benefits to the extent they were applicable and available. Always a professional, even Delilah could not contain her shock that David had declined the low-cost disability insurance offered by Goliath. That changed immediately, and David signed up for Goliath's short-term and long-term disability offerings the next day.

Likewise, Delilah recommended that Abby engage with a benefits agent and administrator to consider and implement various benefit plans for Slingshot. She noted that these plans would allow Abby and her team to access various benefits, including disability and life insurance, in an inexpensive and sometimes tax-efficient manner.

Establish a Plan to Achieve Financial Independence

A serious problem that Delilah could see almost immediately was the couple's overexposure to Goliath stock. In addition to owning Goliath stock in his retirement plan, David already had been granted some nonqualified stock options and incentive stock options at Goliath, and he had been participating in the company's ESPP, which enabled him to make regular purchases of Goliath stock at discounted prices. All of this, combined with the fact that David was now being offered restricted stock and additional options upon becoming an officer of Goliath, meant that David needed a clearer strategy for investing in Goliath stock—and other assets.

After reviewing all of the Goliath equity awards and the complex plans that governed them, Delilah carefully explained how they worked to David and Abby—legally, economically, and from a tax perspective. This led to a discussion of the couple's overall asset allocation and investment strategy. She presented them with a Monte Carlo analysis that illustrated the probability of the couple achieving financial independence by age 60 if they began an aggressive monthly savings program and adopted a specific asset allocation and investment strategy. She explained that, in her opinion, and based on the couple's current and expected future circumstances, financial independence meant that David and Abby would need to have the following by age 60:

- $10 million of investable assets, enough to sustain their current lifestyles for the rest of their projected lifetimes (with each of David and Abby projected to live until age 90)
- No long-term debt other than the mortgage debt on their current home, as amortized to reflect the regularly scheduled repayments that would be made in the interim
- All education-related and other major expenses paid or provided for in full

Based on the couple's holdings, and assuming a regular savings plan going forward, Delilah then recommended that the couple restructure their current investment holdings to do two things:

- Create a cash reserve sufficient to cover six months of living expenses
- Implement an overall asset allocation strategy, exclusive of their cash reserves, as follows (Fig. 13.2):

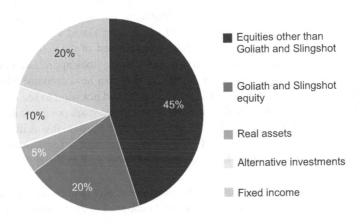

Fig. 13.2 An asset allocation plan for Abby and David

In turn, David would need to sell some of his accumulated Goliath stock and reinvest the proceeds in other assets, consistent with the new asset allocation plan. Delilah advised using a staggered sales approach to protect against major fluctuations in value, to be conducted only after obtaining approvals from Goliath's legal department. She also advised a strategy that reduced the tax impact of these gains by making the sales in David's tax-deferred retirement plan when appropriate.

With regard to David's stock options, Delilah recommended that David hold his stock options and be prepared to exercise them at some point in the future consistent with the couple's overall asset allocation strategy, tax circumstances, and investment outlook on Goliath's stock. When they did exercise any options, they would prioritize the exercise of David's incentive stock options, as they offered a more favorable tax result in the event that David held the underlying stock long enough. While holding off on exercising the options, Delilah did agree that David should continue to make discounted purchases of Goliath's stock under the company's ESPP.

With regard to the restricted stock that was granted to David, Delilah advised David not to make a Section 83(b) election. Yes, he would thereby forfeit the opportunity for long-term capital gain in the future, but Delilah felt that the costs and risks of making the election on the Goliath stock were too great at the time. She explained that if he made the election, he would be required to pay ordinary income tax on the substantial value of the stock as of the date of grant and that if the stock subsequently were forfeited because he left Goliath, or if the stock ultimately declined in value, he could be stuck having to settle for a less valuable capital loss.

Now David had heard something about "trading plans" at some point in the past. He knew that he was subject to special rules for making sales of his Goliath stock; and he also knew that a group of other executives had implemented plans to facilitate regular sales of their stock; but David wasn't among that group. David was just always too busy for these things.

Delilah changed that too. She worked with David and Goliath to create a Rule 10b5-1 trading plan that ensured that David would make regular sales of his stock in a manner that also complied with David's obligations to observe the securities rules against insider trading. This strategy would ensure that David's Goliath holdings would not become overly concentrated relative to the rest of the couple's portfolio and would also allow them to take profits gradually as the stock appreciated in value.

Delilah was also concerned about Abby's holdings in her company, Slingshot. Under the proposed asset-allocation strategy, Delilah did not want to see more than 20% of the couple's portfolio tied up in their concentrated stock positions in Goliath and Slingshot. The Slingshot stock was especially risky because it was illiquid and difficult to value. Abby's income had been ramping up, after a few slower-growth years while she simultaneously focused on her business and on the couple's growing children.

In fact, Abby seemed increasingly well positioned to capitalize on the information age and the growing needs of businesses to adapt to it. Her company now had 14 employees and had just leased a newly renovated office; and she was now thinking about further professionalizing the business with a dedicated management team, as she and David had the sense that it was getting too large and complicated to continue to run it the way it had been run in its earlier years.

Abby had not accumulated much capital within Slingshot. She had put a limited amount of money away in an individual retirement account, but she had never set up a formal retirement plan for her business; and she usually found herself reinvesting her profits back into her business. She even found it necessary to secure a line of credit from a bank, which she had to guarantee personally, to ensure that she always had enough cash to pay her employees during periods of lagging cash flow.

Delilah made several suggestions with regard to Slingshot:

- Immediately make an S election in order to reduce the magnitude of double taxation, take advantage of favorable tax provisions relating to pass-through entities, and mitigate the effect of payroll taxes on distributable income
- Work with Slingshot's benefits administrator to bolster its use of tax-deferred retirement plans
- Hire a third-party consultant to conduct a strategic-planning exercise for the business

- Establish a clear discipline about how and when, if ever, the company's line of credit would be used
- Put in place a plan for Abby to make sales of Slingshot stock to key employees as they became ready to be owners

David and Abby had joked that they were "cash poor" because their money was tied up in their home, their retirement accounts, and in Goliath and Slingshot equity—and they were only now finishing the repayment of their student loans. They even had to borrow against David's retirement account to update the older kitchen and bathrooms in their home.

Delilah also addressed David and Abby's debt and cash-flow strategy. Delilah's plan called for David and Abby to refinance their current home mortgage to reflect the lower interest-rate environment and give the couple a new, 30-year repayment period. Delilah looked at the possibility of paying points to reduce the interest rate further but concluded that, given the current environment and the possibility of rates falling further, her clients were best served with a no-point, no-closing-costs refinancing. Delilah explained that their mortgage had no prepayment penalties and that, in the future, she might recommend accelerating the repayment schedule, depending on future circumstances.

Delilah also advised that, while they were refinancing their mortgage, it also was the perfect time for David and Abby to obtain a home equity line of credit. Whether or not they needed it at the time, their credit was relatively strong and their incomes were high, so it made sense to lock up a credit line, even though it would only be used for emergencies or to exploit various opportunities in the future. Importantly, by locking up this credit facility now, it would be there for the couple in the future even if circumstances changed for them in a way that impaired their creditworthiness.

With regard to the couple's student loans, Delilah put the couple on an accelerated repayment schedule to finish paying them off within a year. She explained that these were not tax-favored loans because the interest rates were relatively high and the interest was not currently tax deductible.

Lastly, Delilah strongly encouraged David and Abby not to borrow against their retirement accounts in the future. She advised them to continue paying off the loan that they took out against David's retirement plan and that their retirement savings would need to grow unfettered in order to achieve financial independence according to their plan.

Minimize the Risks to Which the Couple Was Subject

The above steps were designed to maximize the couple's earning position while best positioning them to achieve financial independence. Yet, they simultaneously offered David and Abby a plan to mitigate some of the investment and business-related risks associated with their positions at Goliath and Slingshot. Still, Delilah was keenly aware of other defensive steps that the couple needed to take—as soon as possible. Most of these steps involved the use of insurance.

First, Delilah recommended that David and Abby allow her to get some quotes for supplemental disability insurance policies. David would now have his disability policy at work, but it had limitations, and Delilah wanted him to have more coverage if not too costly. She also wanted Abby to have some disability coverage—both outside of and within Slingshot. She recommended that Abby install a low-cost disability benefit within Slingshot for her and her employees.

Delilah then offered a comprehensive review of David and Abby's property and casualty insurance policies. She reviewed and made changes not only to their coverage limitations but also to their deductibles and, in some cases, the insurance carriers themselves when she was concerned about the financial strength of any carrier. Her analysis demonstrated that the couple was under-insured in several respects and over-insured in others and that they were able to save some money on premiums while improving and re-prioritizing their overall coverage. The couple also needed a low-cost umbrella policy to ensure that they would be protected in the event of a catastrophe.

On the topic of life insurance, David had a friend who had convinced him to buy a whole-life insurance policy a few years ago.

David had known that he needed to buy some life insurance, but he didn't really know how much or what type he needed. His friend told him that he needed a $5 million whole-life policy, which would cost him about $50,000 per year. David knew that he could have purchased less expensive term insurance, but his friend had said something about whole-life insurance being partly for investment purposes. David never took the time to evaluate his choices and bought the policy from his friend, having never investigated his real needs for insurance and how he could have obtained more efficient policies.

Delilah recommended that David cash out the whole life policy, which had a value of about $35,000, and replace it with 15-year, level-premium term insurance with a face amount of $5 million. She estimated that the cost of this insurance would be about $5,000 per year and advised David and Abby to invest the cash value and some of the annual savings as part of their investment plan. She advised them to take the remainder of the annual savings and acquire a 10-year, level-premium insurance policy for $1 million on Abby's life for use in replacing her income and providing for additional childcare help in the event of her early death.

Lastly, Delilah recommended that David and Abby secure some level of long-term-care insurance for their aging parents. While she often preferred to avoid the expense of this costly insurance, especially when there were sufficient family assets to cover the cost of any long-term-care needs, she believed that David and Abby were not yet ready to bear these expenses if one of their parents needed help.

Optimize Their Current and Future Tax Circumstances

With regard to taxes, Delilah worked with David and Abby to understand better all of the ways that they could reduce their tax liabilities. It was clear that the couple had never really strategized about taxes. It was also clear that they didn't fully understand the tax landscape. Some of the basic suggestions she made, in addition to the ones mentioned above, included:

- Reduce Abby's tax burden by separating her compensation and profit distributions from Slingshot after making an election to be an S corporation
- Maximize their use of tax deferral opportunities
- Review all expenses, especially Abby's business-related expenses, to identify expenses that should be deducted
- Review their portfolio annually for opportunities to harvest tax losses
- Begin purchasing some tax-exempt municipal bonds as part of their fixed-income allocation
- Set aside an account to fund quarterly estimated tax payments as necessary (and reduce interest and penalties payable to the government)

She also referred them to an experienced accountant who could help them not only with return filings but also with tax-mitigation strategies. She and the accountant could then coordinate their efforts in the future. For example, she and the accountant could look for opportunities within David and Abby's investment portfolio each year to harvest tax losses and, when appropriate, repurchase sold securities in accordance with the wash-sale rules.

Establish a Plan for the Couple's Legacy, Including Their Children and Their Favorite Charities

When Delilah began speaking with David and Abby, she soon realized that the couple, like many busy couples, had been too busy to think clearly about specifically providing for their children and the causes they cared about most. Of course, David and Abby loved their children and wanted to support their favorite causes; but they always thought there would be some time in the future when they finally would get around to doing the right thing.

That time was now! First, the couple needed to go through a complete estate planning process. This would require analyzing all of the couple's holdings and how they were titled, as well as working with an estate-planning attorney. The key steps would include:

- Drafting wills for each of David and Abby, providing for the care and custody of their children and the distribution of their assets upon death
- Creating revocable and irrevocable trusts for each of David and Abby, including:
  - trusts designed to minimize estate taxes, ensure the passage of assets for the benefit of the surviving spouse and children, and protect against the claims of future spouses and creditors
  - trusts designed to hold the couple's life insurance policies, shelter the proceeds from estate taxation, and ensure the appropriate distribution of the proceeds

- Reviewing and reconsidering how all assets were held (*e.g.*, as joint tenants, tenants by the entirety, tenants in common, or individually) to limit probate exposure, provide for orderly distribution at death, and minimize estate taxes
- Executing powers of attorney for each of David and Abby, affording each spouse the power to make legal decisions in the event of a catastrophe involving the other spouse
- Executing healthcare proxies and directives for each of David and Abby, affording each spouse the power to make healthcare decisions in the event of a medical emergency involving the other spouse
- Reviewing all beneficiary designations for all insurance policies and accounts with the goal of minimizing taxes, avoiding probate, and maximizing efficiency in the event of a death

Along with the estate planning process, the couple needed to put in place a plan to pay for their children's education. Delilah illustrated her projections for how much it would cost to educate the couple's children, accounting for inflation and even the possibility of attending graduate school. The number was somewhat of a shock to David and Abby, but Delilah selected a state-sponsored Section 529 plan based on a variety of factors particular to the couple and showed that if they made monthly contributions to the accounts and also segregated a portion of their current holdings, then they had a good chance to reach their goals.

Finally, David and Abby needed to adopt a charitable-gifting plan. They first needed to identify the charities that they cared about the most. They then needed to set up a donor-advised fund that would allow them to control the timing of their charitable deductions, which might not necessarily coincide with the timing of their actual contributions to the charities. The donor-advised fund would also enable the couple to donate appreciated Goliath stock and avoid ever having to pay taxes on the gain!

They had a good amount of work ahead of them to implement the plan, but they knew that Delilah was there to help them. She had a checklist and a clear timeline for implementation, prioritized by urgency. When they left Delilah's office, David and Abby already had peace of mind.

The Future

Of course, life is not predictable. Two years after David's big promotion, Goliath acquired one of its competitors, Samson Assembly Corp., and, well, you already know what happened next. Goliath's stock plunged. A national bank unexpectedly filed for bankruptcy, setting off shockwaves in the global markets and triggering a major economic recession. Goliath was unprepared for the consequent tightening of the credit markets and was forced to sell itself to a competitor for a small fraction of its historic value. David was laid off about a month later, and yes, David still had a heart attack (and survived).

But the rest of the story is actually a happy one. The couple was well prepared not only to withstand these setbacks but also to *thrive* in their aftermath.

David received the more extensive severance package for which Delilah and his employment lawyer had negotiated—two weeks per year of employment at the rate of his current base salary, increased as though it included a proportionate amount of any short-term incentive payments he received during the prior year. Vesting on his equity incentives was accelerated, and, while their value was greatly diminished, David and Abby were well diversified, so they were not devastated by the loss in value attributable to the awards or David's other Goliath stock. In fact, the couple had been using the Goliath stock to make charitable contributions, further reducing their concentrated position and insulating them from some of the decline. David's trading plan likewise had ensured that he was constantly diversifying away from Goliath.

David was now covered by Goliath's disability insurance policies, and the couple was grateful that they had changed their thinking on these policies. David would now receive 60% of his total annual compensation—subject to some limitation but free of taxes—for as long as it took for him to get back to work (or until the policy eventually expired). He also had the supplemental disability policy that Delilah recommended, offering him an additional 10%, again free of income taxes.

They had just paid off the loan against their retirement account, and they had paid down their student loans on an accelerated basis as Delilah had suggested; so, fortunately, all the bad news came at a time when the couple was dealing with a reduced debt burden.

Sure enough, David and Abby still had to pay taxes on the vested stock options that David had accumulated and not exercised. During Goliath's distressed sale, the acquiring company had agreed to pay out cash to all holders of vested, "in-the-money" stock options; and while most of the stock options were underwater and therefore worthless, some of David's options had been valuable enough to earn him a cash payout. They also had to pay capital gain tax on the unrestricted shares of Goliath stock David owned outside of his retirement plan. With regard to David's restricted stock, however, David and Abby were especially grateful for the advice Delilah had given them. Because David refrained from making a Section 83(b) election on that stock, he avoided having to pay ordinary income tax on the higher value at the time of grant, with only a capital loss to compensate him for the subsequent decline in value. Instead, he paid ordinary income tax only on the lower value at the time of vesting, saving the couple a great deal in taxes.

With regard to their home, because of the recession, their mortgage was now greater than the value of their home; but fortunately, Delilah had them refinance it prior to David losing his job, and they were locked in at a lower interest rate. The recession might ultimately lead to lower mortgage rates, so there might be another opportunity to refinance the mortgage at a lower rate—and the disability insurance policy made the couple creditworthy even if it took David some time to recover and get a new job.

The couple was also grateful that they acquired long-term, level-premium, term life insurance. They were set from an insurance perspective for many years to come because they acquired their policies while they were both completely healthy. Better still, Delilah had recommended that they take the optional "disability rider" on David's insurance policy, so his premiums would now be paid for him until he could get back to work!

As for Abby, it was now up to her to be the sole earner for a while, and she was freed up to do so because the couple could afford to hire some help with childcare. Her business was at an inflection point, but Delilah had been advising her all along. She had led a comprehensive strategic planning process, had brought in some minority partners, and had a completely unused line of credit available to provide her any capital she might need to expand her business—even in the face of a general recession.

So the couple could rely on Abby's earnings. And they also had David's extended severance, the proceeds of the Goliath transaction, and their tax-free disability insurance payments—together with six months of cash reserves and a fully available home equity line of credit just in case!

Yet, David was not the only one in the family with health issues. David's aging mother, who already had become frail, was now moving rapidly downhill. She was moving towards an Alzheimer's diagnosis, and she needed to move into an assisted-care facility. But, with Delilah's guidance, the family now had long-term care insurance that would pay for up to three years of long-term care at an excellent facility.

Yes, the couple had suffered the shock of David's heart attack and the loss of his job, along with enduring an economic recession; but they spent their time worrying about getting David back into shape and about taking care of his mother and father. They did not waste valuable time and effort worrying about their long-term finances. Their investments were properly diversified. In fact, because their investments were properly diversified and structured to be uncorrelated, some of their investments actually became more valuable during the recession, though the equity portion of their portfolio declined.

While Goliath had failed them, their investment plan remained largely intact. At times during the recession, Abby called Delilah to ask about selling some of the equities, which seemed to keep declining. Delilah, however, warned that selling these positions, which she considered to be solid long-term investments, would be a mistake. She told Abby to remain focused on the long-term and not to succumb to the mistakes made by so many of trying to time the markets or acting on short-term emotional impulses.

In the end, David fully recovered and got another job—at a company called Old Eden Manufacturers, located in Bethlehem, Connecticut. Abby built Slingshot into a regional powerhouse and ultimately sold it to a public company, Gideon Consolidators, Inc., for which she became an executive. She and her fellow Slingshot owners received millions in the transaction, and she got to keep a larger portion of the proceeds after taxes because her S election allowed her to avoid, in part, the second level of taxation that would have applied in the absence of the election.

As for the recession, it lasted for about a year, but the couple's portfolio began to recover even before the recession ended, ultimately erasing its losses and again producing attractive returns. David's mother eventually passed away, but she lived her remaining years in comfort and with dignity, constantly surrounded by her family and friends. In her honor, David and Abby became proud supporters of an Alzheimer's charity, funded by their donor-advised fund and the charitable trust that Delilah suggested when Abby sold Slingshot.

They were the power couple again. They were happy, and their children were happy. Most of all, they had peace of mind—the kind necessary to find real meaning and joy in their lives for the rest of their days.

Index

Note: Page numbers followed by 'n' refer to notes.

© The Colony Group 2018
M. J. Nathanson et al., *Personal Financial Planning for Executives and Entrepreneurs*, https://doi.org/10.1007/978-3-319-98416-2

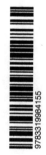